Here I Stand

G2476 To Stand –

denotes an upright and active position.

Published by Clow Company Ltd

First Edition

ISBN 978-0-473-42952-2

Here I Stand

Word4v203

Date: 23 April 2018, 07:51:21 AM

I thought it would be good to write down the fundamental facts of what I believe. I hope that God will use what I have written to show more of his love, interest and friendship with us.

Andrew Clow

Contents

1.0 Introduction

"If the foundations be destroyed, what can the righteous do?"
Psalm 11:3

1.1 The Rock

I think many Christians suffer real problems because they do not properly understand what they believe. It reminds me of the scripture 'my people are destroyed for lack of knowledge'[1]. I have based my outline on Hebrews 6:1-2.

> "Therefore leaving the principles[2] of the doctrine[3] (word)[4] of Christ, let us go on unto perfection; not laying again the foundation of repentance from dead works, and of faith toward God,
>
> Of the doctrine[5] of baptisms, and of laying on of hands, and of resurrection of the dead, and of eternal judgment."
>
> Heb 6:1-2

The topics I cover are those developed in Derek Prince's 'Foundation Series'[6]. Although the writer of Hebrews continues the discussion going 'on unto perfection', these notes deal mainly with 'the beginning of the word of Christ'. Some parts I have digressed slightly, where I thought it would be of benefit to the reader. There are six main topics:

1. Repentance [away] from dead works
2. Faith toward God
3. Doctrine of Baptisms
4. Laying on of hands
5. Resurrection [standing up] of the dead
6. Eternal judgement

The first two topics are necessary and sufficient for salvation[7]. Knowledge of the remaining four topics is not required for salvation (with the exception that Christ was crucified for our sins and was resurrected). The writer of Hebrews 6:1-2 was, I think, interested in separating the first two topics from the remaining ones, because they concern placing a foundation. Never the less, all six topics have the same foundation (or basis), which if permitted we shall now come to.

Reading Matthew 7:24-27

Christ is likened to a rock. Paul speaking to the Corinthians said

---

[1] Hosea 4:6

[2] G746 (prop. abstract) a *commencement* or (concrete) *chief* (through idea of being first):- principles

[3] G3056 "something *said*", by implication a *topic* (subject of discourse)

[4] please see 'Appendix B. Notation', page 229

[5] G1322 *instruction* (the act or the matter); from G1321 to *teach*

[6] refer 'Appendix A. Recommended Reading and References'

[7] It is by hearing the word of God that a man is saved. "So then faith cometh by hearing, and hearing by the word of God." Rom 10:17. Jesus is the Word "And the Word was made flesh, ..." John 1:14

"For other foundation can no man lay[8] than that is laid[9], which is Jesus Christ."

1Cor 3:11

The Corinthian brethren had already laid the foundation Jesus Christ. If we compare the scripture with Mat 7:24-27 we see that Jesus is the rock upon which we can build a secure life. How many people forget that a Christian's life is not based on a set of rules, but on a person - Jesus Christ.

[8] G5087 to *place* in a passive or horizontal posture

[9] G2749 to *lie* outstretched (properly reflexive and utterly prostrate)

2.0 Repentance

"Therefore by the deeds of the law there shall no flesh be justified in his sight: ..."
Rom 3:20

2.1 The Law

A good place to start talking about justification and faith is the law.

> "Wherefore the law was our schoolmaster to bring us unto Christ, that we might be justified by faith."
>
> Gal 3:24

To be justified by the law, a man must do the works of the law.

> "Now therefore hearken, O Israel, unto the statutes and unto the judgments, which I teach you, for to do them, that ye may live, and go in and possess the land which the Lord God of your fathers giveth you."
>
> Deut 4:1

> "Ye shall therefore keep my statutes, and my judgments: which if a man do, he shall live in them: I am the Lord."
>
> Lev 18:5

> "For Moses describeth the righteousness which is of the law, That the man which doeth those things shall live by them."
>
> Rom 10:5

> "(For not the hearers of the law are just before God, but the doers of the law shall be justified."
>
> Rom 2:13

No one except Jesus is justified by the law.

> "... both Jews and Gentiles, that they are all under sin;
>
> As it is written, There is none righteous, no, not one: There is none that understandeth, there is none that seeketh after God.
>
> They are all gone out of the way, they are together become unprofitable; there is none that doeth good, no, not one."
>
> Rom 3:9-12; cf. Ps 14:1-3 & 53:1-3

Skipping a bit. In reference to the words above, the scripture says.

> "Now we know that what things soever the law saith, it saith to them who are under the law: that every mouth may be stopped, and all the world may become[10] guilty[11] before God.
>
> Therefore by the deeds of the law there shall no flesh be justified in his sight: for by the law is the knowledge of sin."
>
> Rom 3:19-20

---

[10] *cause to be*

[11] *under* (a just) *sentence*

> "For all have sinned, ... "
>
> Rom 3:23

> "But we are all as an unclean thing, and all our righteousnesses are as filthy rags; and we all do fade as a leaf; and our iniquities, like the wind, have taken us away.
>
> Isaiah 64:6

Although the law can appear to be the way to God it is not. By good deeds, by much prayer, Bible study, beautiful singing, scripture memorisation, witnessing, preaching, being friendly to people, raising of hands, feelings, will power, church attendance - efforts of our own, no one will be saved. God never intended that people come to him based on their own hard work and effort. I think God sees the efforts many good Christians make to be accepted by him, and is sad.

Reading Luke 18:9-14

We can only come to God trusting in his mercy.

2.2 Repentance from Dead Works

The New Testament Greek word[12] most commonly translated as 'repent' means to change ones mind. A decision. Not an emotion.

In the Old Testament a Hebrew word[13] translated as 'repent' means literally 'to turn', 'to turn back'. The New testament emphasises the inward decision of repentance, the old testament the outward expression of this decision. Together, repentance is an inner change of mind, resulting in an outward turning back, or turning around, to face in a completely new direction.

Repentance is kind of like a new years resolution. By itself, like most peoples new years resolutions, it can not prevent you from sinning. We can make the choice to go in the direction God wants but without God's help we don't get very far. Never the less, it is a prerequisite for salvation, and it is something God wants to see.

Reading Luke 15:11-24

This story illustrates a man coming to his senses and returning to the God who loves him. Repentance is seen here by an inward decision "I will arise and go to my father.", and an action "He arose and went to his father."

The word 'repent' that is used in the King James Bible, may[14] signify regret[15]. An example of a person who showed regret without repentance is given in Hebrews 12:17 where Esau crying sought to repent, but could not.

> "For ye know how that afterward, when he would have inherited the blessing, he was rejected: for he found no place of repentance[16] [way to change his decision], though he sought it carefully with tears."
>
> Hebrews 12:17

---

[12] -G3340 from G3326 ["amid"] and G3539 [to *exercise* the *mind* (*observe*) i.e. fig. to *comprehend, heed*]; to *think differently* or *afterwards*, i.e. *reconsider* (morally *feel compunction*):- repent.
-G3341 from G3340 (subj.) compunction (for guilt, includ. reformation); by implication *reversal* (of [another's] decision):- repentance.

[13] H7725 A primitive root; to *turn* back (hence, away) trans. or intrans., lit. or fig. (not necessarily with the idea of *return* to the starting point); generally to *retreat*; often adverbially *again*.

[14] The word 'repent' in the King James can be a translation of a number of words including G3340, G3338, H5162 & H7725. Therefore, the meaning of the original text can differ from one place to another even though the same word 'repent' is used in the King James Bible.
In the New Testament, 'repent' is a translation of G3340 (except for 2Cor 7:8 & Heb 7:21 where it is of G3338) & 'repentance' is a translation of G3341 except for Rom 11:29.

[15] In the King James, in the old testament, 'repent' usually means 'to sigh' (H5162). H5162 was translated in the New Testament Greek as G3338, "The Lord sware, and will not (regret), Thou art a priest ..." (Psalm 110:4,Heb 7:21).
-G3338 from G3326 and the middle of G3199; to *care afterwards*, that is, *regret:* - repent (self).
-H5162 A prim. root; properly *to sigh*, i.e. *breathe* strongly; by implication to *be sorry*.
H5162 does not necessarily require an action to be associated with it. But because of its intensity, often the person does take some action as a consequence of it. e.g. H7725 meaning *to turn* is often associated with H5162. cf. Exod 13:17 "Lest peradventure the people repent (to sigh/regret) (H5162) when they see war, and they return (H7725) ..."; Joel 2:14 "Who knoweth if he will return (H7725) and repent (to sigh/regret) (H5162) ...".

[16] G3341 see footnote 12

There comes a point where a person must choose. For most people, they have their whole lifetime to choose salvation, however some people within their lifetime, have made a decision concerning salvation, which like Esau's can not be changed. (Don't worry about the details I'd almost stake my life it's not you.)

Repentance reminds me of the following scripture.

> "I have surely heard Ephraim bemoaning himself thus; Thou hast chastised me, and I was chastised, as a bullock unaccustomed to the yoke: turn thou me[17] , and I shall be turned; for thou art the Lord my God.
>
> Surely after that I was turned, I repented; and after that I was instructed, I smote upon my thigh: I was ashamed, yea, even confounded, because I did bear the reproach of my youth.
>
> Is Ephraim my dear son? is he a pleasant child? for since I spake against him, I do earnestly remember him still: therefore my bowels are troubled for him; I will surely have mercy upon him, saith the Lord."
>
> Jer 31:18-20

We have turned to walk after our own ways, but God has a direction he wants to lead us in. God never forces people to turn, but he offers his direction freely. God longs to have mercy upon us, but we must repent first.

> "Who is a God like unto thee, that pardoneth iniquity, and passeth by the transgression of the remnant of his heritage? he retaineth not his anger for ever, because he delighteth in mercy[18].
>
> He will turn again, he will have compassion upon us; He will subdue[19] our iniquities; and thou wilt cast all their sins into the depths of the sea."
>
> Micah 7:18-19

Reading Hosea 14:1-4

This is an excellent example of repentance.

> "O Israel, return unto the Lord thy God; for thou hast fallen by thine iniquity."

Here Israel had departed from God and God asks Israel to return. The thing that took them away was iniquity. 'thou hast fallen by thine iniquity'. But God calls Israel heavenward to himself.

How could Israel return?

> "Take with you words, and turn to the Lord: say unto him, take away all iniquity, and receive us graciously ..."

The first step we must take back to God is repentance. We can not ask for God's forgiveness without repenting.

---

[17] H7725

[18] kindness

[19] *tread* down

If we look back to Heb 6:1 the first topic is "repentance from dead works". We have seen that repentance is a decision to change the way we live. I could repent from cleaning my teeth, which would mean I wouldn't clean my teeth any more (not!!!). We are to repent from dead works. Dead works include sin.

> "Let everyone who names the name of Christ depart from iniquity."
>
> 2Tim 2:19

As a personal opinion I think dead works also include those which endeavour to justify us by the law.

Repentance is not something we do once and then it is over.

> "Set thee up waymarks, make thee high heaps: set thine heart toward the highway, even the way which thou wentest: turn again, O virgin of Israel, turn again to these thy cities."
>
> Jer 31:21

God speaks here of a path which Israel had trodden, and asks them to walk in it again. In my experience we turn away from God, sometimes in small things, sometimes in big. We should always turn to God, not run away when we sin. I remember someone saying 'always keep short accounts with God'. Don't let sin ruin your relationship with God. Ask for his mercy and set thine heart again toward the highway.

> "And an highway shall be there, and a way, and it shall be called The way of holiness; the unclean shall not pass over it; but it shall be for those: the wayfaring men, though fools, shall not err therein.
>
> No lion shall be there, nor any ravenous beast shall go up thereon, it shall not be found there; but the redeemed shall walk there: ..."
>
> Isaiah 35:8-9

Reading Psalm 103:8-14

Lastly I think it is important to realise that repentance begins with God.

> " ... the riches of his goodness and forbearance and longsuffering; not knowing that the goodness of God leadeth thee to repentance?"
>
> Rom 2:4

> "No man can come to me, except the Father which has sent me draw him: and I will raise him up at the last day."
>
> John 6:44

> " ... and him that cometh to me I will in no wise cast out."
>
> John 6:37

It is God who leads us to repentance and to Christ. Accepted this drawing leads us to saving faith and eternal life; rejected, it leaves the sinner to continue on his way to the grave and the unending darkness of an eternity apart from God[20].

God gave everything he had to bring us back to himself. The statement Paul makes concerning himself is true for us today.

> " ... the Son of God, who loved me, and gave himself for me."
> Gal 2:20

---

[20] From Derek Prince's Foundation Series. Please see 'Appendix A. Recommended Reading and References'

3.0 Faith towards God

"For if, when we were enemies, we were reconciled to God by the death of his son, much more, being reconciled, we shall be saved by his life. "

Rom 5:10

3.1 What is Faith?

The second topic is faith towards God. In general Faith is:

New Testament[21]:

A conviction of truth, reliance on something by an inward certainty.

A few examples of the New Testament Greek word for faith are:

"Jesus answered and said unto them, Verily I say unto you, if ye have *faith*, and doubt not, ye shall not only do this which is done to the fig tree, ..."
Mat 21:21

"..., so worship I the God of my fathers, *believing* all things which are written in the law and the prophets: ..."
Acts 24:14

"That the trial of your *faith*, being much more precious than of gold ..."
1Pet 1:7

"... before him whom he *believed*, even God, who quickeneth the dead, and calleth those things which be not as though they were."
Rom 4:17

Note that both in the new and old testaments, the respective Greek or Hebrew word is often translated as either 'faith' or 'believe'. The Hebrew word for faith means:

Old Testament[22]:

To trust. It is associated with the following ideas: of something being secure, firmness (as in an object being firmly fixed to something - not wobbling), permanent, true, reliable.

Some examples are:

"... when his [he who hates][23] voice is gracious, do not *believe* him ..."
Prov 26:25[24]

"And Moses answered and said, But, behold, they will not *believe* me, nor hearken unto my voice: for they will say, The Lord hath not appeared unto thee."
Ex 4:1

---

[21] G4102 πίστις *pis'-tis* from G3982*; persuasion, i.e. credence;* moral *conviction (*of ...), especially *reliance* upon ... G3982 pi'-tho; A prim. verb; to convince (by argument, true or false); ...

[22] H539 אמן *aw-man'*; A prim. root; properly to *build up* or *support;* to *foster* as a parent or nurse; fig. to *render* (or *be) firm* or faithful, to *trust* or believe, to be *permanent* or quiet; morally to be *true* or certain; ...

[23] see notation regarding the use of brackets Appendix B, page 229

[24] Literal Translation of the Holy Bible, by Jay P. Green

> "Ye are my witnesses, saith the Lord, and my servant whom I have chosen: that ye may know and *believe* me, and understand that I am he: before me there was no God formed, neither shall there be after me.
>
> I, even I, am the Lord; and beside me there is no saviour."
>
> Isaiah 43:10-11

Faith in the Bible usually refers to man's trust in God. Paul speaking of his faith says

> "For the which cause I also suffer these things: nevertheless I am not ashamed: for I know whom I have *believed*, and am persuaded that he is able to keep that which I have committed unto him against that day."
>
> 2Tim 1:12

Really believing God and getting to know him should go hand in hand. We don't trust a set of rules, our trust is in Jesus Christ. Remember Hebrews 6:1

> "... and of faith toward God, ..."

3.2 Righteousness

3.2.1 Righteousness by the Law

First, I would like to review a few scriptures

> "Ye shall therefore keep my statutes, and my judgments: which if a man do, he shall live in them: I am the Lord."
>
> Lev 18:5

> "And it shall be our righteousness, if we observe to do all these commandments before the Lord our God, as he hath commanded us."
>
> Deut 6:25

Righteousness through the Law of Moses is achieved by keeping the commandments God gave in the Old Testament[25].

God found a fault with the covenant he made with Israel, not that there was anything wrong with the law. For the law is holy, just and good. But the covenant was unable to allow us to even come near God.

> "For finding fault with them [that first covenant], he [God] saith, Behold, the days come, saith the Lord, when I will make a new covenant with the house of Israel and with the house of Judah: Not according to the covenant that I made with their fathers in the day when I took them by the hand to lead them out of the Land of Egypt; because they continued not in [broke] my covenant, and I regarded them not, saith the Lord."
>
> Heb 8:8-9

> "But now the righteousness of God without the law is manifested, being witnessed by the law and prophets;"
>
> Rom 3:21

God made another way of getting righteousness.

---

[25] Some churches today have different rules, but the basis of righteousness is still working to achieve our own righteousness by fulfilling the Law. Typical symptoms are feeling God does not accept us. That God is far away, and his expectation of us is too great.

3.2.2 The purpose of the Law

> 22 But the scripture hath concluded all under sin, that the promise by faith of Jesus Christ might be given to them that believe[26].
>
> 23 But before faith came, we were kept[27] under the law, shut up[28] unto the faith which should afterwards be revealed.
>
> 24 Wherefore the law was our schoolmaster to bring us unto Christ, that we might be justified by faith.
>
> 25 But after that faith is come, we are no longer under a schoolmaster.
>
> 26 For ye are all the children of God by faith in Christ Jesus.
>
> Gal 3:22-25

In old times, a wealthy child would have a trainer (or schoolmaster) to look after him and teach him things until he was about 8 years old. A tutor then took over the child's education. At this time the trainers job was complete. His only remaining duty was to bring the child to their personal tutor for further education.

The trainer is the law, and the tutor is Christ Jesus. As when the child became of age, and began to be taught by the tutor, so it is with us, when we first trust Jesus. The law is no longer our teacher. However, when we sin it serves to bring us back through repentance to Christ, that we might again be justified by faith.

> "But after that faith is come, we are no longer under a (trainer[29]) [the Law]. For ye are all the children of God by faith in Christ Jesus." Gal 3:25-26

---

[26] or 'to those believing'

[27] guard/watch [to prevent escaping], fig. to hem in, protect.

[28] to shut/close together, i.e. *include* or (fig.) *embrace* in a common subjection to [the law]

[29] G3807
From G3816 and a reduplication form of G71; a *boy leader*, that is, a servant whose office it was to take the children to school;

3.2.3 Where does faith come from?

Reading Luke 8:5-15

The basis of what we believe is the fact that the Bible was written by God.

> "All scripture is given by inspiration of God, and is profitable for doctrine, for reproof, for correction, for instruction in righteousness: that the man of God may be perfect, thoroughly furnished unto all good works."
>
> 2Tim 3:16-17

In the reading (Luke), Jesus is speaking about believing (faith) in the word that comes from God. The person who sows the seed is Jesus.

> “He that soweth the good seed is the Son of man”
>
> Mat 13:37

> “The seed is the word of God." Luke 8:11

The ground is the heart of the person receiving the word.

> “But that on the good ground are they, which in an honest and good heart, having heard the word, keep it, and bring forth fruit with patience.”
>
> Luke 8:15

The scripture states that believing the word results in salvation.

> “Those by the wayside are they that hear; then cometh the devil, and taketh away the word out of their hearts, <u>lest they should believe [the word] and be saved</u>.”
>
> Luke 8:12

I heard someone say that the Bible is like a letter written by God to Christians. God must like us a lot to write such a big letter. When we trust (believe) what is written in a letter, we trust the person who wrote it.

> “In whom (Christ) ye also trusted, after that ye heard the word of truth, the gospel of your salvation: ...”
>
> Eph 1:13

3.2.4 Righteousness by Faith

What are we supposed to believe so that we may obtain righteousness and thereby be saved?

For salvation we must trust the record God gives.

> "... Jesus came into Galilee, preaching the gospel of the kingdom of God, and saying, The time is fulfilled, and the kingdom of God is at hand: repent ye, and believe the gospel."
>
> Mark 1:14-15

The record we are to believe is the gospel.

> 1 Moreover, brethren, I declare unto you the gospel which I preached unto you, which also ye have received, and wherein ye stand;
>
> 2 By which also ye are saved, if ye keep in memory what I preached unto you, unless ye have believed in vain.
>
> 3 For I delivered unto you first of all that which I also received, how that Christ died for our sins according to the scriptures;
>
> 4 And that he was buried, and that he rose again the third day according to the scriptures:
>
> 1Cor 15:1-4

Verses 1-2 show that the brethren were saved by the Gospel[30]. Verses 3-4 declare the good news. This record consists of three facts:

(1) Christ took the punishment for our sins on the cross

(2) That he died and was buried

(3) That he stood up again in the flesh

These facts are recorded in Matthew, Mark, Luke and John[31].

> "... he that believeth not God hath made him a liar; because he believeth not the record that God gave of his Son. And this is the record, that God hath given to us eternal life, and this life is in his Son. He that hath the son hath life; and he that hath not the son of God hath not life."
>
> I John 5:10-12

---

[30] 'Gospel' is often a translation of 'bringing or announcing of good tidings' or 'a good message.' I suppose its like the telegrams which are read out at a wedding when a friend or relative is unable to be present, but they wish to congratulate and encourage the bride and groom.

[31] For example, that Christ was raised from the dead is shown in each of the Gospels. The following verses all refer to Christ after he was crucified and had died.

"And they came and held him by the feet ..." Mat 28:9

"he is risen [referring to the body]; he is not here: behold the place where they laid him." Mark 16:6

"And he took it [a share of steeped fish and of an honeycomb], and did eat before them." Luke 24:42

"Reach hither thy finger, and behold my hands; and reach hither thy hand, and thrust it into my side: ..." John 20:27

"For God so loved the world, that he gave his only begotten Son, that whosoever believeth in him should not perish, but have everlasting life. For God sent not his Son into the world to condemn the world; but that the world through him might be saved.

He that believeth on him is not condemned: but he that believeth not is condemned already, because he hath not believed in the name of the only begotten Son of God."

John 3:16-18

It is important to believe that Christ stood up again after his death. Jesus said after he was resurrected

"Behold my hands and my feet, that it is I myself: handle me, and see; for a spirit hath not flesh and bones, as ye see me have."

Luke 24:39

Reading Romans 4:1-8

In Romans four, the writer asks "how was Abraham justified?"

"For what saith the Scripture? Abraham believed God, and it was counted unto him for righteousness."

Rom 4:4

Abraham was justified by faith,

"But to him that worketh not, but believeth on him that justifies the ungodly, his faith is counted for righteousness."

Rom 4:5

People often condemn others who don't work as lazy. There are however times when we should not work. Abraham did not work for righteousness, but trusted God, and God counted his trust for righteousness.

"Even as David also describes the blessedness of the man, unto whom God imputeth righteousness without works, Saying, Blessed are they whose iniquities are forgiven, and whose sins are covered. Blessed is the man to whom the Lord will not impute sin."

Rom 4:6-7

Praise the Lord we're clean. The precious blood of Christ, as of a lamb without blemish and without spot, who truly was foreordained before the foundation of the world, buys us righteousness we could never obtain by ourselves. Hallelujah!, that God would consider us worth rescuing, so that of us it is said

"... to whom the Lord will not impute sin." Rom 4:8

I love you Lord.

The next scripture shows that we can obtain righteousness by faith in the same way that Abraham did.

"And being fully persuaded that, what he had promised, he was able also to perform. And therefore it was imputed to him for righteousness. Now it was not written for his sake alone, that it was imputed to him; but for us also, to whom it shall be imputed, if we believe on him that raised up Jesus our Lord from the dead; who was delivered for our offences, and was raised again for our justification."

Rom 4:21-25

This scripture shows righteousness as a result of believing.

The gospel is outlined

(1) God raised up Jesus our Lord from the dead

(2) Jesus was delivered for our offences and raised for our justification

Paul refers to a scripture in the old testament explaining how Abraham obtained righteousness as a result of believing God[32]. He continues to say we can receive righteousness if we believe God. Immediately after saying this, Paul records the facts declared in 1Cor 15:3-4 as the gospel. When we believe the record in God's word of Jesus death burial and resurrection, we trust God by trusting what he says (the Bible) is true.

"But continue thou in the things which thou hast learned and hast been assured of, knowing of whom thou hast learned them;

And that from a child thou hast known the holy scriptures, which are able to make thee wise unto salvation through faith which is in Christ Jesus.

All scripture is given by inspiration of God, and is profitable for doctrine, for reproof, for correction, for instruction in righteousness:

That the man of God may be perfect, thoroughly furnished unto all good works."

2Tim 3:14-17

The following scripture also shows righteousness may be obtained through faith.

"But the righteousness which is of faith speaketh on this wise, ...

The word is nigh thee, even in thy mouth, and in thine heart: that is, the word of faith, which we preach; That if thou shalt confess with thy mouth the Lord Jesus, and shalt believe in thine heart that God hath raised him from the dead, thou shalt be saved.

For with the heart man believeth unto righteousness; and with the mouth confession[33] is made unto salvation."

Rom 10:6-10

---

[32] Gen 15:6

[33] G3670 homologeō

From a compound of the base of G3674 and G3056; to *assent*, that is, *covenant, acknowledge:* - con- (pro-) fess, confession is made, give thanks, promise.

G3674 homou

Genitive case of ὁμός homos (the *same*; akin to G260) as adverb; *at* the *same* place or time: - together.

G3056 logos

From G3004; something *said* (including the *thought*)

It declares that we are to trust in Christ, that he through his death and resurrection will give us righteousness. It is through believing this record God gave that we obtain righteousness, and will be saved in the day of judgment.

> "Who hath believed our report? and to whom is the arm of the Lord revealed? ...
>
> All we like sheep have gone astray; we have turned every one to his own way; and the Lord hath laid on him the iniquity of us all.
>
> He was oppressed, and he was afflicted, yet he opened not his mouth: he is brought as a lamb to the slaughter, and as a sheep before her shearers is dumb, so he openeth not his mouth.
>
> (From prison and from justice was he taken, and his generation who shall consider?) for he was cut off out of the land of the living: for the transgression of my people was he stricken."
>
> Isaiah 53:1,6-8

3.3 Living faith

Reading James 2:14-26

Works are a result of faith. You can have good works without faith in God, but it is impossible to have faith in God without good works.

> JAM 2:26 For as the body without the spirit is dead, so faith without works is dead also.

If a person is alive, he'll walk around, eat, talk etc. The body's actions are a result of the spirit abiding in the man. Similarly good works follow automatically if there is faith.

Today many people get the cart before the horse. Counsellors look at a man's sinful actions and say we must get him to do x, y or z, when the real problem is with the heart.

> "For with the heart man believes ..." Rom 10:10

When the heart is right, the actions follow.

> "For out of the heart proceed evil thoughts, murders, adulteries, fornications, thefts, false witness, blasphemies: These are the things which defile a man: ..."
>
> Mat 15:19-20

If the heart is set on the Lord, a Christian naturally does good.

> "This I say then, Walk in the Spirit, and ye shall not fulfil the lust of the flesh."
>
> Gal 5:16

It is a God inspired "shall not" that enables us to walk in obedience to our Father.

> "But let us, who are of the day, be sober, putting on the breastplate of faith and love; and for an helmet, the hope of salvation. For God hath not appointed us to wrath, but to obtain salvation by our Lord Jesus Christ,
>
> Who died for us, that, whether we wake or sleep, we should live together with him."
>
> 1Thes 5:8-10

4.0 Baptisms

"..., Of the doctrine of baptisms, ..." Heb 6:2

4.1 John's Baptism

Reading Mark 1:1-5

> MAR 1:4 John did baptize in the wilderness, and preach the baptism of repentance for the remission of sins.
>
> MAR 1:5 And there went out unto him all the land of Judaea, and they of Jerusalem, and were all baptized of him in the river of Jordan, confessing their sins.

John was sent to prepare 'the way of the Lord'.

> MAR 1:14 Now after that John was put in prison, Jesus came into Galilee, preaching the gospel of the kingdom of God,
>
> MAR 1:15 And saying, The time is fulfilled, and the kingdom of God is at hand: repent ye, and believe the gospel.

Repentance must always come before faith. We must confess that we have done wrong before God will forgive us.

> 1JOHN 1:10 If we say that we have not sinned, we make him a liar, and his word is not in us.

Reading Acts 19:1-6

Paul found disciples who, he thought had been baptised in the name of Jesus. He asked them whether they had received the Holy Spirit. They said no, they hadn't heard of the Holy Spirit. Paul guessed something was wrong, so he asked them what they had been baptized into. He corrected the situation by proclaiming the Gospel and baptising the disciples in the name of Jesus.

> MAT 28:18 And Jesus came and spake unto them, saying, All power is given unto me in heaven and in earth.
>
> MAT 28:19 Go ye therefore, and teach all nations, baptizing them in the name of the Father, and of the Son, and of the Holy Ghost:
>
> MAT 28:20 Teaching them to observe all things whatsoever I have commanded you: and, lo, I am with you alway, even unto the end of the world. Amen.

Note that in the above scripture, there is no mention of the baptism of repentance. If we look at Acts 8:38-39 we see that Philip baptised the Eunuch only once. John's Baptism of repentance has been superseded by baptism in the name[34] of the Father, and of the Son, and of the Holy Ghost.

---

[34] it says name, not names, because “The Lord our God is one Lord” (Mark 12:29). There is only one God. The Father, the Son and the Holy Ghost are not three God's.

4.2 Water Baptism

> "Know ye not that so many of us as were baptised into Jesus Christ were baptised into his death?"
>
> Romans 6:3

Before we deal with water baptism, it is useful to examine some background material so that the references we will be using from the Bible may be placed in context.

4.2.1 Born of the Spirit

Man has three parts: the spirit, the soul and the body.

> "And the very God of peace sanctify you wholly [completely]; and I pray God your whole spirit and soul and body be preserved blameless unto the coming of our Lord Jesus Christ."
>
> 1Thes 5:23

Reading John 1:1-13

> "But as many as received him, to them gave he power to become the sons of God, even to them that believe on his name:
>
> Which were born, not of blood, nor of the will of the flesh, nor of the will of man, but of God."
>
> John 1:12-13

Reading John 3:1-9

Nicodemus asked Jesus "How can a man be born when he is old?"[35] Jesus answers this important question in verses 14-18 (John 3).

> "... whosoever believeth in him should not perish, but have eternal life."
>
> John 3:15

The Bible compares believing the gospel to the birth of a child.

> "Whosoever believeth that Jesus is the Christ is born of God: ..."
>
> 1John 5:1

It is a result of faith that we are born of the Spirit. If we compare the previous scripture (1John 5:1) with the following scriptures;

> "God is a Spirit: ..." John 4:24

[35] John 3:4

"… that which is born of the Spirit is spirit" John 3:6

It is evident that the child born of God is a spirit. Some astounding things are said about the child born of God.

> "Whosoever is born of God doth not commit sin; for his [God's] seed remaineth in him: and he can not sin, because he is born of God."
> 1John 3:9

> "For whatsoever is born of God overcometh the world: and this is the victory that overcometh the world even our faith."
> 1John 5:4

It is a result of faith in Christ: belief in his death for our sins and in his resurrection, that we are born of the spirit. The part of us thus born is perfect in every way, however it is not fully grown, but a babe.

> "And I, brethren, could not speak unto you as unto spiritual, but as unto carnal, even as unto babes in Christ. I have fed you with milk, and not with meat: for hither to ye were not able to bear it, neither yet now are ye able."
> 1Cor 3:1-2

It may be asked what a child born of the spirit is to feed on.

> "Wherefore laying aside all malice, and all guile, and hypocrisies, and envies, and all evil speakings,
>
> As new born babes, desire the sincere milk of the word, that ye may grow thereby:
>
> If so be ye have tasted that the Lord is gracious."
> 1Peter 2:1-3

Malice, guile, hypocrisies, envies, evil speakings are things that can taint the milk, making it go sour and unpalatable. The word is vital for newly born Christians. Babies don't eat a lot, but they do eat regularly. They don't feed on solid food either. Some books in the Bible are easier to understand than others. Most people like the stories about how David slew Goliath [1Sam 16-17], how Moses was hidden in a fissure in the rock as God passed by [Exod 32-34], the story of Adam and Eve [Gen 1-5] and of Jesus' birth [Mat 1-2, Luke 1-2]. I also like 1John, Jonah, and Elijah the prophet [1Kings 16:25-22:53, 2Kings 1-2]. Other References may be found in the footnote[36]. I suppose the crucifixion and resurrection of Christ should not be missed. This is recorded at the end of Matthew, Mark, Luke and John.

[36] Other reading: The story of Noah and the ark [Gen 6-9], Colossians, Ephesians, Philippians, 1Thessalonians, 1 and 2 Timothy, 1Peter, James.

4.2.2 Redemption

The word 'redeem' means to buy something which was yours. An example of the use of this word in the old testament is when a person sold a house in a walled city. That person had the right for one year to buy back the house. If he did so, it would be said that he had redeemed his house.

> LEV 25:29 And if a man sell a dwelling house in a walled city, then he may redeem it within a whole year after it is sold; within a full year may he redeem it.
>
> LEV 25:30 And if it be not redeemed within the space of a full year, then the house that is in the walled city shall be established for ever to him that bought it throughout his generations: it shall not go out in the jubilee.

God never forgets us. It is he that made us. At the first we were his. And praise the Lord we are and ever will be his if we hold fast the Gospel firm unto the end.

> PSA 139:13 For thou hast possessed my reins: thou hast covered me in my mother's womb.
>
> PSA 139:14 I will praise thee; for I am fearfully and wonderfully made: marvellous are thy works; and that my soul knoweth right well.
>
> PSA 139:15 My substance was not hid from thee, when I was made in secret, and curiously wrought in the lowest parts of the earth.
>
> PSA 139:16 Thine eyes did see my substance, yet being unperfect; and in thy book all my members were written, which in continuance were fashioned, when as yet there was none of them.
>
> PSA 139:17 How precious also are thy thoughts unto me, O God! how great is the sum of them!
>
> PSA 139:18 If I should count them, they are more in number than the sand: when I awake, I am still with thee.

We have been sold through sin.

> ISA 50:1 Thus saith the LORD, Where is the bill of your mother's divorcement, whom I have put away? or which of my creditors is it to whom I have sold you? Behold, for your iniquities have ye sold yourselves, and for your transgressions is your mother put away.
>
> ISA 50:2 Wherefore, when I came, was there no man? when I called, was there none to answer? Is my hand shortened at all, that it cannot redeem? or have I no power to deliver? behold, at my rebuke I dry up the sea, I make the rivers a wilderness: their fish stinketh, because there is no water, and dieth for thirst.
>
> "... : but I am carnal, sold under sin."
> Rom 7:14

4.2.3 Redemption of the Body

Our bodies have been sold under sin and in this lifetime, they are not redeemed by God.

> "And not only they [the whole of God's creation], but ourselves also, which have the first fruits of the Spirit, even we ourselves groan within ourselves, waiting for the adoption, to wit, the redemption of our body."
> Rom 8:23[37]

> "... sin that dwelleth in me. For I know that in me (that is, in my flesh,) dwelleth no good thing: for to will is present with me; but how to perform that which is good I find not."
> Rom 7:17-18

Our flesh is without strength to save us, because of sin which dwells in our bodies. Jesus was born, but not with sin in his body. His body I suppose, is the only one in creation which sin hasn't corrupted.

> "... , God sending his own Son in the likeness of sinful flesh, ..."
> Rom 8:3

> "… : the Spirit indeed is willing, but the flesh is weak (strengthless)."
> Mat 26:41

> Wherefore, as by one man sin entered into the world, and death by sin; and so death passed upon all men, for that all have sinned: …
> Rom 5:12

> "… ; but with the flesh [I serve] the law of sin."
> Rom 7:25

> "That as sin hath reigned unto death, ..."
> Rom 5:21

I suppose sin is like a kingdom, in which we once lived. The laws and decrees of sin held authority over us.

Reading 1Cor 15:50-58

Our bodies will be changed at the resurrection. This corruptible body must put on incorruption. At this time, our bodies will be redeemed.

In view of all this, Paul asks the following question:

---

[37] All of creation waits [like a covering sheet being taken off an ornamental vase, or a stage curtain opening] for the appearance of the sons and daughters of God (cf. 'manifestation' Rom 8:18). I suppose as people wait for the parents to bring out their new born child, so creation waits for God and his sons and daughters to be revealed.

> "O wretched man that I am! who shall deliver me from the body of this death?" Rom 7:24

It is Jesus who delivers us.

> "who shall deliver me from the body of this death? I thank God through Jesus Christ our lord. So then ..." Rom 7:24-25

OK, with God's help we've finished the background material. We will now begin discussion of water baptism, and later return to the matter of dealing with sin. Water baptism doesn't save us from sin, but it does represent how Jesus has made a way for us to come to God the Father through his death and resurrection. This way leads to the Holy of Holies and ends sin.

4.3 Death and Resurrection with Christ

Reading Rom 6:1-18 [died, buried and living with him]

The word baptise is a transliteration of a Greek word meaning to completely cover with water; to make whelmed (i.e. fully wet). The original translators did not wish to obviously contradict the religious practices of the time, so instead of translating it as 'immerse' they wrote the phonetics of the Greek word in English 'baptizo'. This was then anglicised as 'baptise'.

A water baptism is a ceremony where a person is immersed completely in water, and then comes up out of the water. An example of this is when Jesus was baptised.

> MAR 1:9 And it came to pass in those days, that Jesus came from Nazareth of Galilee, and was baptised of John in Jordan.
>
> MAR 1:10 And straightway coming up out of the water, he saw the heavens
>
> opened, and the Spirit like a dove descending upon him:
>
> MAR 1:11 And there came a voice from heaven, saying, Thou art my beloved Son, in whom I am well pleased.

Water baptism symbolises our death with Christ on the cross. The ceremony of water baptism depicts what has already happened in the life of a believer. How he has been identified with Christ in his death, burial and resurrection. The baptism is similar to a sea burial conducted by the Navy for a man killed in battle. A Christian is immersed in water symbolising his death with Christ, then as Christ rose from the dead, so we come up out of the watery grave, resurrected to God.

We have died with Christ.

> "I am crucified with Christ: ..."
> Gal 2:20
>
> “Knowing this, that our old man is crucified with him, ...”
> ROM 6:6
>
> "For ye are dead, and your life is hid with Christ in God."
> Col 3:3

Colossians 3:3 tells how we have died, and at the moment we are hidden with Christ. We are hidden together with him in his death and in his life.

> ROM 6:8 Now if we be dead with Christ, we believe that we shall also live with him: ...

We have been resurrected with Christ.

"But God, who is rich in mercy, for his great love wherewith he loved us, even when we were dead in sins, hath quickened us [made us alive] together with Christ, (by grace ye are saved;) and hath raised us up together[38], and made us sit together in heavenly places in Christ Jesus:

That in the ages to come he might shew the exceeding riches of his grace in his kindness toward us through Christ Jesus. For by grace are ye saved through faith; and that not of yourselves: it is the gift of God:

Not of works, lest any man should boast."
Eph 2:4-9

HOS 6:2 After two days will he revive us: in the third day he will raise us up, and we shall live in his sight.

"Buried with him[39] [Christ] in baptism, wherein also ye are risen with him ..."
Col 2:12

It is because we have been crucified with Christ, that we have been reconciled to God.

"And you, that were sometime alienated and enemies in your mind by wicked works, yet now hath he reconciled *in the body of his* flesh through death, to present[40] you holy and unblameable and unreprovable in his sight: ..."
Col 1:21-22

It is through trust in Christ that we are saved. We will be tempted until our bodies are redeemed at the resurrection. Never the less when we stand by faith with God, through his help and mercy, we reign and endure temptations.

“Who shall lay anything to the charge of Gods elect? It is God that justifieth.[41]”
Romans 8:33

God is for us, he loves us.

“Nay, in all these things we are more than conquerors[42] through him that loved us.”
Rom 8:37

He has rescued us from death, and brought us back to himself.

---

[38] cf. Col 2:12-13

[39] G4197 *to inter in company with* fig. to assimilate spiritually (to Christ by a sepulture as to sin). From G4862 *union* (i.e. with or together) and G2290 –to celebrate funeral rights i.e. to inter (i.e. put a dead body in the ground).

[40] G3936
From G3844 and G2476; to *stand beside*, i.e. (as this is trans. with the dir. obj = "you") to *exhibit, proffer*, (specially) *recommend*, (fig.) *substantiate (i.e. support or prove truth of)*; [ref Strong's and Oxford Dictionaries]

[41] G1344 to render just or innocent.

[42] 5245 to vanquish beyond, i.e. gain a decisive victory: - *more than conquer*.
from
-5228 a primary preposition; “over”. General ideas are: above, beyond, superior to, more than.
-3528 ‘to subdue’ (from 3529)
-3529 nike conquest (abstr.), i.e. fig. means of success:- victory.

"*Who his own self bare our sins in his own body (onto) the tree*[43]*, that we, being dead to sins, should live unto righteousness*: by whose stripes ye were healed. For ye were as sheep going astray; but are now returned unto the Shepherd and Bishop of your souls."

1Pet 2:24,25

4.3.1 The End of the Law through Death.

Reading Rom 7:1-6

"... the law hath dominion over a man as long as he liveth"

Comparing us to a woman re-marrying after the death of her husband, it says

"… ye also are become dead to the law by the body of Christ; that ye should be married to another, even to him who is raised from the dead, ..."

Rom 7:4

We were married to the law, but because we have died, we were able to (and did) marry Christ. This means the law has no more authority over us.

"But now we are delivered from the law, that being dead wherein we were held; ..."

Rom 7:6

"… that like as Christ was raised up from the dead by the glory of the Father, even so we also should walk[44] in newness of life."

Rom 6:4

We have been redeemed from under the law with the precious blood of Christ.

"But when the fulness of the time was come, God sent forth his Son, made of a woman, made under the law, to redeem them that were under the law, that we might receive the adoption of sons."

Gal 4:4-5

It is not God's plan that we should return to the law.

"For Christ is the end[45] of the law [as a means] for righteousness to every one that believeth."

Rom 10:4

---

[43] or *Timber*

[44] Love is a choice that we continually make.

"... when Jesus knew that his hour was come that he should depart out of this world unto the Father, having loved his own which were in the world, he loved them unto the end." John 13:1

[45] or *terminus*. From a primary word tellō (to set out for a definite point or goal)

Note also Mat 5:17-20. Jesus completed/fulfilled the law on our behalf, because we could not[186].

4.3.2 The New Covenant

Reading Hebrews chapter 8 to chapter 10v24

We are under a new covenant. For those who believe, the law is at the end of its usefulness.

> "For I will be merciful to their unrighteousness, and their sins and their iniquities will I remember no more. In that he saith, A new covenant, he hath made the first old. Now that which decayeth and waxeth old is ready to vanish away."
>
> Heb 8:12-13

Under this new covenant, we receive mercy.

> "For by grace are ye saved through faith; ..."
>
> Eph 2:8

There is only one way of standing before God with a pure conscience. It doesn't matter how good we are.

> "Christ is become of no effect unto you, whosoever of you are justified by the law; ye are fallen from grace."
>
> Gal 5:4

It is through Christ's sacrifice for our sins on the cross, that we are able to draw nigh to God.

> "But this man [Jesus Christ], after he had offered one sacrifice for sins for ever, sat down on the right hand of God; from henceforth expecting till his enemies be made his footstool. For by one offering he hath perfected for ever them that are sanctified. Whereof the Holy Ghost also is a witness to us[46]: ... , This is the covenant that I will make with them ... and [saith the Lord] their sins and iniquities will I remember no more. Now where remission of these is, there is no more offering for sin."
>
> Heb 10:12-18

Jesus made one sacrifice and through it perfected us forever. God said that he wouldn't remember our sins any more. There is no point in giving sacrifices for sins because God does not and will not remember our sins.

Reading Heb 9:1-8

> "The Holy Ghost this signifying. that the way into the holiest of all was not yet made manifest, while as the first tabernacle [or the Temple] was yet standing: ..."
>
> Heb 9:8

The veil of the temple used to be the way to enter into the holiest place on earth, where God dwelt. But when Jesus died, the veil was ripped in two[47]. We now enter into the holiest place,

---

[46] Jer 31:31-34 'Behold, the days come, saith the Lord, that I will make a new covenant with the house of Israel, ...'

[47] "And, behold, the veil of the temple was rent in twain from the top to the bottom; ..." Mat 27:51 (also in Mark

through Christ's death and resurrection. Through faith in our Lord we are able to stand in the Holy of Holies.

> "Having therefore, brethren, boldness to enter into the holiest by the blood of Jesus, By a new and living way, which he hath consecrated for us, through the veil, that is to say, his flesh; And having an high priest over the house of God; Let us draw near ... "
>
> Heb 10:19-22

> "Seeing then that we have a great high priest, that is passed into the heavens, Jesus the Son of God, let us hold fast our profession.
>
> For we have not an high priest which cannot be touched with the feeling of our infirmities; but was in all points tempted like as we are, yet without sin.
>
> Let us therefore come boldly unto the throne of grace, that we may obtain mercy, and find grace to help in time of need."
>
> Heb 4:14-16

Who are the ones Paul is talking about who need to come to God to find mercy?

> "Let us …"

God watches over us and looks after us.

> Blessed be God, even the Father of our Lord Jesus Christ, the Father of mercies, and the God of all comfort; who comforteth us in all our tribulation, that we may be able to comfort them which are in any trouble, by the comfort wherewith we ourselves are comforted of God."
>
> 2Cor 1:3-4

The safest place to be is in the sanctuary, in God's presence.

> "He that dwelleth in the secret place of the most High shall abide under the shadow of the Almighty. I will say of the Lord, He is my refuge and my fortress: my God; in him will I trust."
>
> Psalm 91:1-2

Distinguishing between the law and faith towards God, has been a problem since the beginning of the church.

Reading Gal 4:19-5:6

Abraham had two sons. One of a bondwoman, and one of the free. One corresponds to the law, the other to the new covenant through faith in Christ's death and resurrection.

This message was written to people desiring to be under the law.

> "Tell me, ye that desire to be under the law, do ye not hear the law?"
>
> Gal 4:21

15:38 & Luke 23:45)

Paul says that the law "gendereth to bondage", and that "the son of the bondwoman shall not be heir with the son of the free woman."

There is no mixing of the law and Faith.

> "So then, brethren, we are not children of the bondwomen, but of the free."
> Gal 4:31

The difference between legalism (working under the law) and faith is love. If we are under the law, we are in slavery. Christ hath made us free so that whatever we do, would be a result of love (Gal 5:6). Many Christians have a yoke "which neither our forefathers nor we were able to bear[48]".

> "I do not frustrate the grace of God: for if righteousness come by the law, then Christ is dead in vain."
> Gal 2:21

Righteousness never comes by fulfilling a set of rules. It is Christ's death that saves us.

> "For if that [the ministry of a guilty verdict and death] which <u>is done away</u>[49] was glorious, much more, that which remaineth is glorious."
> 2Cor 3:11

We can't spend our time looking back at the law to see if we're justified. Done away. God never expects us to work for righteousness. The law is done away, when Christ died he cried, "It is *finished*"[50], the veil ripped in two. Never look back to the law as the means of coming to God.

---

48 Acts 15:10-11

49 Literally 'to *be* (*render*) *entirely idle* (*useless*)'. [cf. Luke 13:7 'cumbereth', Rom 6:6 'destroyed', Rom 7:2 'loosed', Gal 5:4 'no effect']

50 Jesus died at 3pm in the afternoon. He cried out once, "My God, my God, why hast thou forsaken me?" And then he said "I thirst". A person ran and gave him to drink by putting a sponge soaked in vinegar on a stick and lifting the sponge up to his lips. He then cried out the last time "It is finished." The last words of Jesus were "Father, into thy hands I commend my spirit", he then bowed his head, and gave up the ghost (cf. Appendix E, page 246). The veil of the Temple was torn in half from top to bottom and there was an earthquake. The day was dark from 12pm in the afternoon until Jesus death. I suppose the winds came and drove the clouds away when Christ died.
<u>Note</u>:
The word G3908 'commend' (into thy hands I commend my spirit) is also (sometimes 1Tim 1:18, 2Tim 2:2, 1Pet 4:19) translated as 'commit'. It means 'place alongside' i.e. present to. It is derived from a word which means 'place in a passive or horizontal posture'. Taking a few liberties, a person who takes something dear to them and lays it down in front of someone would be 'committing'. I suppose this is like a small church service where, after worshipping God, one kneels before the altar, and presents ones life to God.
"Wherefore let them that suffer according to the will of God *commit* the keeping of their souls to him in well doing, as unto a faithful Creator." 1Pet 4:19

4.4 Spirit vs. the Flesh

We have a conflict. The Spirit is perfect. The flesh is thoroughly sinful. Our mind may be subject to one of two kingdoms: that from above, or from below. It is possible to be subject to God through Christ, or to the natural things of this world.

> "Because the carnal mind is enmity against God: for it is not subject to the law of God, neither in deed can be." Rom 8:7

We are stuck in the middle, with both the spirit and the body vying for our attention[51].

> ROM 6:12 Let not sin therefore reign in your mortal body, that ye should obey it in the lusts thereof.
>
> ...
>
> ROM 6:15 What then? shall we sin, because we are not under the law, but under grace? God forbid.
>
> ROM 6:16 Know ye not, that to whom ye yield[52] yourselves servants to obey, his servants ye are to whom ye obey; whether of sin unto death, or of obedience[53] unto righteousness?

4.4.1 Freedom from Sin

> "Jesus answered them, Verily, verily, I say unto you, Whosoever committeth sin is the servant of sin."
> John 8:34

God offers us an alternative to serving sin.

Reading Isaiah 55:1-11

> Ho, every one that thirsteth, come ye to the waters, and he that hath no money; come ye, buy, and eat; yea, come, buy wine and milk without money and without price.
>
> Wherefore do ye spend money for that which is not bread? and your labour for that which satisfieth not? hearken diligently unto me, and eat ye that which is good, and let your soul delight itself in fatness.

---

[51] "Turn your eyes upon Jesus, look full in his wonderful face, and the things of earth will grow strangely dim, in the light of his glory and grace." -song, author Helen Howarth Lemmel, public domain.

[52] Greek 3936
to *stand beside (*from G3844 'near' and G2476 'to stand')
cf. "present (G3936) your bodies a living sacrifice, … unto God, ..." Rom 12:1
& "...; even so now yield (G3936) your members servants to righteousness ..." Rom 6:19.
Also can signify 'to present a person or thing', or 'to be at hand (or ready) to aid' in addition to its literal meaning.

[53] G5218 *attentive hearkening* (by implic.) *compliance* or *submission*
From G5219
G5219 From G5259 and G191; to *hear under* (as a *subordinate*), that is, to *listen attentively*; by implication to *heed* or *conform* to a command or authority: - hearken, be obedient to, obey.

Incline your ear, and come unto me: hear, and your soul shall live; and I will make an everlasting covenant with you, even the sure mercies of David.

Isaiah 55:1-3

We know that in time past we sinned against God.

“... ye were without Christ, being aliens[54] from the commonwealth of Israel, and strangers from the covenants of promise, having no hope, and without God in the world: ...”

Eph 2:12

"To open their eyes, and to turn them from darkness to light, and from the power of Satan unto God, that they may receive forgiveness of sins, and inheritance among them which are sanctified by faith that is in me."

- The Lord Jesus (Acts 26:18)

When we first believed in Christ, Jesus set us free.

"If the son therefore shall make you free, ye shall be free indeed."

John 8:36

ROM 6:6 Knowing this, that our old man is crucified with him, that the body of sin might be destroyed, that henceforth we should not serve sin.

ROM 6:7 For he that is dead is freed[55] from sin.[56]

"For sin shall not have dominion over you: ..."

Rom 6:14

I remember some church services where the speaker would talk about holiness and dedication to God. Often, this brings no benefit, but the acknowledgement again of our sin and helplessness.

"... for to will[57] is present with me; but to fully work good[58], I do not find."

Rom 7:18[59]

They used to call the front of the church the altar. And we could at the end of the service go up and be prayed for, and we could ask God for help. Those were great times where God would draw near.

---

[54] G526 to *estrange away*, i.e. (passively and fig.) to be *non-participant*. From G575 and a derivative of G245.
G575 a primary particle; “*off*” i.e. *away* (from something near), in various senses (of place, time, or relation; lit. or fig.). In composition (as a prefix) it usually denotes separation, departure, cessation, completion, reversal, etc.
G245 *another's* i.e. not ones own; by extension *foreign, not akin, hostile.*

[55] rendered just or innocent [equitable in character or act, right (as self evident)]

[56] “The one that has died, has been justified from sin. ... Count yourselves dead indeed to sin, but alive to God in Christ ... Accordingly, do not let sin rule in your mortal body, that ye should obey it ... but yield yourselves unto God, ... For sin shall not have dominion over you: ...” Rom 6:7,11-13 [a translation]

[57] to *determine* - i.e., *choose* or *prefer* (lit. or fig.); by implication to *wish*, i.e. *be inclined* to, future tense - to *be about to*; by Hebraism to *delight in.*

[58] properly *beautiful*, but chiefly (fig.) *good*

[59] a translation. KJV is "... for to will is present with me; but how to perform that which is good I find not."

"For a day in thy courts is better than a thousand."
Psalm 84:10

I think much of the reason for God's actions was the sincerity of the congregation in dedicating their whole life to God.

I suppose the greatest love we can show to God is to lay down our life.

> "Greater love hath no one than this, that someone lay down them self their own life[60] for their friends."
> John 15:13[61]

Before Jesus came we had to obey sin, but now we are free to choose to present ourselves to God. When we dedicate our body to God, and lay it down before him, sin will not rule over us. God knows that when he has our bodies, he has what is in the body: our soul and our spirit - He has us, safe in his arms[62].

4.4.2 Under Christ

> If by any means I might attain unto the resurrection of the dead. Not as though I had already attained, either were already perfect: but I follow after, if that I may lay hold of that for which also under Christ Jesus, I am laid hold of.
> Phil 3:11-12[63]

Praise the Lord, it is not just our efforts which save us. God mercifully has laid hold of us by the scruff of the neck and pointed us in the direction of home. He loves us, but sometimes we need a bit of help to get our bearings straight.

I believe we have been crucified with Christ and now we have a choice who we serve. We can dedicate our bodies to serving God, or we can serve the things of this world.

> "Now the works of the flesh[64] are manifest, which are these; Adultery, fornication, uncleanness, lasciviousness, idolatry, witchcraft, hatred, variance, emulations, wrath, strife, seditions, heresies, envyings, murders, drunkenness, revellings, and such like: of the which I tell you before, as I have also told you in time past, that they which do such things shall not inherit the kingdom of God.
> Gal 5:19-21

It is the body ('our members' or 'the flesh') that does works. There is a key to being free from sin. This key is to present not just our works, but our 'members' (i.e. our bodies and effectively ourselves) to God[65].

---

[60] or *breath.*

[61] a translation

[62] I suppose laying down our life includes laying down our heart, and soul, and mind and strength before God, and putting our trust in him to look after us.

[63] a translation

[64] flesh (as stripped of the skin)

[65] I believe it is only a combination of death with Christ at the cross, and serving God continually out of love that it is possible to be free from sin.

> "... even so now yield your members[66] servants to righteousness unto holiness."
> Romans 6:19

> Neither yield ye your members as instruments of unrighteousness unto sin: but yield yourselves unto God, as those that are alive from the dead, and your members as instruments of righteousness unto God.
> Rom 6:13

The way that they should be presented to God is as a sacrifice. God is able to take the offering (or sacrifice) we make of our bodies and to sanctify us, and make us holy.

> I invite you near therefore brothers, by the pity of God (the judge), that ye present your whole body as a living sacrifice sacred fully agreeable to God, which is your logical service. And don't become like this age[67] but otherwise refresh your intellect[68] that ye may trial[69] the determination of God which is good and well agreeable and perfect.
> Rom 12:2 [a translation]

This living sacrifice resembles our baptism with Christ when we first believed: how we died, and were raised with Christ.

> "Buried with him[70] (Christ) in baptism, wherein also ye are risen with him ..."
> Col 2:12

> I am crucified with Christ: nevertheless I live; ... I live by the faith of the Son of God, who loved me, and gave[71] himself for me.
> Gal 2:20

By faith we can die daily and have all our life totally sanctified "being made conformable unto his death[72]". We can look to Jesus. If we present our body and lay it down before him as a living sacrifice, we can trust God that he will see to it that the evil works of the body are put to death. It is at the cross that sin loses its grip on us.

> "For he that is dead is freed from sin." Rom 6:7

I think it is together with God that we have victory over sin. When we dedicate our body, our works, hopes and dreams to God, and lay them down before him, sin shall not rule over us.

"I need thee every hour; stay thou near by; temptations lose their power when thou art nigh."
A song, authors: Annie S. Hawks & Robert Lowry

66 a *limb* or *part* of the body
67 perpetuity
68 intellect
69 G1381 *to test* (lit. or fig.); by implication '*to approve*'
70 G4197 *to inter in company with* fig. to assimilate spiritually (to Christ by a sepulture as to sin). From G4862 *union* (i.e. with or together) and G2290 –to celebrate funeral rights i.e. to inter (i.e. put a dead body in the ground).
71 or *surrender* ['*near i.e. from beside* (lit. or fig.)' & '*to give*']. Often translated as 'betray', when someone else gives someone over to the jailers or their enemies.
72 Philippians 3:10

> "Neither yield ye your members as instruments of unrighteousness ... but yield yourselves unto God, as those that are alive from the dead, and your members as instruments of righteousness unto God. For sin shall not have dominion over you: for ye are not under the law ..." Rom 6:13-14

> "But now being made free from sin, and become servants to God, ..."[73]
> Rom 6:22

I think it is good to present our bodies as a living sacrifice over and over, so that the power of Christ may rest upon us, and so that we may know him[74].

> "I protest by your rejoicing which I have in Christ Jesus our Lord, I die daily."
> - Paul the Apostle (1Cor 15:31)

I believe it is possible to live so full of the Holy Spirit, and continually engaged in the work of the Lord, that all things of this world are crucified and all ones life is holy, sanctified and consecrated unto the Lord.

When we come to God through Jesus Christ, we meet God at the foot of the cross[75]. It is in his holy presence we find that we are free. It is then we see that God has fought for us, and all our old enemies are dead, and can not arise[76]. It is then we stand victorious with Christ Jesus our Lord and peace abounds like a river and righteousness as the waves[77] of the sea.

> "... in[78] thy presence is fullness of joy; ..." Psalm 16:11

> "Rejoice[79] in the Lord, O ye righteous: for praise is comely[80] for the upright.
> Psalm 33:1; (cf. Psalm 147:1)

> "Now the Lord is that Spirit[81]: and where the Spirit of the Lord is, there is Liberty[82]."
> 2Cor 3:17

Hallelujah. Praise the Lord.

> "He also exalteth the horn of his people, the praise of all his saints; even of the children of Israel, a people near unto him. Praise ye the Lord."
> Psalm 148:14

---

73 I think although we are the sons and daughters of God by faith in Christ, we also work as servants for our Father [cf. Mat 21:28-32 & '... as a man spareth his own son that serveth him.' Mal 3:17]

74 Philippians 3:8-10

75 Consider the work of the cross: perfect in every respect, perfect in every aspect.

76 cf. Exod 14:21-30 [passing through the sea]

77 Isaiah 48:18

78 properly "nearness", near

79 properly to *creak (or emit a loud and harsh sound)*, i.e. to *shout* (usually for joy).

80 to be comfortable, beautiful, like how one makes something to be at home.

81 a *current* of air, i.e. *breath* (blast) or a *breeze* by analogy or figuratively a *spirit*

82 *freedom* from G1658
G1658 *unrestrained* (to *go* at pleasure), i.e. (as a citizen) *not a slave* (whether freeborn or manumitted) or (generally) *exempt* (from obligation or liability)

4.5 Obedience to the Father

> But God be thanked, that ye were the servants of sin, but ye have obeyed from the heart that form of doctrine which was delivered you.
>
> Rom 6:17

Obedience is a result of what is in the heart. I believe that as Christians, we are supposed to follow after the Spirit. If we do, we are free to do anything we want.[83]

> "But if ye be led of the Spirit, ye are not under the law." Gal 5:18

4.5.1 The Spirit of the Law

What does the Spirit expect of us? We are no longer under the law. However God still wants us to obey the spirit of the Law.

> MAR 12:29 And Jesus answered him, The first of all the commandments is, Hear, O Israel; The Lord our God is one Lord:
>
> MAR 12:30 And thou shalt love the Lord thy God with all thy heart, and with all thy soul, and with all thy mind, and with all thy strength: this is the first commandment.
>
> MAR 12:31 And the second is like, namely this, Thou shalt love thy neighbour as thyself. There is none other commandment greater than these.
>
> MAT 22:40 On these two commandments hang all the law and the prophets.

Reading Luke 10:30-37 [Jerusalem to Jericho - real love]

> MAR 12:32 And the scribe said unto him, Well, Master, thou hast said the truth: for there is one God; and there is none other but he:
>
> MAR 12:33 And to love him with all the heart, and with all the understanding, and with all the soul, and with all the strength, and to love his neighbour as himself, is more than all whole burnt offerings and sacrifices.
>
> MAR 12:34 And when Jesus saw that he answered discreetly, he said unto him, Thou art not far from the kingdom of God. And no man after that durst ask him any question.

---

[83] Does a man who follows the Spirit keep the law? He neither 'keeps it', nor 'not keeps it'. He is dead and the law is 'done away' (2Cor 3:11). A man who believes in Christ has ceased to be a murderer, an adulterer or a covetous man. Will a man who loves God be unfaithful to him? In the measure that he loves God, he will be faithful. Cf. p97-98, chapt. 10 “Life in the Spirit” in “Ever increasing Faith” by Smith Wigglesworth revised edition 1971, printed 1992.

ROM 13:8 Owe no man any thing, but to love one another: for he that loveth another hath fulfilled the law.

ROM 13:9 For this, Thou shalt not commit adultery, Thou shalt not kill, Thou shalt not steal, Thou shalt not bear false witness, Thou shalt not covet; and if there be any other commandment, it is briefly comprehended in this saying, namely, Thou shalt love thy neighbour as thyself.

ROM 13:10 Love worketh no ill to his neighbour: therefore love is the fulfilling of the law.

ROM 7:6 But now we are delivered[49] from the law, that being dead wherein we were held; that we should serve in newness of spirit, and not in the oldness of the letter.

The spirit of the law is Love. If the Gospel is not preached with love as a central theme, we have missed the mark.

Brethren, I write no new commandment unto you, but an old commandment which ye had from the beginning. The old commandment is the word which ye have heard from the beginning.
1John 2:7

For this is the message that ye heard from the beginning, that we should love one another.
1John 3:11

And this is his commandment, That we should believe on the name of his Son Jesus Christ, and love one another, as he gave us commandment.
1John 3:23

And above all these things put on charity, which is the bond of perfectness.
Col 3:14

And we have known and believed the love that God hath to us. God is love; and he that dwelleth in love dwelleth in God, and God in him.
1John 4:16

God is love. Should not children grow up to be like their father? The greatest of all things is love. Love is what God is really looking for. Man looks on the outward appearance - the works that we do. If we walk in love, we fulfil the spirit of the law.

4.5.2 Faith and Love work.

Faith comes from the heart.

> For with the heart man believeth unto righteousness; and with the mouth confession is made unto salvation.
>
> Rom 10:10

Love is what gives faith its motivation to act.

> For in Jesus Christ neither circumcision availeth any thing, nor uncircumcision; but faith which worketh by love.
>
> Gal 5:6

Obedience out of love and faith results in works.

> He that hath my commandments, and keepeth them, he it is that loveth me: ...
>
> John 14:21

I think obedience comes from love. Love doesn't come from obedience.

> For this is the love of God, that we keep his commandments: and his commandments are not grievous.
>
> 1John 5:3

Only works which result from love are of any value.

> Though I speak with the tongues of men and of angels, and have not charity, I am become as sounding brass, or a tinkling cymbal.
>
> And though I have the gift of prophecy, and understand all mysteries, and all knowledge; and though I have all faith, so that I could remove mountains, and have not charity, I am nothing.
>
> And though I bestow all my goods to feed the poor, and though I give my body to be burned, and have not charity, it profiteth me nothing.
>
> 1Cor 13:1-3
>
> JOH 15:4 Abide in me, and I in you. As the branch cannot bear fruit of itself, except it abide in the vine; no more can ye, except ye abide in me.
>
> JOH 15:5 I am the vine, ye are the branches: He that abideth in me, and I in him, the same bringeth forth much fruit: for without me ye can do nothing.

In the above two verses, Jesus says that it is out of friendship with him that we do works. The works come as a result of remaining with Jesus. If a vine has a twig grafted to it, the twig grows into a branch and will eventually produce fruit. Today we expect fast food, instant coffee, quick stop petrol. Some things take time. I wish leaders would have some patience with new believers. We all make mistakes. New Christians take time to grow into maturity. As we grow in love, we will become more obedient to the Lord.

> He that hath my commandments, and keepeth them, he it is that loveth me: ...
> John 14:21

Many leaders look on the outward appearance - the works that we do. They see their congregation lacking in works, so they endeavour to get people to do more works. God is not interested in the outward appearance. The real problem is with the heart - often a lack of love for the Lord, or unbelief in the Gospel.

4.5.3 There Remains therefore a Rest for the People of God.

> HEB 4:9 There remaineth therefore a rest to the people of God.
>
> HEB 4:10 For he that is entered into his rest, he also hath ceased from his own works [those which justify him by the law], as God did from his.

When we finish trying to gain acceptance with God by our efforts, we enter into his rest.

> “Now the end of the commandment is charity out of a pure heart, and of a good conscience, and of faith [in God] unfeigned [unpretended]: ...”
> 1Tim 1:5
>
> Knowing this, that the law is not made for a righteous man, but for the lawless and disobedient, for the ungodly and for sinners, for unholy and profane, for murderers of fathers and murderers of mothers, for manslayers, ...
> 1Tim 1:9

The end has not changed, but the means of achieving it has. No longer do we work to fulfil rules, but from our hearts we serve the living God. If we sin, we don't do anything to make up for it - we repent and rest in God's forgiveness.

> “For this is the covenant that I will make with the house of Israel after those days, saith the Lord; I will put my laws into their mind, and write them in their hearts: and I will be to them a God, and they shall be to me a people: ...”
> Heb 8:10
>
> PSA 103:13 Like as a father pitieth his children, so the LORD pitieth them that fear him.
>
> PSA 103:14 For he knoweth our frame; he remembereth that we are dust.

God knows we make mistakes.

> MAT 11:28 Come unto me, all ye that labour and are heavy laden, and I will give you rest.
>
> MAT 11:29 Take my yoke upon you, and learn of me; for I am meek and lowly in heart: and ye shall find rest unto your souls.
>
> MAT 11:30 For my yoke is easy, and my burden is light.

Serving God out of love is not hard work.

4.5.4 What does God expect of me?

Reading Micah 6:2-8

> MIC 6:8 He hath showed thee, O man, what is good; and what doth the LORD require of thee, but to do justly, and to love mercy, and to walk humbly with thy God?

If we do things resulting from love for God and man, and hate evil, I believe we will get a good reward.

There are plans which are different for each one.

> TI2 1:9 Who hath saved us, and called us with an holy calling, not according to our works, but according to his own purpose and grace, which was given us in Christ Jesus before the world began,

> EPH 2:10 For we are his workmanship, created in Christ Jesus unto good works, which God hath before ordained that we should walk in them.

We are all members of the body of Christ (the Church-see Eph 4:12-16). Each member has a different purpose. Each member does different things at different times. Thank God that he doesn't want us to do exactly what everyone else is doing.

I think that if we would try and imagine the best plan for our lives, the one God has chosen is even better.

> ISA 55:7 Let the wicked forsake his way, and the unrighteous man his thoughts: and let him return unto the LORD, and he will have mercy upon him; and to our God, for he will abundantly pardon.

> ISA 55:8 For my thoughts are not your thoughts, neither are your ways my ways, saith the LORD.

> ISA 55:9 For as the heavens are higher than the earth, so are my ways higher than your ways, and my thoughts than your thoughts.

God gives guidance through the written word and by his spirit - by prophecy and by the still small voice of the Holy Spirit.

> This charge I commit unto thee, son Timothy, according to the prophecies which went before on thee, that thou by them mightest war a good warfare;
>
> Holding faith, and a good conscience; which some having put away concerning faith have made shipwreck:
>
> TI1 1:18-19

All scripture is given by inspiration of God, and is profitable for doctrine, for reproof, for correction, for instruction in righteousness:

That the man of God may be perfect, thoroughly furnished unto all good works.
TI2 3:16-17

God can and does speak to us individually.

And thine ears shall hear a word behind thee, saying, This is the way, walk ye in it, when ye turn to the right hand, and when ye turn to the left.
Isaiah 30:21

"My sheep hear my voice, and I know them, and they follow me: ..."
John 10:27

I remember my pastor saying the Word and the Spirit are like two oars on a rowing boat. If we only use one or the other, we will end up going around in circles.

God wants to instruct all his children in the way of righteousness, but it is easy not to listen and to follow after the flesh.

"My son [or my daughter], ..." Prov 23:26

Notice that this is written to Christians, it is not written to unbelievers.

"... give me thine heart, and let thine eyes observe my ways[84]." Prov 23:26

PRO 4:1 Hear, ye children, the instruction of a father, and attend to know understanding.

PRO 4:2 For I give you good doctrine, forsake ye not my law.

We need to look to God for advice. It is God who gives the best counsel, and he's very patient and merciful. He will never turn us away when we come to him 'along the line of faith'. After all we are his sons and daughters.

Knowing God's will helps us make decisions.

COL 1:9 For this cause we also, since the day we heard it, do not cease to pray for you, and to desire that ye might be filled with the knowledge of his will in all wisdom and spiritual understanding;

COL 1:10 That ye might walk worthy of the Lord unto all pleasing, being fruitful in every good work, and increasing in the knowledge of God;

---

[84] H1870 From H1869; a *road* (as *trodden*); fig. a *course* of life or *mode* of action, often adverbial.
H1869 A primitive root; to *tread*; by implication to *walk*; also to *string* a bow (by treading on it in bending).

4.5.5 The Father

> HEB 12:5 And ye have forgotten the exhortation which speaketh unto you as unto children, My son, despise not thou the chastening of the Lord, nor faint when thou art rebuked of him:
>
> HEB 12:6 For whom the Lord loveth he chasteneth, and scourgeth every son whom he receiveth.
>
> HEB 12:7 If ye endure chastening, God dealeth with you as with sons; for what son is he whom the father chasteneth not?
>
> ...
>
> HEB 12:11 Now no chastening for the present seemeth to be joyous, but grievous: nevertheless afterward it yieldeth the peaceable fruit of righteousness unto them which are exercised thereby.

God disciplines us with the objective of teaching us obedience, which results in righteousness. This righteousness is not of the Law of Moses. No longer are we under God's harsh wrath which is upon everyone who seeks him through the Law.

The end of the cross is not primarily to have obedient Christians, but to have sons and daughters who know their Heavenly Father.

> MAT 13:44 Again, the kingdom of heaven is like unto treasure hid in a field; the which when a man hath found, he hideth, and for joy thereof goeth and selleth all that he hath, and buyeth that field.
>
> MAT 13:45 Again, the kingdom of heaven is like unto a merchant man, seeking goodly pearls:
>
> MAT 13:46 Who, when he had found one pearl of great price, went and sold all that he had, and bought it.

We are his treasure. We trust in the living God who gave everything to have us back.

Reading Exod 19:3-6

The Lord speaking to the Children of Israel said

> "... I bare (or lifted) you ..."
>
> "... and brought you unto ..."

What does it say? Not to the Law, not to the land, not to the promises, but to –

> "… myself." Exod 19:4

God is not so interested in what we do as in us[85]. The most important thing to God is us.

> ZEC 2:8 For thus saith the LORD of hosts; ... for he that toucheth you toucheth the apple of his [the Lords] eye.

> "Greater love hath no man than this, that a man lay down his life for his friends."
> John 15:13

> "Who died for us, that, whether we wake or sleep, we should live together with him."
> 1Thes 5:10

I know of only one person who died for me because he loved me.

[85] One of the worst lies around is that God cares more about what we do than us. Often we can get caught up in what we are doing (even though it may be good) and forget God.

4.6 Some Guidelines

Reading Acts 8:26-40

> And as they went on their way, they came unto a certain water: and the eunuch said, See, here is water; what doth hinder me to be baptized?
>
> And Philip said, If thou believest with all thine heart, thou mayest.
>
> And he answered and said, I believe that Jesus Christ is the Son of God.
> Acts 8:36-37

The only condition for water baptism is that we believe the Gospel.

> "... Christ also suffered for us, leaving us an example, that ye should follow his steps: ..."
> 1Peter 2:21

I was about thirteen when I was baptized. I was not particularly impressed with the idea. My Mum however 'encouraged me' to be baptized. My Dad was not a Christian, so I had the option not to be baptized. I eventually conceded that if Christ needed to be baptised, and he expected me to follow him, then I would be baptised also. The first word the Lord spoke to me by prophecy when I was baptised was

> "A step today of obedience ..."

God does command us to be baptised. One is usually hesitant when someone says ‘God commands you to do this” (and generally it is not without good reason that one hesitates). Examine the scriptures, and follow your conscience. One can be apprehensive, but I think as a Father, we can trust God. He only wants the best for us. He knows better than us the reasons for telling us to obey him by being water baptised.

> "... be baptised everyone of you in the name of Jesus Christ ..." Acts 2:38

It appears to me that (in Acts) there was no delay longer than a few days between a person believing and them being baptised.

> "And now why tarriest thou? arise, and be baptised, ..."
> Acts 22:16

> "And he took them the same hour of the night, and washed their stripes; and was baptised, he and all his, straightway."
> Acts 16:33

> "Therefore we are buried with him by baptism into death: ..."
> Rom 6:4

How long do we wait before a burial service? Surely no one waits more than a few weeks? I reckon Christians should be baptised not long after they are saved. If they believe in Christ’s death and resurrection, they are qualified to be baptised.

4.6.1 Water Baptism and Salvation

Water baptism is not required for salvation. Salvation comes by believing the word.

> "For whosoever shall call upon the name of the Lord shall be saved."
> Rom 10:13[86]

> "Whosoever believeth on him shall not be ashamed (put to shame)."
> Rom 10:11[87]

Reading Romans 10:6-17

> "But the righteousness which is of faith speaketh on this wise, ... The word is nigh thee, even in thy mouth, and in thy heart: that is, the word of faith, which we preach; That if thou shalt confess with thy mouth the Lord Jesus, and shalt believe in thine heart that God hath raised him from the dead, thou shalt be saved. For with the heart man believeth unto righteousness; and with the mouth confession is made unto salvation."
> Rom 10:6,8-10

In verse 14 the writer makes plain that the following steps are essential to salvation.

A)	God must send someone to preach	
B)	The preacher must speak the word	
C)	Someone must hear the word	
D)	Someone must believe the word	(the heart)
E)	Someone must call out to the Lord	(the mouth)

I remember a university lecturer once saying. For a student to learn something is quite remarkable. First I must speak it. If everyone is talking, they won't hear it. If everyone's quiet they may hear it, but they may not be paying attention. Even if they have both heard and were paying attention, it doesn't mean they understood. If they do understand, there's still a possibility by the time the exam comes, they'll have forgotten it.

Salvation comes first by the word being sent, and then by a person hearing it, and then (as a matter of choice) believing it.

> "... faith cometh by hearing, and hearing by the word of God."
> Rom 10:17

[86] Acts 2:21, Joel 2:32
[87] Rom 9:32-33; Isaiah 8:14 & 28:16, 1Cor 1:23

"Therefore being justified by faith, we have[88] [not 'will one day have', but 'now have'] peace with God ..."
Rom 5:1

"He that believeth on him is not condemned: ..." John 3:18

"Whosoever believeth that Jesus is the Christ is born of God: ..."
1John 5:1

Believing occurs in the heart, not in that which is seen.

"For with the heart man believeth unto righteousness; ..."
Rom 10:10

The mouth invariably speaks what is in the heart. One can say things which one doesn't believe in ones heart, but eventually what we believe in our hearts, we will say.

"... for out of the abundance of the heart the mouth speaketh."
Mat 12:34

Saying "Jesus save me", makes no difference if we don't mean it.

"... man looketh on the outward appearance, but the Lord looketh on the heart."
1Sam 16:7

Reading Acts 10:34-48

Water Baptism is not required for salvation. In the above story, we read that the Gentiles were saved by the 'hearing of faith'. Paul preaching to those gentiles said

To him give all the prophets witness, that through his name whosoever believeth in him shall receive remission of sins.
Acts 10:43

Note that believing is sufficient to receive remission of sins.

It is evident from the following scripture, that the word saved the Gentiles.

Who shall tell thee words, whereby thou and all thy house shall be saved.
Acts 11:14

And when there had been much disputing, Peter rose up, and said unto them, Men and brethren, ye know how that a good while ago God made choice among us, that the Gentiles by my mouth should hear the word of the gospel, and believe.
Acts 15:7

Believing is not a result of baptism.

---

[88] literally, to *hold*

ACT 15:8 And God, which knoweth the hearts, bare them witness, giving them the Holy Ghost, even as he did unto us;

ACT 15:9 And put no difference between us and them, purifying their hearts by faith.

These Christians were not water baptized, yet their sins had been forgiven.

We read in Mat 3:13-15

MAT 3:13 Then cometh Jesus from Galilee to Jordan unto John, to be baptized of him.

MAT 3:14 But John forbad him, saying, I have need to be baptized of thee, and comest thou to me?

MAT 3:15 And Jesus answering said unto him, Suffer it to be so now: for thus it becometh us to fulfil all righteousness. Then he suffered him.

"Suffer it to be so now: for thus it becometh us to fulfil all righteousness."

Did Jesus need to be baptized to save him from sin? I think <u>not</u>.

"For by grace (ye are) saved *through faith*; ..." Eph 2:8

The scripture applies to us also.

"... for thus it becometh us to fulfil all righteousness." Mat 3:15

Let us now look at some scriptures which could be misinterpreted as saying the opposite.

A)

"He that believeth and is baptized shall be saved; but he that believeth not shall be damned."
Mark 16:16

Note this scripture says nothing about a person who believes and has not been baptised.

B)

Then Peter said unto them, Repent, and be baptized every one of you in the name of Jesus Christ for the remission of sins, and ye shall receive the gift of the Holy Ghost.
Acts 2:38

The prerequisite for baptism is believing.

"And as they went on their way, they came unto a certain water: and the eunuch said, See, here is water; what doth hinder me to be baptized? And Philip said, If thou believest with all thine heart, thou mayest."
Acts 8:36-37

We find (Acts 2:38 above) that repentance, faith and baptism will result in remission of sins. This is true, but it doesn't mean that repentance and faith won't result in remission of sins.

Baptism symbolises Christ's death and resurrection. So we have these scriptures saying repentance and confessing the Gospel sincerely results in the remission of sins.

C)

> PE1 3:20 Which sometime were disobedient, when once the longsuffering of God waited in the days of Noah, while the ark was a preparing, wherein few, that is, eight souls were saved by water.
>
> PE1 3:21 The like figure whereunto even baptism doth also now save us (not the putting away of the filth of the flesh, but the answer of a good conscience toward God,) by the resurrection of Jesus Christ:

The writer elaborates in what way baptism saves us.

> "the answer of a good conscience toward God"

I remember a story of how a boy was being babysitted while his father was away. When he did something wrong, the baby-sitter put a nail in a block of wood. After a while the lad got a bit worried about how many nails there were, knowing that his dad would be coming back soon. He repented, and after a few days of good behaviour the baby-sitter took the nails out of the block of wood. But the wood still had the marks of where the nails had been.

Our conscience is like the piece of wood. When we repent and believe, God takes all our sin away - the nails are taken out. However, the marks of what we have done are still upon our conscience. Through baptism and the cross, even these marks are taken away, and we have ...

> "(... the answer of a good conscience toward God,) (through) the resurrection of Jesus Christ: who is gone into heaven, and is on the right hand of God; ..."
> 1Pet 3:21-22

The power of salvation is in the cross. Looking at all the other scriptures, I conclude that salvation is based on faith.

> ROM 4:3 For what saith the scripture? Abraham believed God, and it was counted unto him for righteousness.
>
> ROM 4:23 Now it was not written for his sake alone, that it was imputed [counted] to him;
>
> ROM 4:24 But for us also, to whom it shall be imputed, if we believe on him that raised up Jesus our Lord from the dead;
>
> ROM 4:25 Who was delivered for our offences, and was raised again for our justification.
>
> ...
>
> ROM 5:1 Therefore being justified by faith, we have peace with God through our Lord Jesus Christ:

4.7 Holy Spirit Baptism

> "Yet now hear, O Jacob my servant; and Israel, whom I have chosen:
>
> Thus saith the LORD that made thee, and formed thee from the womb, which will help thee; Fear not, O Jacob, my servant; and thou, Jesurun, whom I have chosen. For I will pour water upon him that is thirsty, and floods upon the dry ground: I will pour my spirit upon thy seed, and my blessing upon thine offspring: ..."
>
> Isaiah 44:1-3

4.7.1 Introduction

> "This Jesus hath God raised up, whereof we all are witnesses. Therefore being by the right hand of God exalted, and having received of the Father the promise of the Holy Ghost, he hath shed forth this, which ye now see and hear."
>
> Acts 2:32-33

Reading Acts 1:1-5

I was about fifteen when I was baptised in the Holy Spirit, I had heard that it had something to do with 'speaking in tongues'. I had gone up on an altar call at church, and one of the Pastors asked me if I had been baptised in the Holy Spirit. He was a righteous man, and knew God and the scriptures. He asked me if I had heard about the disciples being baptised in Acts. He asked if I was willing for him to pray for me to receive the baptism in the Holy Spirit. Most of this, I took as it came. I had been seeking God, but I had not really looked to be baptised. He laid his hands on me and prayed. After a few minutes he stopped praying and said if any words come to your mind, just speak them. 'Speaking in another tongue', he said is when your spirit bypasses your understanding and talks directly to God. He said the mind is a 'bottleneck' to some of the things a man or woman's spirit wants to say to God. He continued praying and a word did come to my mind. I felt like an idiot to say something when I didn't even know what it meant. Still I didn't want to miss out, so I spoke it. I only spoke this one word a few times, but under the pastors directions I was told to practice my new language.

Well, this all happened shortly before I went to boarding school, and I'm glad it did, because I don't know whether I would still be a Christian today if back then I hadn't been baptised in the Holy Spirit.

The Holy Spirit is 'part' of God.

> "… in the name of the Father, and of the Son, and of the Holy Ghost: ..."
>
> Matthew 28:19

Jesus is the word made flesh.

"That which was from the beginning, which we have heard, which we have seen with our eyes, which we have looked upon, and our hands have handled, of the Word of life; (… which [eternal life] was with the Father, and was manifested unto us;)"
1John 1:1-2

We know that by Jesus the world was made.

JOHN 1:1 In the beginning was the Word, and the Word was with God, and the Word was God. The same was in the beginning with God. All things were made by him, and without him was not anything made, that was made. In him was life; and the life was the light of men.

JOHN 1:14 And the Word was made flesh, and dwelt among us, ... John bare witness of him, …

The only one recorded as being with God during creation was the Spirit of God.

"And the Spirit[89] of God moved[90] upon the face of the waters."
Gen 1:2

Remembering the greatest of all commandments

MAR 12:29 And Jesus answered him, The first of all the commandments is, Hear, O Israel; The Lord our God is one Lord:

MAR 12:30 And thou shalt love the Lord thy God with all thy heart, and with all thy soul, and with all thy mind, and with all thy strength: this is the first commandment.

Our Lord is one Lord. So if we know God the Father, and Jesus, we also know the Holy Spirit. The Holy spirit is not a foreigner to a Christian. And a person may be a Christian without being baptised in the Holy Spirit. Bear with me, and God willing we'll go into one more illustration before looking more closely at the scriptures.

There were two neighbours. They both had gardens. One man had a hose which he used to water his garden, the other had a watering can. The man with the hose was quicker at watering his garden. Suppose the man with the hose neglected to water his garden, while the man with the watering can diligently watered his garden. The garden of the man with the hose would die while that of the man with the watering can would look great.

The water is the Holy Spirit. God has given every believer the Holy Spirit. The man with the watering can is the man who believes and has not been baptised. The man with the hose is the man who believes and has been baptized in the Holy Spirit. With the baptism comes a greater measure of the Holy Spirit. From the illustration, we see that just because a man has been baptised in the Spirit, it doesn't mean he's a 'good' Christian.

When I first heard this story I was annoyed that God hadn't baptised me in the Holy Spirit. This was down right unfair that someone else should have an advantage over me concerning getting

[89] H7307 *wind.* By resemblance *breath,* ... [or] *spirit* (but only of a rational being). From a root meaning *to blow.*
[90] To brood i.e. by implication be relaxed, to move gently, flutter.

treasure in heaven. Well, No God's not unfair and, No someone else did not have an advantage concerning getting treasure in Heaven.

Our reward is based on how we administer the things we have been given by God. The reward a person gets will be based on how much they achieved, and what God gave them to achieve it with. A man who knows nothing about the baptism will get the same reward as someone who has worked equally hard with the baptism of the Holy spirit.

The Holy Spirit wants to help us with the task God has appointed us. We can accomplish much more watering with a hose. Who wants to limit themselves to a small work for God, when he offers us through the baptism of the Holy Spirit extra help not only in our works, but throughout life? Don't be satisfied with the watering can, God wants us to use the hose.

4.7.2 Salvation and receiving the Spirit.

Salvation by Faith

Reading Hebrews 6:10-20

> In which [the promise] more abundantly God willing to show unto the heirs of the promise the immutability[91] of his counsel, He confirmed (interposed[92]) with an oath[93], that through two unchangeable things, in that it was impossible for God to lie, we might have strong[94] consolation[95], who have fled away to lay hold with strength upon the hope (anticipation, expectation) lying in front: which we hold as an anchor of the soul[96], both secure and stable[97], and which entereth into the interior of the veil, where the fore-runner is for us entered, even Jesus ...
>
> Heb 6:17-20 [a translation]

God wants us to be utterly confident, knowing the certainty of the salvation where with he saved us. Our Father promised with an oath that he would send **Jesus** to save us. God **Never** lies. God's plan of salvation will never change. God has never failed anyone who calls out to him. He never will.

> "For whosoever shall call upon the name of the Lord shall be saved."
>
> Rom 10:13, Acts 2:(16-)21, Joel 2:(28-)32

---

[91] unchangeability
[92] cf. Gen 26:28 'an oath between us'
[93] a fence/restraint.
[94] mighty
[95] G3874 *imploration, hortation, solace*. From G3870 meaning to 'call near' (cf. Luke 15:28, G3870 'entreat'). The Holy Spirit is known as the 'comforter' G3875 (*intercessor, consoler*), also I suppose derived from the same 'call near'. G3874 'consolation', I suppose by definition, only comes by someone drawing near. Because God loved us, he was willing to (and did) draw near to exhort us (cf. Heb 12:5 G3874 translated as 'exhortation') and give us hope.
[96] breath (as in 'breathing' creature)
[97] Joshua 1:5 'I will not fail (*slacken* [derived from 'to mend by stitching']) thee, nor forsake (to *loosen, relinquish*) thee.' cf. Deut 4:29-31

If you need saving in anything, Jesus saves[98]. God has not changed his mind. God's plan has not changed, if you need food, cry out to Jesus. If you need friends, ask God. Ask and ye shall receive. What kind of Father deserts you when you are in trouble? We too often say God can't be bothered, God's not interested, God doesn't care. Oh that God would reveal his power, that men's faith and hope might rest in the Father of mercies and the God of all comfort. God gives a damn, he sent his only son, don't you hear me. God cares. God doesn't want things to go wrong. God wants you to have a good future. God wants you to know his power. God wants to talk to you like he talked to Adam in the evenings. God's plan is to bring you back to himself. He doesn't want to steal things off you, his plan is not to destroy your life with misery or to consume you with grief. What kind of Gospel do you believe? Do you believe? God sends Jesus to save us **Today!, NOW! Ask and ye shall receive that your joy may be full. He is able and wants to do more than you can ask. More than you can think. More than you can dream. Praise The LORD!!! Praise GOD! Selah.**

We must admit our guilt, and turn to God, honestly intending to leave our sin and to follow after God. If we do this, and believe, we may by calling to Jesus for help, be saved.

> HOS 14:1 O Israel, return unto the LORD thy God; for thou hast fallen by thine iniquity.
>
> HOS 14:2 Take with you words, and turn to the LORD: say unto him, Take away all iniquity, and receive us graciously: so will we render the calves of our lips.

We don't say a particular set of words to save us. Jesus himself is the person we must come to. It is he that saves.

> JER 3:12 Go and proclaim these words toward the north, and say, Return, thou backsliding Israel, saith the LORD; and I will not cause mine anger to fall upon you: for I am merciful, saith the LORD, and I will not keep anger for ever.
>
> JER 3:13 Only acknowledge thine iniquity, that thou hast transgressed against the LORD thy God, and hast scattered thy ways to the strangers under every green tree, and ye have not obeyed my voice, saith the LORD.
>
> JER 3:14 Turn, O backsliding children, saith the LORD ...

When we repent and cry out to God for forgiveness, he will save us.

> For whosoever shall call upon the name of the Lord shall be saved.
> Rom 10:13

---

[98] The word Jesus comprises of two parts:

1. saved - to be open, wide or free, by implication safe, to free or help, get victory.
2. God to exist, breath.

Hence the meaning of Jesus is 'God Saviour'. Praise the Lord, that Jesus came to set me in a wide open place, free and safe.

"Offer unto God thanksgiving; and pay thy vows unto the most High: and call[99] upon me in the day of trouble: I will deliver thee, and thou shalt glorify me."
Psalm 50:14-15

God's word is infallible.

PSA 12:6 The words of the LORD are pure words: as silver tried in a furnace of earth, purified seven times.

Our salvation is through faith.

"Verily, verily, I say unto you, He that believeth on me hath everlasting life."
John 6:47

"For if, when we were enemies, we were reconciled to God by the death of his Son, ..."
Rom 5:10

It is Christ's death and resurrection that saves us, through the 'hearing[100] of faith'. It is through this gospel that a man who hears and believes, is saved.

"For after that in the wisdom of God the world by wisdom knew not God, it pleased God by the foolishness of preaching to save them that believe."
1Cor 1:21

The cross is despised by men. It was through Christ's weakness that he died. There is no great act or feat of strength required to be saved, neither is there an intellectual challenge. We are saved by repenting (forsaking our sin and returning to God) and believing that Christ was crucified as punishment for our sin and that he rose again.

Christ purchased us with his blood.

"For as much as ye know that ye were not redeemed [ransomed] with corruptible things, as silver and gold, ... but with the precious blood of Christ, ..."
1Peter 1:18-19

"Therefore being justified by faith, ..." Rom 5:1

---

[99] H7121 A prim. root (rather identical with [H7122 'to *encounter*'], through the idea of *accosting* a person met); to *call* out to (i.e. properly *address* by name, but used in a wide variety of applications)

[100] 8 But what saith it? The word is nigh thee, even in thy mouth, and in thy heart: that is, the word of faith, which we preach;
9 That if thou shalt confess with thy mouth the Lord Jesus, and shalt believe in thine heart that God hath raised him from the dead, thou shalt be saved.
10 For with the heart man believeth unto righteousness; and with the mouth confession is made unto salvation.
11 For the scripture saith, Whosoever believeth on him shall not be ashamed.
...
14 How then shall they call on him in whom they have not believed? and how shall they believe in him of whom they have not heard?
...
17 So then faith cometh by hearing, and hearing by the word of God.
Rom 10:8-11,14,17

"... then, being now justified by his blood, ..." Rom 5:9

Both faith and Christ's blood are required for salvation. Christ did his part on Calvary[101], it is up to a man to believe the record God gave in the Bible concerning our Lord.

ROM 4:25 Who was delivered for our offences, and was raised again for our justification.

God paid the price in his blood, whether or not a man chooses to believe.

ROM 3:25 Whom God hath set forth to be a propitiation [atonement] through faith in his blood, to declare his [God's] righteousness for the remission of sins that are past, through the forbearance of God;

"Giving thanks unto the Father, which hath made us meet to be partakers of the inheritance of the saints in light: Who hath delivered us from the power of darkness, and hath translated us into the kingdom of his dear Son: In whom we have redemption through his blood, even the forgiveness of sins: ..."
Col 1:12-14

We sinned against God. For our transgression we were sentenced to die.

“For all have sinned, and come short of the glory of God; ...”
Rom 3:23

“As it is written, There is none righteous, no, not one: ...”
Rom 3:10

God took no pleasure in making the judgment. Nevertheless, death was the ultimate penalty for our sin, and death was the price which had to be paid.

"... the soul that sinneth, it shall die." Ezek 18:4

It is through faith in Christ we are saved. It is he that bought us from under the kingdom of darkness into the light. It was with Christ's life that the price was paid for our sin.

God sought for a way to bring us back to himself.

Reading Heb 8:7-13

God seeing that the law was powerless to save, because it was weak through our sin, sought for another way, that we might come to God. God wanted to pay attention to us, but by the law, he could not.

"... I will make a new covenant ... not according to the covenant that I made with their fathers in the day when I took them by the hand to lead them out of the land of Egypt; because they continued not in my covenant, and I regarded them not, saith the Lord."
Heb 8:8-9

[101] Mat 27:33,Mark 15:22,Luke 23:33 & John 19:17.

That way was through the cross.

> "Blotting out the handwriting of ordinances that was against us, which was contrary to us, and took it out of the way, nailing it to his cross;"
> Col 2:14

> "For what the law could not do, in that it was weak through the flesh, God sending his own Son in the likeness of sinful flesh, and for (concerning) sin, condemned sin in the flesh: ..."
> Rom 8:3

Salvation is by Faith. In other words, salvation is by choosing to believe God's record:

- that Christ through the sacrifice he made at the cross has removed our sins, and
- that Christ was resurrected.

While this is an intellectual choice, it also marks the beginning of a friendship with God when we first:

- say sorry to him and
- ask him to forgive us for all that we have done wrong.

when we do this, God accepts us and sends his Spirit into our heart(s).

> Then will I sprinkle clean water upon you, and ye shall be clean: from all your filthiness, and from all your idols, will I cleanse you.
>
> A new heart also will I give you, and a new spirit will I put within you: and I will take away the stony heart out of your flesh, and I will give you an heart of flesh.
>
> And I will put my spirit within you, ...
> Ezek 36:25-27

Receiving the Spirit

Paul asked certain disciples

> "Have (you) received the Holy Ghost since (you) believed?" Acts 19:2

It is possible to believe and not have received the baptism of the Holy Ghost.

If a man believes, he is saved - irrespective of whether he has been baptised. e.g. Jesus talking to Thomas said "because thou hast seen , thou hast believed, blessed are they who have not seen, and yet have believed." The baptism at Pentecost was still weeks away, yet Thomas had believed.

> Verily, verily, I say unto you, He that heareth my word, and believeth on him that sent me, hath everlasting life, and shall not come into condemnation; but is passed from death unto life.
> John 5:24

In John the scripture likens the Holy Spirit to water.

> JOH 7:37 In the last day, that great day of the feast, Jesus stood and cried, saying, If any man thirst, let him come unto me, and drink.
>
> JOH 7:38 He that believeth on me, as the scripture hath said, out of his belly shall flow rivers of living water.
>
> ...
>
> JOH 7:39 (But this spake he of the Spirit, which they that believe on him should receive: for the Holy Ghost was not yet given; because that Jesus was not yet glorified.)

Water is often used in the Bible to represent the Holy Spirit, whether it be dew on the grass, or a thick cloud, or a spring, or a river[102]. The following scripture declares that God pours out his Spirit. It is reasonably safe to say that the Spirit comes from above, as it is rather difficult to pour things in any direction except downwards.

> ACT 2:16 But this is that which was spoken by the prophet Joel;
>
> ACT 2:17 And it shall come to pass in the last days, saith God, I will pour out of my Spirit upon all flesh: and your sons and your daughters shall prophesy, and your young men shall see visions, and your old men shall dream dreams:
>
> ACT 2:18 And on my servants and on my handmaidens I will pour out in those days of my Spirit; and they shall prophesy:

Receiving the baptism of the Holy Spirit is like standing underneath a waterfall.

> "For I will pour water upon him that is thirsty, and floods upon the dry ground: ..."
> Isaiah 44:3[103]

Who gets the water? If someone is really thirsty, they will ask for a drink, even when one isn't offered. God doesn't always say do this or that. Using our initiative and asking God for help is a good thing. God goes beyond giving us a cup of water. He pours water on top of us.

> "And God is able to make <u>all</u> grace <u>abound</u> toward you; that ye, <u>always</u> having <u>all</u> sufficiency in <u>all</u> things, may <u>abound</u> to <u>every</u> good work:"
>
> 2Cor 9:8

God wants to provide more than we can use.

> "But my God shall supply all your need <u>according to</u> his riches in glory by Christ Jesus."
>
> Phil 4:19

---

[102] Psalm 133 -dew; Exod 40:38 a cloud; Jer 2:13, Ps 114:8 a fountain; Ezek 47:1-9,Psalm 1:3, Ps 105:41 river.

[103] The word spirit used in this verse (ref. complete verse Isaiah 44:3) is:
H7307 *roo'-akh wind*; by resemblance *breath*, ... [or] *spirit* (but only of a rational being).
From a prim. root H7306 (to *blow*).

Reading Acts 8:12-17 [Philip preaches Christ to them of the city of Samaria]

The believers would have confessed that Jesus was the son of God[104], even before Peter and John had prayed for them. It says:

> "... prayed for them, that they might receive the Holy Ghost: (For as yet he was fallen upon none of them: ..."

I believe that they had received the Holy Ghost by faith, but they had not received the Holy Spirit in the manner or quantity indicated by the words "as yet he was fallen upon none of them."

The disciples in Samaria had received the Holy Spirit in a small way like a person might receive a cup of water, but the Holy Ghost had not fallen from above.

> ACT 8:16 (For as yet he [the Holy Spirit] <u>was fallen</u> upon none of them: only they were baptized in the name of the Lord Jesus.)
>
> In whom [Christ] ye also trusted, after that ye heard the word of truth, the gospel of your salvation: in whom also after that ye believed, ye were sealed with that holy Spirit of promise, which is the earnest of our inheritance until the redemption of the purchased possession, unto the praise of his glory.
> Eph 1:13-14

The word sealed (in Eph. above) is as in a wax seal placed upon a letter. In the Old days, a king would mark the wax while it was still warm with his signet ring. This indicated that it was his letter, and prevented it from being tampered with whilst in transit to its destination. When we believe, we are sealed with 'that Holy Spirit of promise'. We are the letter. Our destination is to be with the Lord, our Father. When we stand before his throne, God will see the seal of the holy Spirit and know that we are his.

Reading John 20:14-23

After Jesus was glorified, the Holy Spirit was given. In the reading from John, Jesus commands the disciples to receive the Holy Ghost.

> "… he breathed on them, and saith unto them, Receive ye the Holy Ghost: …"
> John 20:22

It was at this point the Holy Spirit was given. Thus the scripture was fulfilled for the disciples which says

[104] 'heard that Samaria had received the word of God, ...'. If they had received the word into their heart and believed, there would result a confession of that which was in their hearts.
'We having the same spirit of faith, according as it is written, I believed and therefore have I spoken, we also believe and therefore speak;' 2Cor 4:13
'For out of the abundance of the heart, the mouth speaketh.' Mat 12:34; Luk 6:45

".. and, lo, I am with you alway, even unto the end of the world. Amen."
Matthew 28:20 (last verse of Matthew).

Jesus said this after his resurrection. Jesus' body did leave the disciples, yet the Lord our God is one Lord, and this scripture was fulfilled by the Holy Spirit coming when Jesus breathed on the disciples.

CO2 13:5 ... Know ye not your own selves, how that Jesus Christ is in you, except ye be reprobates[105]?

God sent his spirit into our hearts when we first believed. If a man believes, God dwells in him by His Spirit.

JO1 4:15 Whosoever shall confess that Jesus is the Son of God, God dwelleth in him, and he in God.

JO1 4:13 Hereby know we that we dwell in him, and he in us, because he hath given us of his Spirit.

We receive the spirit by faith at salvation[106]. The baptism in the Spirit most often occurs at a different time.

GAL 3:26 For ye are all the children of God by faith in Christ Jesus.

When we believe, God calls us his children and sends his Spirit into our hearts, whereby we cry Daddy, Father.

"And because ye are sons, God hath sent forth the spirit of his son into your hearts, crying, Abba, Father."
Gal 4:6

Receiving the spirit occurs when we become sons, and sonship occurs when we believe in Jesus our Saviour[107].

---

[105] Previously shown to be *not acceptable* e.g. a car that was inspected and is not able to pass a warrant of fitness test.
[106] Gal 3:2 'This only would I learn of you, Received ye the Spirit by the works of the law, or by the hearing of faith?' It is evident from the question that the answer is that 'a man receives the Spirit by the hearing of faith'. This hearing refers to hearing and believing the word of God i.e. the gospel. In the parable of the sower, the seed which is sown is the word of God. But God is a spirit (John 4:24), so we are born by the Word of God and by his Holy Spirit, the Spirit of Faith (2Cor 4:13 'We having the same spirit of faith, ...').
[107] It is a doctrine of devils to say that a man doesn't receive the Holy Spirit until he receives the baptism. To say this is to say that a man who has not received the baptism is not saved. This doctrine stands against the gospel - salvation by faith in Christ Jesus. This doctrine says people who believe will not be saved.
"... Now if any man have not the Spirit of Christ, he is none of his [Christ's]." Rom 8:9,
see John 6:47 & John 5:24
Satan is always telling people who are going to hell everything's all right. The devil endeavours to kill Christians, to cause them to lose heart by deceiving them into believing everything is wrong, when in fact their steps in life are prepared by God himself. There is hope. God is reliable. The devil is a liar (John 8:44).
"Because he hath set his love upon me, therefore will I deliver him: I will set him on high, because he hath known my name. He shall call upon me, and I will answer him: I will be with him in trouble; I will deliver him, and honour him. With long life will I satisfy him, and shew him my salvation." Psalm 91:14-16

4.7.3 Seeking baptism in the Holy Spirit.

Reading Luke 11:9-13

> ACT 2:38 Then Peter said unto them, Repent, and be baptized every one of you in the name of Jesus Christ for the remission of sins[108], and ye shall receive the gift of the Holy Ghost.
>
> ACT 2:39 For the promise is unto you, and to your children, and to all that
>
> are afar off, even as many as the LORD our God shall call.
>
> And, being assembled together with them, commanded them that they should not depart from Jerusalem, but wait for the promise of the Father, which, saith he, ye have heard of me. For John truly baptized with water; but ye shall be baptized with the Holy Ghost not many days hence.
> Acts 1:4-5

"but wait for the promise of the Father"

The promise is the baptism in the holy Spirit. This promise is for every believer.

> "For the promise is unto you, and to your children, and to all that are afar off, even as many as the Lord our God shall call."
> Acts 2:39

Reading Acts 2:1-40

> "This Jesus hath God raised up, whereof we all are witnesses. Therefore being by the right hand of God exalted, and having received of the Father the promise of the Holy Ghost, he hath shed forth this, which ye now see and hear."
> Acts 2:32-33

God does not have favourites. This also applies to who he chooses to baptise. It is God's plan to baptise every Christian in the Holy Spirit. But of course, he won't without our consent.

> ACT 10:34 Then Peter opened his mouth, and said, Of a truth I perceive that God is no respecter of persons:
>
> ACT 10:35 But in every nation he that feareth him, and worketh righteousness, is accepted with him.

Recently, God has been very generous in pouring out His holy Spirit. Many people are baptised in the holy Spirit without putting much effort into seeking God for it. God sees the heart, and he is just, he better than anyone else knows what he is doing. Don't let Satan lie to you. God wants you to be baptised in the holy Spirit.

[108] cf. Page 55, section '4.6.1 Water Baptism and Salvation', Comment on interpretation (part 'B')

ROM 8:31 What shall we then say to these things? If God be for us, who can be against us?

ROM 8:32 He that spared not his own Son, but delivered him up for us all, how shall he not with him also freely give us all things?

Praise the Lord!

MAR 1:9 And it came to pass in those days, that Jesus came from Nazareth of Galilee, and was baptized of John in Jordan.

MAR 1:10 And straightway coming up out of the water, he saw the heavens opened, and the Spirit like a dove descending upon him:

MAR 1:11 And there came a voice from heaven, saying, Thou art my beloved Son, in whom I am well pleased.

Christ is our example

LUK 9:23 And he said to them all, If any man will come after me, let him deny himself, and take up his cross daily, and follow me.

MAR 8:34 And when he had called the people unto him with his disciples also, he said unto them, Whosoever will come after me, let him deny himself, and take up his cross, and follow me.

He wants us to follow him. It will cost us everything, but I think it's worth it.

Jesus was baptised in the Holy Spirit after he came up out of the water. I believe this is the pattern intended for most believers. If we want the baptism in the Holy Spirit, I believe that we've got to attend to our responsibilities before we can expect God to baptise us in the Holy Ghost.

"Repent, and be baptised every one of you in the name of Jesus Christ for the remission of sins, and ye shall receive the gift of the Holy Ghost."
Acts 2:38

God commands us to be water baptised. If we are disobedient, we can not expect God to give us the baptism in the Holy Spirit. However, God does sometimes baptise people in the Holy Spirit before they are water baptised[109].

The Holy Spirit and the Bible are the most precious things that I have. God does not treat the baptism lightly. If we want the baptism, we must value and respect the gift God gives us.

God is not stingy, or disinterested in us. Parents like to give gifts to their children. God wants us to look after the gift which he gives us.

God is our Father. He wants us to have the baptism.

---

109 Cornelius and his family and friends are examples (Acts 10:1-48, particularly verses 44 & 47), see also Acts 15:7-9.

"... how much more shall your Heavenly Father give the Holy Spirit to them that ask him?"

Luke 11:13

I think God wants us to seek after the baptism. If we ask and seek after it, it proves that we believe that the gift is precious. It also helps us appreciate the gift when we receive it.

“Ask, and it shall be given you; seek, and ye shall find; knock, and it shall be opened unto you: For everyone that asketh receiveth; and he that seeketh findeth; and to him that knocketh it shall be opened.”

Mat 7:7-8

4.7.4 Gifts and Ministries

Introduction

Reading 1Cor12:1-31

Both gifts and ministries have the opportunity to be misused. Many people misuse them today - some through ignorance, and others for their own gain. What is the key to using them successfully? Paul describes this in the next chapter - the more excellent way, the way of love. Love does cover a multitude of sins. A little bit of patience and mercy when people make mistakes doesn't go amiss. God is our refuge. When things go wrong we can always turn to him.

God gives instruction, which if we heed, helps us stand firm in the day of adversity.

> PRO 4:10 Hear, O my son, and receive my sayings; and the years of thy life shall be many.
>
> PRO 4:11 I have taught thee in the way of wisdom; I have led thee in right paths.
>
> PRO 4:12 When thou goest, thy steps shall not be straitened; and when thou runnest, thou shalt not stumble.
>
> PRO 4:13 Take fast hold of instruction; let her not go: keep her; for she is thy life.

Ministries

When our Lord went up into heaven, he gave gifts to us.

> "When he [Christ] ascended up on high, he led captivity captive, and gave gifts unto men."
> Eph 4:8
>
> And he gave some, apostles; and some, prophets; ... till we all come ... unto a perfect man, unto the measure of the stature of the fulness of Christ: ...
> Eph 4:11-13

Praise the Lord! Isn't it great that God's chosen us to be like his son Jesus. That's our destiny.

The gifts spoken of here are positions of employment or offices[110]. These people have been assigned particular jobs. Some have the task of teaching, some prophesying, some looking after a church etc. These people are there to help strengthen the Church.

---

[110] Office has the same meaning as in the following sentence:

> "Mr Jim Bolger holds the office of the Prime Minister of NZ. This position has a tenure of three years, after which candidates are re-elected."

"And he gave some, apostles; and some, prophets; ... For the perfecting of the saints, for the work of the ministry, for the edifying of the body of Christ: ..."

Eph 4:11-12

Beware about being caught up in classifying yourself (or other people) according to the job given by God. I have never met two people exactly the same in character. Our value to God isn't based on our role (or job) in the body of Christ (the church). You are different to everyone that's been and is to come. Your works will be different to everyone that's been and is to come.

CO1 12:4 Now there are diversities of [A] gifts, but the same Spirit.

CO1 12:5 And there are differences (diversities) of [B] administrations [Ministries[111]], but the same Lord.

CO1 12:6 And there are diversities of [C] *operations*[112], but it is the same God which *worketh*[113] all in all.

There are three different items mentioned:

[A]	gifts
[B]	administrations
[C]	operations.

The [B] 'differences of administrations' or 'different ministries' which we encountered in Eph 4:11 are listed again in 1Cor 12:28.

CO1 12:28 And God hath set some in the church, first apostles, secondarily prophets, thirdly teachers, after that miracles, then gifts of healings, helps, governments, diversities of tongues.

Gifts

Well lets move on from Ministries, and take a look at [A] Gifts. Paul says "and concerning spiritual gifts, brethren, I would not have you ignorant."

There are a number of possible ways to communicate with people. A letter, a phone call, a conversation. God does speak to Christians in a number of ways. One vital way is through the Bible. God also speaks to us by his Spirit.

---

[111] G1248 diakonia
attendance (as a servant, etc.); fig. (eleemosynary) *aid*, (official) *service* (especially of the Christian teacher, or technically of the *diaconate*). From G1249
G1249 Probably from διάκω diakō (obsolete, to *run* on errands; compare G1377); an *attendant*, that is, (generally) a *waiter* (at table or in other menial duties); specially a Christian *teacher* and *pastor* (technically a *deacon* or *deaconess*)

[112] G1755 energēma *effect* (in this case something done by God)

[113] G1754 energeō to *be active, efficient*

And thine ears shall hear a word behind thee, saying, This is the way, walk ye in it, when ye turn to the right hand, and when ye turn to the left.
Isaiah 30:21

My sheep hear my voice, and I know them, and they follow me: ...
John 10:27

KI1 19:8 And he arose, and did eat and drink, and went in the strength of that meat forty days and forty nights unto Horeb the mount of God.

KI1 19:9 And he came thither unto a cave, and lodged there; and, behold, the word of the LORD came to him, and he said unto him, What doest thou here, Elijah?

KI1 19:10 And he said, I have been very jealous for the LORD God of hosts: for the children of Israel have forsaken thy covenant, thrown down thine altars, and slain thy prophets with the sword; and I, even I only, am left; and they seek my life, to take it away.

KI1 19:11 And he said, Go forth, and stand upon the mount before the LORD. And, behold, the LORD passed by, and a great and strong wind rent the mountains, and brake in pieces the rocks before the LORD; but the LORD was not in the wind: and after the wind an earthquake; but the LORD was not in the earthquake:

KI1 19:12 And after the earthquake a fire; but the LORD was not in the fire: and after the fire a still small voice.

KI1 19:13 And it was so, when Elijah heard it, that he wrapped his face in his mantle, and went out, and stood in the entering in of the cave. And, behold, there came a voice unto him, and said, What doest thou here, Elijah?

God hardly ever shouts. He's very patient with us.

"Love [God] ... is not easily provoked, ..."[114]
1Cor13:4-5

PSA 103:8 The LORD is merciful and gracious, slow to anger, and plenteous in mercy.

PSA 103:9 He will not always chide: neither will he keep his anger for ever.

PSA 103:10 He hath not dealt with us after our sins; nor rewarded us according to our iniquities.

PSA 103:11 For as the heaven is high above the earth, so great is his mercy toward them that fear him.

PSA 103:12 As far as the east is from the west, so far hath he removed our transgressions from us.

---

[114] 'Charity ... is not easily provoked, ...' KJV.
cf. 1John 4:8 '... for God is love.'

PSA 103:13 Like as a father pitieth his children, so the LORD pitieth them that fear him.

Normally God speaks to me in 'a small still voice' which is inaudible. When we listen to the Holy Spirit, often, he will give us things to do or say. These things are the gifts. It may be to go and pray for someone, to encourage them with a kind word. It might be to surprise someone with a gift. Often God asks us to do things which we consider too scary to do, but always wished we could. It is easy to get proud. God wants what we do (including using the gifts) to be done out of love for him, and our brothers and sisters. The way God speaks can sometimes be different. I heard of one man who used to feel hot and cold running up and down his spine. When he felt this, he knew that God wanted him to speak the words the Spirit said. Sometimes when God wants you to pray for someone, he will give you the same symptoms as the person who needs healing. Your not sick or anything (although you might think so at the time), but God just wants to get your attention and at the same time lets you know what it's like so you can describe what it feels like to the person who's sick.

How many ways does God do things? Doubtless more than I can count. The things God might ask us to say or do can be categorised as follows.

CO1 12:8 For to one is given by the Spirit the word of wisdom; to another the word of knowledge by the same Spirit;

CO1 12:9 To another faith by the same Spirit; to another the gifts of healing by the same Spirit;

CO1 12:10 To another the working of miracles; to another prophecy; to another discerning of spirits; to another divers kinds of tongues; to another the interpretation of tongues:

CO1 12:11 But all these worketh that one and the selfsame Spirit, dividing to every man severally as he will.

Always it is the Holy Spirit who gives the people the gift. I personally think that the Holy Spirit is not limited to giving a fixed number of the above classification of gifts to a person. The Holy Spirit chooses when and what gift he will give. However if you do need one of the gifts in some circumstance, it never hurts to ask. But generally if you need help, ask God for help - the gifts aren't the answer to everything.

Well the third item mentioned is [C] diversities of operations. It's not a gift or ministry - it is this: every person is going to use the [B] ministry or [A] the gifts, in a different way. In fact anyway they choose to. Some people with a bit of common sense - others, well there's always some people who are a right pain in the neck. It should therefore be noted that although a person may exercise many spiritual gifts, it doesn't mean you should trust them. It also does not mean that they know God better than Joe Bloggs down the road.

5.0 Laying on of Hands

"Of the doctrine of baptisms, and of laying on of hands, ..."
Heb 6:2

5.1 Introduction.

> "Therefore leaving the principles of the doctrine of Christ, let us go on unto perfection; not laying again the foundation of repentance from dead works, and of faith toward God,
>
> Of the doctrine[115] of baptisms, and of laying on of hands, and of resurrection of the dead, and of eternal judgment."
>
> Heb 6:1-2

Following the order in Hebrews we come now to the topic of the laying on of hands. Jesus Christ is the beginning of the doctrine of laying on of hands.

> “Therefore leaving the principles[116] of the doctrine[117] of Christ, let us go on unto perfection[118]; ...”
>
> Heb 6:1

In Hebrews 6v2 it speaks of various doctrines. The only reliable basis for these doctrines is Jesus Christ.

> "For other foundation can no man lay than that is laid, which is Jesus Christ."
>
> 1Cor 3:11

Without Jesus Christ these doctrines are incomplete.

> "For it pleased the Father that in him [his dear son] should all fulness[119] dwell; ..."
>
> Col 1:19

I would therefore like to begin discussion of the doctrine of “Laying on of hands” with the gospel of Jesus Christ.

> “In this was manifested the love of God toward us, because that God sent his only begotten Son into the world, that we might live through him.”
>
> 1John 4:9
>
> "But God commendeth his love toward us[120], in that, while we were yet sinners, Christ died for us." Rom 5:8

God loves us whether we are faithless or believing. Through Jesus we have a way today to turn to God for help. At the beginning we came to God through faith in Christ Jesus[121] . If we get lost or

---

[115] G1322 *instruction* (the act or the matter)

[116] G746 archē (from G756); (properly abstract) a *commencement*, or (concrete) *chief* (in various applications of order, time, place or rank)

[117] G3056 log'os (from G3004); something *said* (including the *thought*), by implication a *topic* (subject of discourse): word (e.g. Act 11:1, Mark 8:38, Mark 13:31), saying (John 10:19, Acts 16:36), speech, utterance etc.
G3004 properly to “*lay*” forth, i.e. (fig.) *relate* (in words [usually of systematic or set *discourse; ...*])

[118] G5047 τελειότης teleiotēs (state of) *completeness*. From τέλλω - to set out for a definite point or goal.

[119] G4138 πλήρωμα plērōma *repletion* or *completion*

[120] or 'makes his love *to stand near* toward us'

[121] "For whosoever shall call upon the name of the Lord shall be saved." Rom 10:13

sidetracked we can as at the beginning come to God. The end[122] of the word of the gospel is to know God[123]. I hope that as we consider God's word[124], God will again draw nigh and speak with us by his word and his spirit.

The doctrine of "Laying on of Hands" concerns a ceremony where one person places his hands on another. In this ceremony something is transferred from one person to another. In a similar manner at salvation God offered to us the gift of eternal life[125].

> "... but the gift[126] of God is eternal life through Jesus Christ our Lord."
>
> Rom 6:23

> "And this is life eternal, that they might know thee the only true God, and Jesus Christ, whom thou hast sent."
>
> John 17:3

It is certain everyone receives some things from God even if one does not choose to believe the Gospel. God makes the sunrise and sends rain on the just and unjust alike.

> "... for he [the Highest] is kind unto the unthankful and to the evil."
>
> Luke 6:35

Although God gives many good things to everyone, believing the Gospel entitles us to receive things that otherwise we would have no right to receive. God offers us: forgiveness of sins, eternal life, righteousness, supply of all our needs such as food, health and clothing[127]. No doubt it is impossible to count all the riches God has allocated for us through Christ. Perhaps the clearest definition of what God offered us in salvation was to be his son or daughter.

When we believe in Christ we are adopted as sons (or daughters) by God. I think God places his hand on us when we believe at salvation. When we ask him to come into our hearts, he sends his word and his spirit to rest within us. At this occasion, as we lift our voice to the heavens in prayer, it is as if with our hands we present ourselves to God[128] and ask him to take away our sin.

> "Let us search and try our ways, and turn again to the Lord. Let us lift up our heart with our hands unto God in the heavens."
>
> Lam 3:40-41

"By the which will [God's] we are sanctified through the offering of the body of Jesus Christ once for all." Heb 10:10

[122] "He that saith, I know him, and keepeth not his commandments, is a liar, and the truth is not in him. But whoso keepeth his word, in him verily is the love of God perfected: ..." 1John 2:4-5

"Now the end of the commandment is love out of a pure heart, and of a good conscience, and of faith unfeigned." 1Tim 1:5

Those who know God, keep God's commandments, have the love of God perfected in them and have reached the end of the commandment. I think this is reached when we like Christ have through love laid down our life before God even unto death.

[123] We get to know God by coming to God and spending time with him.

[124] "Draw nigh to God, and he will draw nigh to you." James 4:8

[125] This is an offer to know God.

[126] something that is given out of cheerful good will (cf. Strong's Greek dictionary G5486)

[127] God also promises to give us some things that we want but don't need.

[128] When a child wants to be picked up by one of their parents, they reach up their hands.

The purpose of the gospel is to make a way to come to God. He longs to have us sit next to him, to put his arm around our shoulder and to tell us not to worry because he is here. Never the less God will not see injustice neither watch judgement being perverted and do nothing[129].

> "Touching the Almighty, we cannot find him out: he is excellent in power, and in judgment, and in plenty[130] of justice: he will not afflict."
> Job 37:23

> "Justice and judgment are the habitation[131] of thy throne: mercy and truth shall go before thy face."
> Psalm 89:14

God will by no means acquit the guilty.

> "Keeping mercy for thousands[132], forgiving iniquity and transgression and sin, and that will by no means clear the guilty; ..."
> Exod 34:7

The price[133] that Jesus paid is the reason our guilt[134] could be removed[135].

> "They that trust in their wealth, and boast themselves in the multitude of their riches; None of them can by any means redeem his brother, nor give to God a ransom for him: (For the redemption of their soul is precious, and it ceaseth for ever:)
>
> ...
>
> But God will redeem my soul from the power of the grave: for he shall receive me. Selah."
> Psalm 49:6-8,15

It is only through Jesus Christ that we can come to God.

---

129 It is by God's forbearance that he waits for us to repent, and does not execute judgement swiftly. cf. Rom 2:4; Ecc 8:11; 2Peter 3:4, 3:9

130 H7230 *abundance*

131 H4349 mâkôn From H3559; prop. a *fixture*, i.e. a *basis*; gen. a *place*, esp. as an *abode.*
H3559 kûn A primitive root; prop. to *be erect* (i.e. stand perpendicular);. hence (causatively) to *set up*, in a great variety of applications, whether lit. (*establish, fix, prepare, apply*), or fig. (*appoint, render sure, proper* or *prosperous*)

132 The Jewish Publication Society Bible translates as "Keeping mercy unto the thousandth generation, forgiving iniquity and transgression and sin; ..."

133 "And he is the propitiation (atonement) for our sins: and not for ours only, but also for the sins of the whole world." 1John 2:2 (also cf. 1John 4:9-10)

134 "... that they may receive forgiveness of sins, and inheritance among them which are sanctified by faith that is in me [Jesus]." Acts 26:18
"And you, that were sometime alienated and enemies in your mind by wicked works, yet now hath he reconciled in the body of his flesh through death, to present you holy and unblameable and unreprovable in his sight: ..."
Col 1:21-22

135 "For ye are bought with a price: therefore glorify God in your body, and in your spirit, which are Gods." 1Cor 6:20
God accepted Jesus as payment for our guilt.
"But this man [Jesus Christ], after he had offered one sacrifice for sins for ever, sat down on the right hand of God; from henceforth expecting [or awaiting the arrival of something] till his enemies be made his footstool."
Heb 10:12-13

“Who will have all men to be saved, and to come unto the knowledge of the truth. For there is one God, and one mediator between God and men, the man Christ Jesus; who gave himself a ransom for all, to be testified in due time.”

1Tim 2:4-6

There is no other way to the Father and most of the blessings God gives[136].

"I am the door: by me if any man enter in, he shall be saved, ..."

John 10:9

"Jesus saith unto him, I am the way, the truth, and the life: no man (comes to) the Father, but by me."

John 14:6

Please come with me and we will begin by looking at some of the things that are received and some that are removed when a man becomes a Christian, then at some scriptures in the old testament concerning laying on of hands, and finish by looking at “finding the knowledge of God”[137].

“... The vilest offender who truly believes, in a moment a pardon from Jesus receives. Praise the Lord ... let the earth hear his voice ... Praise the Lord. Let his people rejoice. O come to the Father, through Jesus his son, and give him the glory great things he has done.”

- a song

[136] “... in thy presence is fullness of joy; at thy right hand there are pleasures forevermore.” Psalms 16:11

[137] Derek Prince lecture “Finding the Knowledge of God" concerning Proverbs 2:1-5. I suppose that it is by fellowship with God, listening to what he says, that we get to know him (Prov 2:6).

5.2 Things Transferred at Salvation

5.2.1 My son (daughter)

"Of whom [the Father of our Lord Jesus Christ] the whole family[138] in heaven and earth is named, ..."
Eph 3:15

God made us an offer to become part of his family. When we first believed, God made a covenant with us to be our Father.

"But now in Christ Jesus ye who sometimes were afar off are made nigh by the blood of Christ. (v.13) ... (v.19) Now therefore ye are no more strangers and foreigners, but fellow citizens with the saints, and of the household[139] of God; and are built upon the foundation of the apostles and prophets, Jesus Christ himself being the chief corner stone; ..."
Eph 2:13,19-20

If we confess from our heart that Jesus is the son of God, then we are his children.

"... ye are all the children of God by faith in Christ Jesus." Gal 3:26

and have received the spirit of adoption, which is the Holy Spirit of truth.

"God sent forth his son, ... that we might receive the adoption of sons. And because you are sons, God sent forth the spirit of his son into your hearts, crying Daddy, Father. ... ; but if a son, also an heir of God through Christ."
Gal 4:4-7 [a translation]

5.2.2 The Word and the Spirit

In the beginning God spake and created the heavens and the earth.

"By the word of the Lord were the heavens made; and all the host of them by the *breath*[89] of his mouth."
Psalm 33:6

[138] G3965 paternal *descent* concr. a *group* of families or a whole *race* or *nation*:-family,kindred, lineage. Perhaps the descendants of our Father Abraham.

[139] G3609 *domestic* i.e. (as noun) a *relative, adherent*. from G3624
G3624 a *dwelling* (more or less extensive, lit. or fig.); by implication a *family* (more or less related lit. or fig.)

The *breath*[140] of God's mouth is the Holy Spirit. It is when God's word is combined with the Spirit that life comes.

> "Jesus answered, Verily, verily, I say unto thee, Except a man be born of water and of the Spirit, he cannot enter into the kingdom of God. That which is born of the flesh is flesh; and that which is born <u>of</u> the Spirit is spirit."
>
> John 3:5-6

The word translated here as "water" is like a puddle of water on a rainy day perhaps when the roof in one's house leaks. A Greek speaker would be reminded of the rain which brings water because the word for water is derived from a word meaning to rain[141]. In the old testament, the rain is likened to the word of the Lord.

> "For as the rain cometh down, and the snow from heaven, and returneth not thither, but watereth the earth, and maketh it bring forth and bud, that it may give seed to the sower, and bread to the eater:
>
> So shall my word be that goeth forth out of my mouth: ..."
>
> Isaiah 55:10-11

In another place it says

> "Of his own will begat he [the Father of lights[142]] us with the word of truth, ..."
>
> James 1:18

The Father, the Son, the Holy Spirit, and the Word are one.

> "Hear, O Israel: the Lord our God is one LORD: ..." Deut 6:4

A man is born of the Word[143] and the Spirit when he becomes a Christian.

---

[140] The following italicised words are the same in Hebrew.

> "And the *<u>Spirit</u>* of the Lord came upon him, ..." Judges 3:10
>
> "I will be a lying *<u>spirit</u>* in the mouth of all his prophets." 1Kings 22:22
>
> "I, even I, do bring a flood of waters upon the earth, to destroy all flesh, wherein is the *<u>breath</u>* of life, from under heaven ..." Gen 6:17
>
> "... I will pour out my *<u>spirit</u>* unto you, I will make known my words unto you." Prov 1:23

[141] G5204 *water* (as if rainy) lit. or fig. (from huo a primary verb '*to rain*').

Interestingly, the Hebrew word for "law" ('Torah') is related to rain.

H8451 tôrâh from H3384

> a *precept* or *statute*" especially the *Decalogue* or *Pentateuch*

H3384 yârâh

> A prim. root; properly to *flow* as water (i.e. to *rain*); trans. to *lay* or *throw* (espec. an arrow, i.e. to *shoot*); fig. to *point* out (as if by *aiming* the finger), to *teach*.

[142] G5457 *luminousness* (in the widest application, nat. or artificial, abstr. or concr., lit. or fig.). From an obsol. phaō (to *shine* or make *manifest*, esp. by *rays*)

[143] It is not two separate births, one of the Word and one of the Spirit. It is one birth engendered by one God who is the Word and the Spirit.

> "Being born again, not of corruptible seed, but of incorruptible, by the word of God, which liveth and abideth for ever." 1Pet 2:23
>
> "So then faith cometh by hearing, and hearing by the word of God." Rom 10:17

5.2.3 Removal and burial of sin

> "Come now, and let us reason together, saith the Lord: though your sins be as scarlet, they shall be as white as snow; though they be red like crimson, they shall be as wool."
>
> Isaiah 1:18

God lays his hand upon a man the day that he is saved, and takes their sins, and washes them as clean as snow. Just as dirt is removed from clothing using soap and water, so God removed our sin from us.

> "Blessed is he whose transgression (revolt) is forgiven[144] (lifted), whose (offence) sin is covered[145]."
>
> Psalm 32:1; cf. Rom 4:6-8

> "Thou hast forgiven (lifted) the iniquity[146] (crookedness) of thy people, thou hast covered[147] ... their sin. Selah."
>
> Psalm 85:2

Or in other words, 'Thou hast lifted and covered, the perversity and the offence of thy people.'

Isaiah compares sin being covered with a cloud erasing any existence of their fault.

> "I have blotted out, as (an enveloping dark dense cloud[148], thy revolt), and, as a cloud[149], thy (offences): return unto me; for I have redeemed thee."
>
> Isaiah 44:22

In Micah, we see that God has taken our sin and removed it, casting it into the depths of the ocean so that it is covered by tons of water.

---

[144] forgive / forgiven

Old Testament (OT) - is in a considerable portion of instances a translation of H5375 "to *lift*". H5375 is not always translated as 'forgive' e.g. Ex 25:14 "... the ark may be borne (*lifted*) with them." or Job 7:21 "And why dost thou not pardon (*lift*) my transgression, and take away mine iniquity?".

New Testament (NT) - is with a few exceptions a translation of
G863 to *send forth*, in various applications.
From G575 and ἵημι hiēmi (to *send*; an intensive form of εἶμι eimi (to *go*))
The above definitions correspond respectively to 'forgiven' in Psalm 32:1 (H5375) and in Rom 4:7 (G863)

[145] OT H3680 to *plump*, i.e. *fill up* hollows
NT G1943 to *conceal*, i.e. (fig.) *forgive*

[146] H5771 *perversity* i.e. (moral) *evil*. (from H5753 '*to crook*')

[147] H3680 kaw-saw – a prim. root; *to plump* i.e. *fill up* hollows by impl. *to cover* (for clothing or secrecy). cf. H3780.
H3780 kaw-saw a prim. root; to *grow fat* [i.e. to *be covered* with flesh]

[148] H5645 properly an *envelope*, i.e. *darkness* (or *density*); spec. a (scud) *cloud*; also a *copse*.
H5645 is from H5743 a prim. root. to be *dense*, or *dark*; i.e. to *becloud*

[149] a *cloud* (as *covering* the sky)

Who is a God[150] like unto thee, that pardoneth (lifteth) iniquity, and passeth by (over) the transgression[151] of the remnant[152] of his heritage? he retaineth not his anger for ever, because he delighteth in mercy[153].

He will turn again, he will have compassion upon us; he will subdue[154] our iniquities[155]; and thou wilt cast all (the whole of) their sins[156] into the depths of the [crashing] sea.

Thou wilt perform the truth [reliableness][157] to Jacob, and the mercy[153] to Abraham, which thou hast sworn unto our fathers from the days[158] of old.

Micah 7:18-20

Our sins were removed and buried when Jesus died.

"... but now once in the end of the world hath he [Christ] appeared to put away sin by the sacrifice of himself. And as it is appointed unto men once to die, but after this the judgement: So Christ was once offered to bear the sins of many; ..."

Heb 9:26-28

Reading Isaiah 44:21-23

After sin is removed, it is covered (i.e. buried) with water or dirt. Without shedding blood no covering can be made for sin.

"For the life of the flesh is in the blood: and I have given it to you upon the altar to make an atonement[159] for your souls: for it is the blood that maketh atonement[159] for the soul."

Lev 17:11

---

[150] mighty

[151] revolt

[152] or *remainder*

[153] kindness

[154] H3533 to *tread* down;

[155] crookedness

[156] offences

[157] H571 *stability*; fig. *certainty, truth, trustworthiness*

[158] H3117 'day' is from an unused root that means to *be hot;* a *day* (as the *warm* hours) whether lit. (from sunrise to sunset, or from one sunset to the next), or fig. (a space of time defined by an associated term), [often used adv.]

[159] H3722 to *cover* (spec. with bitumen). N.B. In the KJV 'atonement' is usually a translation of H3722, but sometimes it is a translation of H3725 kippûr *expiation* (a derivative of H3722). It is only a translation of these two words in the Old Testament. On the other hand, H3722 is not always translated as *atonement* e.g. Jer 18:23, Deu 21:8 *forgive(n)*; Isa 6:7, Isa 22:14 *purged*.
Incidentally, H3725 is the word used for the Hebrew celebration of the "Day of Atonement" where the high priest enters only once a year into the holiest to make atonement for the people (Heb 9:7). It is also on that day of the year every fifty years that the trumpets are sounded for the year of Jubilee, where slaves are freed, and land is return to those who lost them through financial problems. Jubilee happens only once or twice in a lifetime. ref also Exod 30:10; Lev 16 (espec. verse 2,3 & v29-34) 'Thus shall Aaron come into the holy place: ...'; Lev 23:27-28; Lev 25:9

This is why Jesus blood was offered upon the altar to God (not the altar in the earthly temple that was built by men, which is a copy of the true temple in heaven). And also, when he arose[160] he entered[161] into the holy of holies to make an atonement in the presence of God for us.

Reading Hebrews 9:22-28

[160] cf. Eph 4:9 first descended, Heb 9:24, John 20:17 'I ascend unto my Father, and your Father; ...'

[161] The blood was sprinkled on the mercy seat which was upon the ark of the covenant within the 2nd veil in the Holy of Holies. cf. Lev 16:15; Exod 26:31-35; Heb 13:10-12 (see also Lev 4:6-7,Lev 4:13-21; Exod 30:1-10)

5.3 Laying on of Hands

The doctrine of "Laying on of hands" says that something unseen is transferred by "Laying on of hands". There are various things which can be transferred. Let us begin by looking at a few examples. The first example is a ritual which was performed under the old testament (the law of Moses). Aaron transferred the iniquities of the nation of Israel to a goat by laying his hands on the head of a goat as he confessed Israel's' sins.

> LEV 16:20 And when he hath made an end of reconciling the holy place, and the tabernacle of the congregation, and the altar, he shall bring the live goat:
>
> LEV 16:21 And Aaron shall lay both his hands upon the head of the live goat, and confess over him all the iniquities of the children of Israel, and all their transgressions in all their sins, putting them upon the head of the goat, and shall send him away by the hand of a fit man into the wilderness:
>
> LEV 16:22 And the goat shall bear upon him all their iniquities unto a land not inhabited: and he shall let go the goat in the wilderness.

When Moses transferred the leadership over Israel to Joshua he publicly laid hands on Joshua. This ceremony was in a fashion similar to that of a king being crowned (except of course no crown was involved).

> NUM 27:15 And Moses spake unto the LORD, saying,
>
> NUM 27:16 Let the LORD, the God of the spirits of all flesh, set a man over the congregation,
>
> NUM 27:17 Which may go out before them, and which may go in before them, and which may lead them out, and which may bring them in; that the congregation of the LORD be not as sheep which have no shepherd.
>
> NUM 27:18 And the LORD said unto Moses, Take thee Joshua the son of Nun, a man in whom is the spirit, and lay thine hand upon him;
>
> NUM 27:19 And set him before Eleazar the priest, and before all the congregation; and give him a charge in their sight.
>
> NUM 27:20 And thou shalt put some of thine honour upon him, that all the congregation of the children of Israel may be obedient.
>
> NUM 27:21 And he shall stand before Eleazar the priest, who shall ask counsel for him after the judgment of Urim before the LORD: at his word shall they go out, and at his word they shall come in, both he, and all the children of Israel with him, even all the congregation.
>
> NUM 27:22 And Moses did as the LORD commanded him: and he took Joshua, and set him before Eleazar the priest, and before all the congregation:

NUM 27:23 And he laid his hands upon him, and gave him a charge, as the LORD commanded by the hand of Moses.

Moses was commanded to put some of his honour upon Joshua.

"... thou shalt put some of thine honour upon him, ..."

Whose honour was it? Moses. Where was some of it commanded to be placed? Upon Joshua. Honour was transferred. This transfer was associated with the laying on of hands.

After this ceremony, it was recorded that Joshua was full of the Spirit of wisdom, and that the reason for this was that Moses had laid his hands on him. A change had occurred. Prior to the laying on of hands he was not full of the spirit of wisdom. If we recall the analogy of a person being a container, then it is seems logical to suggest that Joshua received the spirit of wisdom.

Num 27:18 says that the spirit was in Joshua before Moses laid his hands on him. There is only one spirit of God. That is the spirit of the Lord, "the spirit of wisdom and understanding, the spirit of counsel and of might, the spirit of knowledge and of the fear of the Lord[162]."

There is one body, and one Spirit, even as ye are called in one hope of your calling;

One Lord, one faith, one baptism,

One God and Father of all, who is above all, and through all, and in you all.
Eph 4:4-6

The spirit of wisdom spoken of in Deut 34:9 is the same spirit that was in Joshua before Moses laid his hands on him (Num 27:18). So Joshua had the spirit of wisdom before Moses laid his hands on him. When Moses laid his hands on him, Joshua received the spirit of wisdom adding to what he had.

DEU 34:9 And Joshua the son of Nun was full of the spirit of wisdom; *for* Moses had laid his hands upon him: and the children of Israel hearkened unto him, and did as the LORD commanded Moses.

When Moses spoke to God that his job of leading the children of Israel was too difficult for him, God said that he would take some of the spirit that was upon him, and put it upon some people chosen to help Moses lead. It does not seem unreasonable to suggest that some of the spirit that was upon Moses was transferred to Joshua (Deut 34:9) like some was transferred to those other leaders.

NUM 11:16 And the LORD said unto Moses, Gather unto me seventy men of the elders of Israel, whom thou knowest to be the elders of the people, and officers over them; and bring them unto the tabernacle of the congregation, that they may stand there with thee.

NUM 11:17 And I will come down and talk with thee there: <u>and I will take</u> of the spirit which is upon thee, and will put it upon them; and they shall bear the burden of the people with thee, that thou bear it not thyself alone.

[162] from Isaiah 11:2. The holy spirit is the only spirit which gives good clean and peaceful wisdom.

Another case is recorded in Kings.

> KI2 13:14 Now Elisha was fallen sick of his sickness whereof he died. And Joash the king of Israel came down unto him, and wept over his face, and said, O my father, my father, the chariot of Israel, and the horsemen thereof.
>
> KI2 13:15 And Elisha said unto him, Take bow and arrows. And he took unto him bow and arrows.
>
> KI2 13:16 And he said to the king of Israel, Put thine hand upon the bow. And he put his hand upon it: and Elisha put his hands upon the king's hands.
>
> KI2 13:17 And he said, Open the window eastward. And he opened it. Then Elisha said, Shoot. And he shot. And he said, The arrow of the Lord's deliverance, and the arrow of deliverance from Syria: for thou shalt smite the Syrians in Aphek, till thou have consumed them.
>
> KI2 13:18 And he said, Take the arrows. And he took them. And he said unto the king of Israel, Smite upon the ground. And he smote thrice, and stayed.
>
> KI2 13:19 And the man of God was wroth with him, and said, Thou shouldest have smitten five or six times; then hadst thou smitten Syria till thou hadst consumed it: whereas now thou shalt smite Syria but thrice.

The king wanted to receive something from Elisha before he departed. Joash reminded Elisha of Elijah's departure and how Elisha desperately wanted something from Elijah[163]. Elisha heard, and laid his hands on Joash while Joash held the bow. Victories in battles were given to Joash. This was associated with laying on of hands.

In Genesis 48:8-20, Israel gives a blessing to Joseph's two sons Ephraim and Manasseh by laying his hands on them.

> " And Israel beheld Joseph's sons, and said, Who are these? And Joseph said unto his father, They are my sons, whom God hath given me in this place. And he said, Bring them, I pray thee, unto me, and I will bless them. ... And Israel stretched out his right hand, and laid it upon Ephraim's head, ..."
>
> Gen 48:8-14

So far we have seen examples of honour, the Spirit of Wisdom, victories in earthly battles, sins

---

[163] KI2 2:8 And Elijah took his mantle, and wrapped it together, and smote the waters, and they were divided hither and thither, so that they two went over on dry ground.
KI2 2:9 And it came to pass, when they were gone over, that Elijah said unto Elisha, Ask what I shall do for thee, before I be taken away from thee. And Elisha said, I pray thee, let a double portion of thy spirit be upon me.
KI2 2:10 And he said, Thou hast asked a hard thing: nevertheless, if thou see me when I am taken from thee, it shall be so unto thee; but if not, it shall not be so.
KI2 2:11 And it came to pass, as they still went on, and talked, that, behold, there appeared a chariot of fire, and horses of fire, and parted them both asunder; and Elijah went up by a whirlwind into heaven.
KI2 2:12 And Elisha saw it, and he cried, <u>My father, my father, the chariot of Israel, and the horsemen thereof</u>. And he saw him no more: and he took hold of his own clothes, and rent them in two pieces.
KI2 2:13 He took up also the mantle of Elijah that fell from him, and went back, and stood by the bank of Jordan;
KI2 2:14 And he took the mantle of Elijah that fell from him, and smote the waters, and said, Where is the LORD God of Elijah? and when he also had smitten the waters, they parted hither and thither: and Elisha went over.

and blessings being transferred through the laying on of hands. In the New Testament there are examples of things which we may be involved in concerning the laying on of hands.

5.3.1 Baptism in the Holy Spirit

The Baptism of the Holy Spirit may be transferred through the laying on of hands. Paul came to some people who knew only Johns baptism. He preached the gospel of Jesus death and resurrection. They believed and were baptised. Paul then laid his hands on them and they received the baptism of the Holy Spirit.

> ACT 19:1 And it came to pass, that, while Apollos was at Corinth, Paul having passed through the upper coasts came to Ephesus: and finding certain disciples,
>
> ACT 19:2 He said unto them, Have ye received the Holy Ghost since ye believed? And they said unto him, We have not so much as heard whether there be any Holy Ghost.
>
> ACT 19:3 And he said unto them, Unto what then were ye baptized? And they said, Unto John's baptism.
>
> ACT 19:4 Then said Paul, John verily baptized with the baptism of repentance, saying unto the people, that they should believe on him which should come after him, that is, on Christ Jesus.
>
> ACT 19:5 When they heard this, they were baptized in the name of the Lord Jesus.
>
> ACT 19:6 And when Paul had laid his hands upon them, the Holy Ghost came on them; and they spake with tongues, and prophesied.

God doesn't always use Laying on of hands to give things to us. Laying on of hands is not a requirement for baptism in the Holy Spirit (for example Cornelius Acts 10:30-48).

Cornelius and his household received the Holy Ghost without laying on of hands. It says

> "..., as on us at the beginning." Acts 11:15

Hallelujah! Peter could no doubt have placed his hands on each one of them for them to receive the Holy Ghost. But God was showing that (if he so chooses) his plans are not limited by men's decisions. God gives whatever he wants, to whomsoever he wants, when so ever he wants.

> "And all the inhabitants of the earth are reputed as nothing: and he doeth according to his will in the army of heaven, and amoung the inhabitants of the earth: and none can stay his hand, or say unto him, What doest thou?"
> Dan 4:35[164]

If we are intentionally disobeying God in some area, it will be necessary to repent and say sorry to

[164] "This matter is by the decree of the watchers, and the demand by the word of the holy ones: to the intent that the living may know that the most High ruleth in the kingdom of men, and giveth it to whomsoever he will, and setteth up over it the basest of men." Dan 4:17 cf. Psalm 75:6-7

God, and do what God asks before we can expect to receive the baptism of the Holy Spirit. Remember God's spirit is the Holy Spirit.

Reading Isaiah 6:1-8 ["Woe is me! for I am (cut off[165]); because ..."]

Also note that the Holy Spirit never forces one to do anything. But rather, the Holy Spirit is compared to a dove.

> "And the Holy Ghost descended in a bodily shape like a dove upon him, and a voice came from heaven, which said, Thou art my beloved Son; in thee I am well pleased."
>
> Luke 3:22

Although the Holy spirit is like a harmless dove, remember the Father, the Son and the Holy Ghost are one.

> "Hear, O Israel: the Lord our God is one Lord: ..."
>
> Deut 6:4; Mark 12:29

God watches over how we treat the Holy Spirit.

> "And I will come near to you to judgment; and I will be a swift witness against the sorcerers, and against the adulterers, and against false swearers, and against those that oppress the hireling in his wages, the widow, and the fatherless, and that turn aside the stranger from his right, and fear not me, saith the Lord of hosts.
>
> For I am the Lord, I change not; therefore ye sons of Jacob are not consumed."
>
> Malachi 3:5-6

I believe the usual order is to believe in Christ, make a request to the church ministers for the baptism ceremony in water and be baptised, then ask God for the gift of the Holy Spirit. If one does not receive the baptism of the Holy Spirit after a few weeks, it may require diligence, and patience petitioning God until one receives the baptism. This is even though God longs to give the baptism of the Holy Spirit to you.

> "For the promise is unto you, ... even as many as the Lord our God shall call."
>
> Acts 2:39

I am sad to say that involvement in things concerning the Holy Spirit is often surrounded by confusion. Yet this is not God's intention.

> "For God is not the author of confusion, but of peace, as in all churches of the saints."
>
> 1Cor 14:33

The leaders of a church supervise what happens in a church meeting so that there is no disorderly or improper behaviour. However, like so many things in this world, often the way God wants things to be, and the way they are, are two different things.

---

165 H1820 prim. root; to be *dumb* or *silent*, hence to *fail* or *perish*; trans. to *destroy:* - cease, be cut down (off), destroy, be brought to silence, be undone, X utterly. Cf. Ps. 115:17 '... neither any that go down into silence.'

"… the kingdom of God is ... righteousness[166], and peace, and joy[167] in the Holy (Spirit)."

Rom 14:17

Peter and John laid hands on the disciples and they received the baptism of the Holy Spirit. Note that it is not permissible for people to charge money for the baptism in the Holy Spirit.

ACT 8:14 Now when the apostles which were at Jerusalem heard that Samaria had received the word of God, they sent unto them Peter and John:

ACT 8:15 Who, when they were come down, prayed for them, that they might receive the Holy Ghost:

ACT 8:16 (For as yet he was fallen upon none of them: only they were baptized in the name of the Lord Jesus.)

ACT 8:17 Then laid they their hands on them, and they received the Holy Ghost.

ACT 8:18 And when Simon saw that through laying on of the apostles' hands the Holy Ghost was given, he offered them money,

ACT 8:19 Saying, Give me also this power, that on whomsoever I lay hands, he may receive the Holy Ghost.

ACT 8:20 But Peter said unto him, Thy money perish with thee, because thou hast thought that the gift of God may be purchased with money.

Ananias was sent to Saul so that Saul might receive his sight, and be filled with the Holy Spirit. He too did this with laying on of hands.

ACT 9:17 And Ananias went his way, and entered into the house; and putting his hands on him said, Brother Saul, the Lord, even Jesus, that appeared unto thee in the way as thou camest, hath sent me, that thou mightest receive thy sight, and be filled with the Holy Ghost.

5.3.2 Healing

The custom of placing your hands on a sick person, for the purpose of healing them, is done because health or virtue is transferred. Hands were laid on Saul so that he would receive his sight.

ACT 9:12 And hath seen in a vision a man named Ananias coming in, and putting his hand on him, that he might receive his sight.

“...putting his hand on him, that ...” - what?

“... that he might receive his sight.”

---

166 *equity* (of character or act)

167 *cheerfulness*

God is the one who gives the gift of healing. At the end of the day, everything we have was given to us by God.

> "... and what hast thou that thou didst not receive?" 1Cor 4:7

If he gives healing to us, we may as obedient servants administer what we have been given, freely to those who need it.

> MAT 10:8 Heal the sick, cleanse the lepers, raise the dead, cast out devils: freely ye have received, freely[168] give.

What were they to do? Heal the sick, cleanse the lepers, raise the dead, cast out devils.

Jesus gave them authority to heal.

> "And when he had called unto him his twelve disciples, he gave them power against unclean spirits, to cast them out, and to heal[169] all manner of sickness[170] and all manner of disease[171]."
>
> Mat 10:1

When you give something, you transfer something. It seems to match that laying on of hands is associated with healing being imparted.

> “And these signs shall follow them that believe; ... they shall lay hands on the sick, and they shall recover.” Mark 16:17-18

There is a classic example of virtue being transferred, resulting in healing (Mark 5:25-34). A woman who had an issue of blood came and touched Jesus clothes. Jesus immediately knew that virtue had been transferred.

> "And Jesus, immediately knowing in himself that virtue had gone out of him, turned him about in the press [the crowd], and said, Who touched my clothes?"
>
> Mark 5:30

Admittedly it wasn’t Jesus laying hands on her, but still something unseen was transferred and it was associated with an outward action similar to laying on of hands.

Does any man deserve to be healed? Yet it is our right to be healed. Isn’t God merciful? I know that we may get sick. But God never wants us to be sick. He loves us.

> "And it was, that the father of Publius [Publius was the chief of the Island Melita] was lying down suffering from fevers and dysentery, to whom Paul having entered and praying, laying on his hands, cured him. Then, this happening, also the rest of those having infirmities in the Island came up and were healed; who also, with many honours, honoured us. And, on our sailing laid on the things for the supplies."
>
> Acts 28:8-10[172]

---

[168] G1432 *gratuitously* i.e. as a free gift

[169] G2323 to *wait upon* menially, i.e. (fig.) to *adore* (God), or (specially) to *relieve* (of disease)

[170] G3554 *malady* [English word 'malady' is from French to be 'sick' or Latin 'have illness']

[171] G3119 *softness*, i.e. *enervation* [lack of vigour] (*debility* [weakness])

[172] A translation cf. "The Interlinear Bible" by Jay P Green

"And there sat in a window a certain young man named Eutychus, being fallen into a deep sleep: and as Paul was long preaching, he sunk down with sleep, and fell down from the third loft, and was taken up dead. And Paul went down, and fell on him, and embracing him said, Trouble not yourselves; for his life is in him.

... And they [the disciples in Troas, Turkey] brought the young man alive, and were not a little comforted."

Acts 20:9-11

"and were not a little comforted."

Hallelujah! Comforted by the power of God. Our trust should not rest only in words, but in God that he will do something to save us when we need help. It is a fundamentally flawed attitude to treat the scriptures as only having sentimental value.

"For the kingdom of God is not in word, but in power." 1Cor 4:20

Reading Luke 7:1-17

5.3.3 Christ took our sins and sicknesses

"And ye know that he [Jesus] was manifested to take away[173] our sins; and in him is no sin." 1John 3:5

Christ took our sins from us and carried them to his death on the cross. In the old testament there are illustrations[174] of this in the description of the sacrifices made by the priest as he prepared[175] to approach God in the holy sanctuary. Previously[176] we saw a ceremony where by "laying on of hands" sin was transferred to a goat and then the goat carried the sin into the wilderness.

"And Aaron shall lay both his hands upon the head of the live goat, ... and the goat shall bear upon him all their iniquities[177] unto a land not inhabited (a desert or waste land): ..."

Lev 16:21-22[178]

Sin may be carried by a man. We see this early in Genesis, when Cain bemoans the punishment that was upon him because of the iniquity he had.

"My (perversity[177]) is greater than I can bear (literally *to lift*).[179]"

Gen 4:13

If he could have had his iniquity removed, then the punishment that he had would also be removed.

---

[173] G142 'to lift'

[174] "For the law having a shadow of good things to come, ..." Heb 10:1

[175] e.g. Leviticus 16

[176] page 85, section '5.3 Laying on of Hands'

[177] H5771 literally *perversity* i.e. (moral) *evil*, from H5753 to *crook* (lit. or fig.). Translated variously in KJV as:- fault, iniquity, mischief, punishment (of iniquity), sin.

[178] cf. Exod 29:14-21 "But the flesh of the bullock, ..."

[179] The KJV is "My punishment[177] is greater than I can bear."

Another example is of someone who sinned in their youth. It appears they were never forgiven of their sin.

> "His bones are full of the sin[180] of his youth, which shall lie down with him in the dust."
> Job 20:11

> "The heaven shall reveal his iniquity; ..."
> Job 20:27

The sin which this person committed when they were young was carried with them in their body to the grave.

When someone sins, their guilt does not depend on whether they know that they commit sin.

> "And if a soul sin, and commit any of these things which are forbidden to be done by the commandments of the Lord; though he wist it not, yet is he guilty, and shall bear his iniquity.
>
> And he shall bring a ram without blemish out of the flock, with thy estimation, for a trespass offering, unto the priest: and the priest shall make an atonement for him concerning his ignorance wherein he erred and wist it not, and it shall be forgiven him.
>
> It is a trespass offering: he hath certainly trespassed against the Lord."
> Lev 5:17-19

The children of Israel carried iniquity in the wilderness because they had seen the miracles God did for them to rescue them out of Egypt, tested God repeatedly, scorned him, refused to listen and went after other Gods.

> "After the number of the days in which ye searched the land, even forty days, each day for a year, shall ye bear your iniquities, even forty years, and ye shall know my [refusal[181]]."
> Num 14:34

Ezra when praying for mercy declared that the children of Israel could not stand before God because of their guilt and shame.

> "And said, O my God, I am ashamed and blush[182] to lift up my face to thee, my God: for our iniquities[183] are increased over our head, and our trespass[184] is grown up unto the heavens.
>
> ...

[180] Lit. "full of his youth or adolescence" cf. Psalm 25:7, Psalm 38:3 & "..., but their iniquities shall be upon their bones, ..." Ezek 32:27

[181] H8569 *alienation*, by implication *enmity* from H5106
H5106 a primary root; *to refuse, forbid, dissuade* or *neutralize*. Translated as :- break, disallow, discourage, make of none effect.

[182] properly to *wound*, but only used figuratively. To *taunt* or *insult*.: be (make) ashamed, blush, be confounded, be put to confusion, hurt, reproach, (do, put to) shame.

[183] H5771 perversity, (moral) evil from H5753 prim. root; *to crook (make crooked, not straight).*

[184] H819 ash-maw; fem. of H817; *guiltiness*, a *fault*, the *presentation of a sin offering*.

O Lord God of Israel, thou art righteous: for we remain yet escaped, as it is this day: behold, we are before thee in our trespasses[184]: for we cannot stand before thee because of this."

Ezra 9:6,15

It appears that the iniquities that they had started off less than their height but now had increased up above them, and that they were in the midst of their trespasses[185].

"Behold, the days come, saith the Lord, that I will make a new covenant with the house of Israel, and with the house of Judah: not according to the covenant that I made with their fathers in the day that I took them by the hand to bring them out of the land of Egypt; which my covenant[186] they brake, although I was an husband unto them, saith the Lord: ..."

Jer 31:31-32

Perhaps the clearest scriptures that Jesus took our sins and our sicknesses are found in Isaiah. Here we can see Jesus took our sins and carried them.

"... ; we have turned everyone to his own way; and the Lord hath laid[187] on him the iniquity[188] of us all[189]."

Isaiah 53:6

"... by his knowledge shall my righteous servant justify many; for he shall bear[190] their iniquities."

Isaiah 53:11

"... because he hath poured out his soul unto death: and he was numbered with the transgressors; and he bare (lit. to lift) the (crime) of many, and made intercession[187] for the transgressors."

Isaiah 53:12

In the new testament Peter says the same, probably based on these scriptures in Isaiah.

"Who his own self bare our sins in his own body on the tree, ..."

1Pet 2:24

Jesus said "After this manner therefore pray ye: Our Father which art in heaven, ... and forgive us our sins; ..."[191].

---

[185] cf. Psalm 38:4 "For mine iniquities are gone over mine head: as an heavy burden they are too heavy for me."

[186] "... for if there had been a law given which could have given life, verily righteousness should have been by the law." Gal 3:21

[187] H6293 to *impinge*

[188] H5771 (from H5753) *perversity* i.e. (moral) *evil* :- fault, iniquity, mischief, punishment (of iniquity), sin H5753 *to crook* lit. or fig :- do amiss, bow down, make crooked, commit iniquity, pervert, (do) perverse (-ly), trouble, X turn, do wickedly, do wrong.

[189] or *whole (in sense of being complete)*

[190] H5445 a primary root *to carry* (lit. or fig.), or (reflex.) *to be burdensome*; specifically *to be gravid*:- bear, be a burden, carry, strong to labour.

[191] Matthew 6:9-13; Luke 11:2-4 (quote is from both Matthew & Luke combined)

The word "forgive[192]" means "to send away".

Reading Psalm 32:3-5 ["When I kept silence, ..."]

If a man repents and asks God to forgive his sin, his sin is removed. This sin is removed by the blood of Christ.

> "And almost all things are by the law purged with blood; and without shedding of blood [there] is no remission[193]."
> Heb 9:22

There were many things which a man could not be justified from in the law of Moses, these included murder, sodomy, witchcraft, cursing parents, blasphemy etc. We are justified from all things by Jesus Christ. There is not one sin omitted.

> "But he, whom God raised again, saw no corruption. Be it known unto you therefore, men and brethren, that through this man is preached unto you the forgiveness of sins: And by him all that believe are justified[194] from[195] all things, from which ye could not be justified by the law of Moses."
> Acts 13:37-39[196]

Jesus was crucified once. There is no more offering for sin. It is finished.

> "... : but now once in the end of the world hath he appeared to put away sin by the sacrifice of himself.
>
> And as it is appointed unto men once to die, but after this the judgment:
>
> So Christ was (offered once) to bear the sins of many; and unto them that look for him shall he appear the second time without sin unto salvation."
> Heb 9:26-28

Reading Matthew 8:1-17

[Leper, centurions servant, Peters wife's mother with fever, many possessed with devils, and all that were sick]

Jesus lifted and carried our sicknesses.

> "surely (firmly) he hath borne (lifted) our griefs[197], and carried our sorrows[198]: ..."
> Isaiah 53:4

---

[192] G863 "*to send forth*" (from G575 and strengthened form of 'to send'). e.g.:-
"Jesus, when he had cried again with a loud voice, yielded up the ghost." Mat 27:50
G575 a prim. particle "*off*", i.e. away (from something near), in various senses (of place, time, or relation; lit. or fig.) In composition (as a prefix) it usually denotes separation, departure, cessation, completion, reversal, etc.

[193] G859 *freedom*; fig. *pardon* (From G863 to *send forth*).

[194] G1344 *to render* (i.e. show or regard as) *just* or *innocent* from [G1349 –*equitable* (in character or act);...]

[195] G575 "*off*", i.e. *away* (from something near)

[196] cf. 1Cor 6:9-11 "And such were some of you: but ye are washed, ..."

Here the Hebrew words translated as 'grief' and 'sorrow' can be used to refer to physical sickness. This is much clearer in the New Testament (Mat 8:17) when Matthew makes a comment about Jesus healing all that were sick[199].

> That it might be fulfilled which was spoken by Esaias the prophet, saying, Himself took[200] our infirmities[201], and bare our sicknesses[202].
>
> Mat 8:17 cf. Isaiah 53:4

God often endures grief with us, as he did with many of the saints because he loves us.

> For he said, Surely they are my people, children that will not lie: so he was their Saviour.
>
> In all their affliction he was afflicted, and the angel of his presence saved them: in his love and in his pity he redeemed them; and he bare them, and carried them all the days of old.
>
> ...
>
> Isaiah 63:8-9

---

[197] H2483 (from H2470) *malady, anxiety, calamity*: disease, grief, (is) sick (-ness).
H2470 a prim. root; prop. *to be rubbed, or worn*; hence fig. *to be weak, sick , afflicted*; or (causat.) *to grieve, make sick*; ...

Examples where H2483 is used:- 1Sa 19:14, 30:13, 1Ki 14:5, 15:23, 17:17, 22:34, Isaiah 39:1, Amos 6:6

[198] H4341 (from H3510) *anguish* or fig. *affliction.*
H3510 a prim. root; properly 'to feel *pain*'; by implic. to *grieve*; fig. to *spoil*: grieving, mar, have pain, make sad (sore), (be) sorrowful.

Anguish - [Oxford English dictionary] severe bodily or mental pain.

Examples where H4341 is used:- 2Ch 6:29, Job 33:19, Jer 51:8, Lam 1:18

[199] "they brought unto him many ... and he ... healed all that were sick" Mat 8:16
Cf. Mat 8:14-19; Luke 4:38-40, Mark 1:29-34 [Peter's wife and many healed];
see also Mat 12:15, Luke 6:17-19 [multitudes healed]

[200] to *take.* Probably objective or active, to *get hold of.*

[201] *feebleness* (of body or mind); by implic. *malady*; moral *frailty*

[202] G3554 of uncert. affin.; *a malady* [rarely fig. of moral *disability*]:- disease, infirmity, sickness.

5.4 The Knowledge of God

"As thou [Father] hast given him [thy Son] power over all flesh, that he should give (life eternal)[203] to as many as thou hast given him. And this is (eternal life), that they might know thee the only true God, and Jesus Christ, whom thou hast sent." – Jesus.

(John 17:2-3)

5.4.1 God is for us

"Verily, verily, I say unto you, Whatsoever ye shall ask the Father in my name, he will give it you. Hitherto have ye asked nothing in my name: ask, and ye shall receive[204], that your joy may be full."

John 16:23-24

Jesus said to the disciples, up to now, you haven't asked the Father for anything. Then he says Ask, so that your joy may be full. Children always need something from their parents. God likes to give us things. He is not stingy or disinterested in us[205]. Remember the end of Job, that the Lord is pitiful, and of tender mercies. God doesn't want bad things for us. He doesn't want us to be heart broken.

This I (make to return to my heart), therefore have I hope. It is of the Lords mercies that we are not consumed, because his compassions fail not. They are new every morning: great is thy faithfulness[206].

...

For the Lord will not cast off forever:

But though he cause grief, yet will he have compassion according to the multitude of his mercies.

For he doeth not afflict (from his heart) nor grieve the children of men.

Lam 21-23,31-33

God is interested in us, and because he loves us, he is interested in the things that worry us as well.

---

[203] *perpetual*. Derived from an obsolete prim. noun (appar. mean continued duration); meaning "ever": translated as (in KJV):- eternal, for ever, everlasting, world (began).

[204] "ye shall receive" is a translation of G2983 to *take* (in very many applications, lit. and fig.) [properly obj. or act., to *get hold* of]. I think of a child asking for a cup, or a toy, and the parents saying yes, you can have it, and then the child takes it for him or her self, but it's not on this occasion handed to them by the parents.

N.B. 'Ask' (which is an imperative, i.e. a command or instruction) is in the present tense and G2983 'receive' (not an imperative) is in the future tense. Cf. Mat 21:22 ['And all things, ...']

[205] Rom 8:31-33 "If God be for us ..."

[206] H530 lit. *firmness*; fig. *security*; moral *fidelity. Fem. of H529.*

H529 from H539 *established* i.e.. fig. *trustworthy*, abstractly *trustworthiness*

H539 אמן 'âman *aw-man'*

A prim root; properly to *build up* or *support*; to *foster* as a parent or nurse; fig to *render* (or *be*) *firm* or faithful, to *trust* or believe, to be *permanent* or quiet; morally to *be true* or certain.

> "Fear not, little flock; for it is your Father's good pleasure to give you the kingdom."
> Luke 12:32

> "My Son, eat thou ... then there shall be a reward[207], and thy expectation[208] shall not be cut off."
> Prov 24:13-14

God promises us a future with him. If someone says there is no future, who is right? God or that evil spirit?

> PSA 30:1 I will extol thee, O LORD; for thou hast lifted me up, and hast not made my foes to rejoice over me.

> PSA 30:2 O LORD my God, I cried unto thee, and thou hast healed[209] me.

Praise the Lord. We can come to God, and he will bind up our grief's and take our sorrows away.

> PSA 147:2 The LORD doth build up Jerusalem: he gathereth together the outcasts of Israel.

> PSA 147:3 He healeth the broken in heart, and bindeth up their wounds.

As a result of believing the gospel God helps us stand. His help to make us stand, and his desire to heal us are based on the same gospel that Jesus came to save us because he loved us.

Reading John 20:1-17 [Mary Magdalene. God has not forgotten.]

Jesus has not changed, he will still stop heaven and earth for us if we ask him.

> "And Jesus answering saith unto them, Have faith in God."

> Mark 11:22

Reading Mark 11:22-24 [mountain removed]

God wants to give us things[210]. However, some things are not easy to obtain.

Reading Mat 7:7-11

[Ask, seek, knock, ... 'if his son ask bread, will he give him a stone?'][211]

---

207 hereafter

208 Literally a cord (as an attachment). Figuratively expectancy. Translated in the KJV as:- expectation [-ted], hope, live, thing that I long for.

209 H7495 A primary root; properly to *mend* (by stitching), i.e. (fig.) to *cure*

210 "For the LORD God is a sun and shield: the LORD will give grace and glory: no good thing will he withhold from them that walk uprightly (refer H8549)." Psalm 84:11

211 cf. Luke 11:1-13

"And it came to pass, that, as he was praying in a certain place, when he ceased, one of his disciples said unto him, Lord, teach us to pray, ... And he said unto them, Which of you shall have a friend, ..."

Luke 11:1,5

The Lord in response to this question mentioned two things. The first is the Lord's prayer, an example of what to say when praying. The second was about not giving up on requests to God, particularly about requesting the gift of the Holy Ghost[212].

I say unto you, Though he will not rise and give him, because he is his friend, yet because of his importunity[213] he will rise and give him as many as he needeth.

And I say unto you, Ask, and it shall be given you; seek, and ye shall find; knock, and it shall be opened unto you.

Luke 11:8-9

On this occasion, the man didn't get what he needed because he was a friend[214]. The emphasis of this parable is that importunity[215] and persistence were what enabled the man to get what he wanted. There are some things God will not give us unless we are determined and persistent.

Reading Luke 18:1-8

[The unjust judge and the widow - It is necessary every time to pray, and not to give up]

5.4.2 Sin deceives

Reading Genesis chapters 2 and 3.

Satan's greatest trick is to lie about the nature of God.

"... (has) God said, ..."

Gen 3:1

Satan questioned God's motive for instructing Adam to keep away from the tree of the knowledge of good and evil.

---

212 Luke 11:13

213 G335 anaideia compound G1 [privation - 'absence of' / without] and G127 [*bashfulness*]; *impudence*, i.e. (by impl.) *importunity*
G127 aidos
perhaps from G1 (as negative particle) and G1492 (through the idea of *downcast* eyes); *bashfulness*, i.e. (towards men) *modesty* or (towards God) *awe*:-reverence; shamefacedness.
Russian translation of G335 is based on word meaning "not" and "- to step back, to retreat, to give up." One root is 'foot'.

214 possibly he would not have got anything if he wasn't

215 Importune - solicit pressingly and repeatedly (Little Oxford Dictionary).
Incidentally, the word H6293 translated as "laid" in ("... and the Lord hath laid on him the iniquity of us all.") Isaiah 53:6 is defined by Strong's Dictionary as "a prim. root; to *impinge*, by accident or violence, or (fig.) by importunity."

"for God doth know that in the day ye eat thereof, then your eyes shall be opened, and ye shall be as Gods, knowing ..."

Gen 3:5

He implied God wanted to hold back blessing. That God wasn't interested in them, but himself. Satan is always out to defame God to his people. When Satan takes away the knowledge of our creator, he has taken away from the relationship we have with him. May God always draw us closer to himself. Sadly they had the source of all good wisdom and knowledge, God himself to talk to.

"For the Lord giveth wisdom: out of his mouth cometh knowledge and understanding."

Prov 2:6

There is both good and bad wisdom.

"But if ye have bitter envying and strife in your hearts, glory not, and lie not against the truth. This wisdom descendeth[216] not from above [from God], but is earthly, sensual, devilish."

James 3:14-15

Not all knowledge is beneficial.

For your obedience is come abroad unto all men. I am glad therefore on your behalf: *but yet I would have you wise unto that which is good, and simple concerning evil.*

And the God of peace shall bruise Satan under your feet shortly. The grace of our Lord Jesus Christ be with you. Amen.

Rom 16:19-20

It is not possible to look at certain things except in the light of the knowledge of God. Jesus is the way, the truth, and the life. Separating Christ from knowledge leads astray. It is impossible to know the truth completely (not leaning towards error), without knowing Christ himself. This is because ultimately the search for truth must lead to a person. The truth is not a set of facts. He is our Lord and saviour Jesus Christ.

Jesus saith unto him, I am the way, the truth, and the life: no man cometh unto the Father, but by me.

John 14:6

Sin is deceitful. We can perhaps see this in the following definitions[217], where mention is made of how it leads astray, and robs us of the things God has planned for us.

Greek 264 properly to *miss* the mark (and so *not share* in the prize), i.e. (fig.) to *err*, espec. (moral.) to *sin*. Perhaps from G1 (as a negative particle) and the base of [G3313 - 'meros'[218]; *a division* or *share*];

---

[216] cometh down

[217] Reference numbers are those of James Strong's Concordance and Greek and Hebrew dictionaries.

[218] from an obsolete but more primary form of meiromai [which means *to get* as a *section* or *allotment*]

Hebrew 2398 a prim. root; properly to *miss*; hence (fig. and generally) to *sin*; by inference to *forfeit, lack, expiate, repent,* (causatively) *lead astray, condemn.*

Sin offers us something that we think we want. The temptation is to exchange something of value for something that is worthless. Sin acts as a decoy to make us walk away from God. It leads on a path that heads away from knowing God.

God will provided for us so that we do not need to sin[219].

> "And **God is able** to make all grace abound toward you; that ye, always having all sufficiency in all things, may abound unto every good work: ..."
>
> 2Cor 9:8; cf. Phil 4:19

An astonishing statement if ever you saw one. But, God is for us. He is our Father, and he loves us.

> "But as God is true, our word toward you was not yea and nay. For the Son of God, Jesus Christ, who was preached among you by us, even by me and Silvanus and Timotheus, was not yea and nay, but in him was yea. For all the promises of God in him are yea, and in him Amen, unto the glory of God by us [including you]."
>
> 2Cor 1:18-20

5.4.3 God Speaks

> "My sheep hear my voice, and I know them, and they follow me: ..."
>
> John 10:27

There are many voices we can listen to. Whether it is a school teacher, or our parents, or a scuba diving instructor. There are also spiritual voices.

> "Beloved, believe not every spirit, but try (test) the spirits whether they are of God: because many false prophets are gone out into the word.
>
> Hereby know ye the Spirit of God: Every spirit that confesseth that Jesus Christ *is come in the flesh*[220] is of God:

---

219 "There hath no temptation taken you but such as is common to man: but God is faithful, who will not suffer you to be tempted above that ye are able; but will with the temptation also make (an exit), that ye may be able to bear it." 1Cor 10:13.

G1545 - an *exit*

see also James 1:1-4 'patience have her (complete) work, that ye may be (complete) and entire, ...'; James 1:12-16 ' Blessed is the man that endureth temptation: ...'; James 5:11 'them happy which endure';

220 "the Greek perfect tense indicates the continuation and present state of a completed past action", i.e. Jesus lives. Jesus is alive in the same body he was born with. Jesus came when he was born cf. Isaiah 9:6; Mat 1:18 [Jesus was born by Mary, and by the Holy Spirit]; Philip 2:5-9; John 8:58; 1Tim 3:16 (see also section '4.7.1 Introduction'). Jesus was born in the flesh, died in the flesh and was resurrected [to stand up again] in the flesh. Jesus Christ is still, even now, in the flesh.

"... it is I myself: handle me and see; ..." Luke 24:39.

" ... , and of one Jesus, which was dead, whom Paul affirmed to be alive." Act 25:19;

cf. John 20:11-18 [Mary Magdalene], Heb 7:14-26 [... he ever liveth to make intercession for them. For such an high priest became us, who is holy, harmless, undefiled, ...] & Rom 5:10-11. [*Footnote is continued on the next page* ...]

And every spirit that confesseth not that Jesus Christ is come in the flesh is not of God: ..."

1John 4:1-3

Reading John 10:1-5 [The shepherd and his sheep]

God will never contradict himself. If something a spirit says is contrary to what is written in the Bible, then we know it was not spoken by God.

Our primary hope for the future is based on God. We trust that God will speak to us, and provide for us. That he will be our friend. I am inclined to believe that it is through hearing God's voice and following his instructions that we receive all that pertains to a good future, hope and life. Hearing God's voice and knowing that it is him that is speaking to us immediately brings confidence that we are not alone and without hope. We can not limit the future to the things which are seen. Neither can we limit it to the things we can do by ourselves. We must hope for God to do

> "... (is able) to do exceeding abundantly above all that we ask or think[221], according to the power[222] that worketh[223] in us[224], ..."
>
> Eph 3:20

> "But as it is written, Eye hath not seen, nor ear heard, neither have entered into the heart of man, the things which God hath prepared for them that love him.
>
> But God hath revealed them unto us by his Spirit: for the Spirit searcheth all things, yea, the deep things of God.
>
> For what man knoweth the things of a man, save the spirit of man which is in him? even so the things of God knoweth no man, but the Spirit of God.
>
> Now we have received, not the spirit of the world, but the spirit which is of God; that we might know the things that are freely given to us of God."
>
> 1Cor 2:9-12

By the Holy Spirit God talks to us, and shows us his plans.

> "Howbeit when he, the Spirit of truth, is come, he will guide you into all truth: for he shall not speak of himself; but whatsoever he shall hear, that shall he speak: and he will shew you things to come.

Jesus is in heaven. "So then after the Lord had spoken unto them, he was received up into heaven, and sat on the right hand of God." Mar 16:19; "..., having a desire to depart, and to be with Christ;" Phil 1:23; Rev 1:17-18. Although Jesus is in heaven some people still see visions or have dreams of him. In some of these visions and dreams Jesus speaks with them. Cf. Acts 7:55 [Stephen]; Acts 9:10 [Ananias]; Acts 18:9-10 [Paul]; Acts 26:19 [Paul]; Rev 1:1-2,13 [John]. However, I suppose it is more frequent for the Holy Spirit to speak e.g. Acts 8:29 [Phillip], Acts 10:19-20 [Peter], cf. Isaiah 30:21.

[221] exercise the mind, i.e. (fig.) to comprehend

[222] *force* or *power* [from G1410 to be *able* or *possible*].

cf. a deep, wide and steadily moving river descending down over a cliff to the water, rock and boulders below

[223] active / 'productive of effect'

[224] 'upon' and 'to us' (combined in KJV as 'in us")

He shall glorify me: for he shall receive of mine, and shall shew it unto you.

All things that the Father hath are mine: therefore said I, that he shall take of mine, and shall shew it unto you."

John 16:13-15

Conversely the enemy would have us lose the knowledge of God.

The best sermon I have heard was about a man telling what he used to do when he was travelling. Before he went to bed, he would set one chair for himself, and two other chairs facing him. At night God would wake him up and he would sit and say, Lord you can have this chair, and Devil you can have this one over here, but you are not to say a word. Then he would begin to say in an American accent "Hallelujah. Praise the Lord." And wait for God to speak.

Although the speaker did not as far as I recall mention it. He prepared both in the natural, and in the spiritual something for God to make him feel welcome and at home. In the natural it was a chair for him to sit down and rest. In the spiritual it was praise and thanksgiving.

"But thou art holy, O thou that inhabitest[225] the praises of Israel."

Psalm 22:3

Many burdens and griefs are lifted when we spend time talking with God. We turn around after we have been communing with God and realise that the grief and sorrow troubling us has been taken away.

"And the Lord of hosts shall stir up[226] a scourge[227] ... and as his rod was upon the sea, so shall he lift it up after the manner of Egypt. And it shall come to pass in that day, that his burden shall be taken away from off thy shoulder, and his yoke from off thy neck, and the yoke shall be destroyed because of the anointing."

Isaiah 10:26-27

"If God be for us, who can be against us?[228]" Rom 8:31

"Beware lest any man spoil you through philosophy and vain deceit, after the tradition of men, after the rudiments of the world, and not after Christ.

For in him dwelleth all the fulness of the Godhead bodily.

And ye are complete in him, which is the head of all principality and power: ..."

Col 2:8-10

All the fullness of life is made complete in a friendship with Christ our Lord who is the head of all principalities and powers. No one dares stand against our heavenly Father.

"None is so fierce that dare stir him (leviathan) up: who then is able to stand before me?"

Job 41:10

---

[225] H3427 A primary root; properly to sit down (specifically as judge, in ambush, in quiet); by implication to *dwell*, to *remain*; causatively to *settle*, to *marry*.

[226] to *wake* (lit. or fig.)

[227] a lash or a whip (noun)

[228] cf. Isaiah 50:7-9 "For the Lord God will help me; ..."

When we stand next to God, no one dares stand against us.

Reading Isaiah 40:21-31

The reason we don't give up is because we trust in our Father, who is the Lord of Hosts.

> "Who can stand before his indignation? and who can abide in the fierceness of his anger? his fury is poured out like fire, and the rocks are thrown down by him.
>
> The Lord is good, a strong hold in the day of trouble; and he knoweth them that trust in him."
>
> Nahum 1:6-7

There will always be battles to fight down here. One of the constant battles is keeping our heart pure.

Reading Psalm 48:1-7

Mount Zion was an inaccessible place due to the cliffs, and also due to the walls of the city. It even mentions how the enemy came to destroy but had such consternation when they saw the city that they gave up and went away. God is our high tower, and our fortress. The greatest victories occur when God fights for us, as he longs to do.

Reading Deuteronomy 32:1-44 [God is our refuge]

The dew takes time to settle, if we quietly wait for God to come and talk to us, he will not disappoint us.

5.4.4 Fruitful in the Knowledge of God

Reading 2Peter 1:1-16

> "Simon Peter ... to those allotted equally with us precious faith through the righteousness of our God and saviour[229] Jesus Christ: Grace and peace increase/multiply to you in the knowledge of God, and of Jesus our Lord, as how, all/everything to us of his divine power which pertains[230] to life and godliness has been given[231], through the knowledge of him who has called us via glory and virtue: ..."
>
> 2Pet 1:1-3 [a translation]

[229] G4990 sōtēr from G4982; a *deliverer*, i.e. God or Christ
G4982 sōzō
From a primary word σῶς sōs (contraction for the obsolete σάος saos, "safe"); to *save*, i.e. *deliver* or *protect* (lit. or fig.)

[230] *forward to* i.e. *toward*

[231] G1433 to *bestow* gratuitously [Bestow v. t. :- deposit, provide with confer (thing) upon (person) as gift.]
from G1435 [G1435 - a *present*; spec. a *sacrifice*.]

Peter talking to those who have obtained faith, goes on to elaborate concerning things which we may obtain from God.

> "And [in that line[232]], giving all *diligence*[233], add[234,235] to your faith virtue; and to virtue knowledge;
>
> And to knowledge temperance; and to temperance patience; and to patience godliness;
>
> And to[236] godliness brotherly kindness; and to brotherly kindness charity[237]."
> 2Peter 1:5-7

> "For in whom these things are not present, he is blind[238], and can not see afar off[239], and forgetfulness taking [the memory that] he was purged from his old[240] sins.
>
> Wherefore the rather, brethren, be diligent to make sure[241] your invitation and selection[242]; for doing these things, not at all will you fall ever.
>
> For so abundantly[243] an entrance shall be supplied[244] unto you into the everlasting kingdom of our Lord and saviour Jesus Christ."
> 2Peter 1:9-11 [a translation]

OK again we see that it is possible for a Christian to fall.

> "For a just man falls seven times, and rises up again[245]: ..." Prov 24:16

We see that just men fall. But it doesn't stop there, nothing will keep down those who seek God through Jesus. For God will cause them to stand.

> Yea, he shall be holden up: for God is able to make him stand.
> Rom 14:4

But some things are said to guarantee that a Christian will never fall. What were those things?

---

232 Literally "that thing itself". I suppose that all things that pertain unto life and godliness include virtue, knowledge, temperance, patience etc.
"... For by grace are ye saved through faith; and that not of yourselves: it is the gift of God: ..." Eph 2:8

233 "speed", i.e. (by implic.) despatch, eagerness, earnestness. From G4692
G4692 to "speed" ("study"), that is, urge on (diligently or earnestly); by implic. to await eagerly

234 G2023 *epichorēgeō*
From G1909 (ἐπί epi) and G5524; to *furnish besides*, that is, fully *supply*, (fig.) *aid* or *contribute*
G5524 chorēgeo
From a compound of G5525 and G71; to be a *dance leader*, that is, (genitive case) to *furnish:* - give, minister.

235 bearing (carrying) in alongside to [your faith ...]

236 The English Standard Version (ESV) Bible translates "to" as "with", e.g. "... , and godliness with brotherly affection, and brotherly affection with love."

237 love

238 *opaque* (as if *smoky*), i.e. (by analogy) *blind* (physically or mentally)

239 to *shut* the *eyes* i.e. blink (see indistinctly)

240 *former* i.e. of the past or an earlier period (e.g. 'in former times', 'more like her former self')

241 From the base of G939 (through the idea of *basality*); *stable* (lit. or fig.): - firm, of force, stedfast, sure.
G939 βάσις basis *bas'-ece* From βαίνω bainō (to *walk*); a *pace* ("base"), i.e. (by implic.) the *foot*

242 I suppose, an outcome of consideration (or review) of a particular choice cf. John 15:16 and 1John 4:19. Yet I suppose there is an invitation to every one (ref. below), and everyone must make their own choice whether to accept it or to choose something else.

"... giving all diligence [A], add [B] to your faith ..." 2Pet 1:5

Item	Ref Number[246]
Virtue	703
Knowledge	1108
Temperance (or self control)	1466
Patience	5281
Godliness	2150
Brotherly kindness	5360
Charity (i.e. Love)	26

Let us look in turn at each of the words. The first word translated as "diligence" in the KJV is

[A] *spoo-day'* Gr. 4710 (from Gr. 4692[247])

and literally means "speed", i.e. (by implication) despatch, eagerness, earnestness. I think of the boss who absolutely wants a job done yesterday. He watches over the workers as they work. He knows watching them won't make it go any faster. But he's keeping his eye on it, so that no obstacle can stand in the way of its completion. He diligently supervises the job to haste its completion.

The second word "add" is a translation of two Greek words.

[B1] epichorēgeō Gr. 2023 to *furnish besides* (that which is already there) i.e. fully supply.

and

[B2] *par-ice-fer'-o* Gr. 3923 to *bear [carry] in alongside,* i.e. *introduce simultaneously.*

The second word '*par-ice-fer'-o'* describes how the first (i.e. furnishing) is done. I suppose it's bringing or carrying in something that is nearby. Something I dare say within our reach or means.

John 1:7, 3:14-17, 12:32; Acts 17:30; 1Tim 2:4, 4:10; 2Pet 3:9; 1John 2:2; Rev 14:6

243 plentifully, has sense of having more than enough, i.e. wealthy, replete, no lack

244 G2023 *furnish besides* - cf. footnote 234 and 2Peter 1:5

245 This reminds me of a song that was played during a rugby league match 'I get knocked down, but I get up again, nothings going to keep me down.'

246 James Strong's Greek Dictionary

247 Gr. 4692 to "*speed*" ("to study"), i.e. *urge* on (diligently or earnestly); by implication to *await* eagerly. Translated as '(make, with) haste unto'

The items that are being carried in and stored (or furnished[248]) are:

[1] Virtue

excellence[249]

[2] Knowledge

lit. '*knowing*' (the act), i.e. (by implic.) knowledge. Derived from the word meaning *to 'know'* (absolute).

to "know"- e.g. be aware (of), feel, (have) know(-ledge)[250], perceive, be sure, understand

[3] Temperance[251]

Strong in a thing (masterful) self controlled.

[4] Patience

Cheerful (or hopeful) endurance, constancy. (from G5278[252])

[5] Godliness

To revere (or adore) well. Devout (earnest, hearty, genuine)[253]

[6] Brotherly Kindness (G5360)

Fond[254] of a brother i.e. someone who was with you and went through the same things from birth. '*Dear* to someone'.

[7] Love

Love, i.e. affection or benevolence (desirous of doing good).

We can bring in virtue, knowledge, self-restraint, patience, godliness, brotherly love and love. I suppose that we can bring in these things all at the same time[255] (together with each other) and stack them away in our storehouse. We have a big wool bale size sack of faith. But the sack isn't full. We however have some other things near by which we could stash safely in that sack, and fill

[248] Furnishings are movable items that one puts into a house to make it more comfortable to live in e.g. fridge, microwave, sofa, coffee table, etc. The items in the list that are to be added to our Faith are, I suppose, similar to furnishings.

[249] properly *manliness* (valour), but it seems to be widely applicable even to inanimate objects cf. Phil. 4:8 "... whatsoever things are ... , ...; if there be any virtue, ..., think on these things."

[250] Learning knowledge requires study, i.e. time and effort

[251] From G1468; *self control* (especially *continence*): - temperance
G1468 From G1722 and G2904; *strong in* a thing (*masterful*), i.e. (fig. and reflex.) *self controlled* (in appetite, etc.): - temperate

[252] G5278 from G5259 and G3306; to *stay under* (*behind*), i.e. *remain*; figuratively to *undergo*, i.e. *bear* (trials), *have fortitude*, *persevere*

[253] The only item which is repeated from 2Peter 1:3 'pertain to life and godliness'. 'Revere' according to the Oxford English dictionary is Regard as sacred or exalted, hold in deep & usually affectionate or religious respect, venerate.

[254] G5384 Properly *dear*, i.e. a *friend*; actively *fond*, i.e. *friendly* (still as a noun, an *associate*, *neighbour*, etc.): - friend.

it out a bit. It's not too difficult for us to go and get them. The scripture says furnish in your faith virtue. So off we go to get some virtue. Then we pop it in the sack, but mate!, there's still plenty of room, lets get some of this knowledge, pack it in there. The sack is no way full yet. OK onwards. We'll pack in a few more goodies in there yet, self-restraint, endurance, godliness, friendliness, love. Its getting pretty chokka in that sack, but its our sack, and we only want the best stuff in there and we want as much as we can get so we can take it with us. Maybe we do get to take something with us, faith, virtue, knowledge of God, self-restraint patience, godliness ... these are the kinds of treasures we can well do with copious quantities of. If we can't take anything with us to heaven when we die, we can sure send it on ahead.

> "... lay up for yourselves treasures in heaven, ..." Mat 6:20

When does treasure begin stacking up in heaven? It is now. We need to see clearly into the future. These things which are discussed here (unpretended faith, virtue - which healed the woman with the issue of blood[256], temperance - which saves us from grief, endurance and cheerful expectation of God's plans for the future, devout - someone who is faithful to God in all that he does, kindness - bearing our brothers and sisters hopes and sadness, [and the best of all] love which never fails), these things help us see a future with God. Praise the Lord, that these things are little everyday things which are bricks and mortar to build a good house for God.

The end of faith, virtue, knowledge, mastery, cheerful endurance, devoutness, brotherly kindness and love is I believe the knowledge of God.

> "For if these things be in you, and abound, they make you that ye shall neither be (not working) nor unfruitful[257] in the knowledge of our Lord Jesus Christ."
>
> 2Peter 1:8

I think the objective is the knowledge of God. One can know God now. We do not have to wait until we reach heaven. The other things mentioned such as seeing afar off, knowledge that we are forgiven, establishing our hearts firmly on Christ, never falling, having an abundant entrance into the everlasting kingdom of God are a result of knowing God.

> “For so an entrance shall be ministered unto you abundantly into the everlasting kingdom of our Lord and Saviour Jesus Christ.”
>
> 2Peter 1:11

This entrance starts now with Jesus and ends with Jesus. It reminds me of the Royal wedding ceremony with a Prince and his new wife. I see the groom standing at the top of the steps of the temple, and the bride running up the steps to her new husband. It is with little effort that those steps are covered as she sees him, reaches the top of those stairs and looks into his eyes. Of that friendship, there will be no end.

---

[255] The first of all the commandments is, Hear, O Israel; The Lord our God is one Lord: and thou shalt love the Lord thy God with all thy heart, and with all thy soul, and with all thy might. Mark 12:29; Deut 6:4. We do not have to wait for large quantities of virtue, self-control, or patience before we begin to fulfil the first and second commandments i.e. to love (which is last on the list of items to be brought in).

[256] “And Jesus, immediately knowing in himself that virtue had gone out of him, turned him about in the press, and said, Who touched my clothes?” Mark 5:30

[257] *barren,* fruitless cf. Tit 3:14

5.4.5 Laying Hold of Eternal Life.

> "... for which [knowing Christ] also I am apprehended[258] of Christ Jesus."
> Phil. 3:12

God laid hold of us. I have watched a rescue boat speed out into the waves to save a drowning person. One of the crew reaches over the side of the boat and grabs the drowning person by their collar with one hand, and lifts them in one movement into the boat. It was with a strong arm[259] that the Lord rescued Israel out of Egypt.

A Quote of Paul the Apostle Concerning the Resurrection

> "But contrariwise, anything which was gain to me, I have counted[260] through Christ, a loss. But, actually accordingly, I count[260] also everything loss through the excellency[261] of knowing Christ Jesus my Lord. The one through whom I lost everything, and count[260] to be that which is chucked to the dogs, so that I can gain Christ, and be found in him, not holding my innocence[262] which is from the law, but that through the faith of Christ, the innocence from God which rests upon faith to know:
>
> (1) him,
>
> (2) and the power[263] (strength, be able, be possible, abundance, might) of his resurrection,
>
> (3) and the participation[264] of the enduring[265] himself went through, being made similar[266] to the death of himself;
>
> if thereby I might arrive at (to/into) from standing up out of the dead. Not that already I have acquired[267], neither am I already complete. But I pursue after if that I may *seize/lay hold*[268] upon that for which I also (beneath[269]) was laid hold[268] of by Christ Jesus.

---

[258] 'laid hold of'

[259] Psalm 89:5-18; Psalm 136 "O give thanks unto the Lord; for he is good: for his mercy endureth for ever."

[260] Middle voice of a (presumed) strengthened form of G71; to *lead*, i.e. *command* (with official authority); figuratively to *deem*, that is, *consider*

[261] G5242 *to hold above* i.e. (fig.) to *excel*

[262] G1343 δικαιοσύνη dikaiosunē *dik-ah-yos-oo'-nay* from G1342; *equity* (of character or act); specially (Christian) *justification:* - righteousness.

G1342 δίκαιος dikaios *dik'-ah-yos* from G1349; *equitable* (in character or act); by implication *innocent, holy* (absolutely or relatively): - just, meet, right (-eous).

G1349 δίκη dikē *dee'-kay* probably from G1166; *right* (as self *evident*), i.e. *justice* (the principle, a decision, or its execution): - judgment, punish, vengeance.

G1166 δεικνύω deiknuō *dike-noo'-o* a prolonged form of an obsolete primary of the same meaning; to *show* (lit. or fig.): - shew.

[263] G1411 δύναμις dunamis *doo'-nam-is* from G1410; *force* (lit. or fig.); specially miraculous *power* (usually by implication a *miracle* itself): - ability, abundance, meaning, might (-ily, -y, -y deed), (worker of) miracle (-s), power, strength, violence, mighty (wonderful) work.

G1410 δύναμαι dunamai *doo'-nam-ahee* of uncertain affinity; to *be able* or *possible:* - be able, can (do, + -not), could, may, might, be possible, be of power.

[264] G2842 κοινωνία koinōnia *koy-nohn-ee'-ah* from G2844; *partnership*, i.e. (lit.) *participation*, or (social) *intercourse*, or (pecuniary) *benefaction:* - (to) communicate (-ation), communion, (contri-), distribution, fellowship.

Brethren, I myself, adding it up reckon that I do *not yet*[270] *possess*[268] it, but one thing truly: that which is behind - I forget and neglect, and that which is in front, I stretch reaching forward to.

Surely, the objective targeted I pursue towards the [gold] *medal*[271] of the invitation calling upward[272] from God in Christ Jesus.

Phil 3:7-14 [a translation]

Paul's primary objective was to know God. For this he was willing to give up everything.

“Let us therefore, as many as be perfect, be thus minded: ...”

1Phil 3:15

I believe that having the objective of knowing God is a characteristic of perfection. And surely there is no intrinsic harm to have this objective when one is not perfect.

“Till we all come in the unity of the faith, and of the knowledge of the Son of God, unto a perfect (complete[273]) man, unto the measure of the stature (maturity[274]) of the fullness of Christ[275]: ..."

Eph 4:13

We should grow to be men. The measure of maturity can probably be in terms of knowing God. We can expect God to talk to us, and help us. The greatest objective any one can have is to know God as their friend. There is no limit to how well one may know God.

1 Afterward he brought me again unto the door of the house; and, behold, waters issued out from under the threshold of the house eastward: for the forefront of the house stood toward the east, and the waters came down from under from the right side of the house, at the south side of the altar.

2 Then brought he me out of the way of the gate northward, and led me about the way without unto the utter gate by the way that looketh eastward; and, behold, there ran out waters on the right side.

3 And when the man that had the line in his hand went forth eastward, he measured a thousand cubits, and he brought me through the waters; the waters were to the ankles.

G2844 κοινωνός koinōnos *koy-no-nos'* from G2839; a *sharer*, i.e. *associate:* - companion, X fellowship, partaker, partner.

265 G3804 πάθημα pathēma *path'-ay-mah* from a presumed derivative of G3806; something *undergone*, that is, *hardship* or *pain*; subjectively an *emotion* or *influence:* - affection, affliction, motion, suffering.

266 G4833 συμμορφόω summorphoō *soom-mor-fo'-o* from G4832; to *render like*, i.e. (fig.) to *assimilate:* - make conformable unto.

G4832 συμμορφός summorphos *soom-mor-fos'* from G4862 and G3444; *jointly formed*, i.e. (fig.) *similar:* - conformed to, fashioned like unto.

267 G2983 λαμβάνω lambanō *lam-ban'-o* A prolonged form of a primary verb, which is used only as an alternate in certain tenses; to *take* (in very many applications, lit. and fig. [probably objective or active, to *get hold* of]

268 'lay hold of' i.e. G2638

G2638 καταλαμβάνω katalambanō *kat-al-am-ban'-o* [From G2596 kata and G2983 '*to take*']; to *take eagerly*, i.e. *seize, possess*, etc. (lit. or fig.). : - apprehend, attain, come upon, comprehend, find, obtain, perceive, (over-) take.

269 2 Sam 22:17; Psalm 18:6,16; Job 2:5

270 G3768 οὔπω *not yet.* Ref. 'The Majority Text Notes' by William G. Pierpont which is an appendix to ‘The Interlinear Bible’ by J. P. Green 1986 (see Appendix ‘A. Recommended Reading and References’).

4 Again he measured a thousand, and brought me through the waters; the waters were to the knees. Again he measured a thousand, and brought me through; the waters were to the loins.

5 Afterward he measured a thousand; and it was a river that I could not pass over: for the waters were risen, waters to swim in, a river that could not be passed over.

6 And he said unto me, Son of man, hast thou seen this?

Ezek 47:1-6

The river represents the Holy Spirit and also, I think, our relationship with God. A toddler likes very shallow water to splash around in. A five year old enjoys venturing into something a bit deeper, but likes to be able to stand up.

But grow in grace, and in the knowledge of our Lord and Saviour Jesus Christ. To him be glory both now and for ever. Amen.

2Peter 3:18

God plans for us to grow up so that we are like Christ.

Eph 4:13 Till we all come in the unity of the faith, and of the knowledge of the Son of God, unto a perfect man, unto the measure of the stature of the fulness of Christ:

1Co 16:13 Watch ye, stand fast in the faith, quit you like men, be strong.

---

271 G1017 lit. an *award* or specially a *prize* in a public games, where there is an external umpire, or adjudicator (cf. 1Cor 9:24 [essentially 'run in this away that you may *obtain*[268]']). Paul says a lot of people compete, and then he says, if you want to win, this is how you do it. An athlete is disciplined in every aspect of life. He does not train erratically, but consistently. He restrains from staying up late, he restrains from too much sweet food, he trains when he doesn't feel like it, he doesn't go to invitations which hamper his training schedule. Paul compares the discipline required by an athlete over his body, to that of a slave driver (1Cor 9:24-27). Cf. "Fight the good fight [contest in an arena] of faith, lay hold on eternal life, ..." 1Tim 6:12 and "run with patience [hopeful endurance] the race [contest]" Heb 12:1

272 G507 ἄνω anō *an'-o* adverb from G473; *upward* or *on the top:* - above, brim, high, up.

G473 ἀντί anti *an-tee'* a primary particle; *opposite*, i.e. *instead* or *because* of (rarely *in addition* to): - for, in the room of. Often used in composition to denote *contrast, requital, substitution, correspondence*, etc.

273 G5046 *tel'-i-os* From G5056;

complete (in various applications of labor, growth, mental and moral character, etc.)

G5056 *tel'-os* From a primary word τέλλω tellō (to *set out* for a definite point or *goal*);

properly the point aimed at as a *limit*, i.e. (by implication) the *conclusion* of an act or state (*termination* [lit., fig. or indef.], *result* [immediate, ultimate or prophetic], *purpose*); specially an *impost* or *levy* (as *paid*). cf. G5411.

274 *maturity* (in years or size)

275 G5547 *anointed* (cf. G5548 "graze" [touch slightly], light upon, etc. to smear or rub with oil, i.e. (by implication) to consecrate to an office or religious service: - anoint.). The word 'Christ' (G5547) i.e. 'anointed' is probably related to the Greek word G5530 which means "to furnish what is needed". It is interesting that anointing with oil, like laying

on of hands, is associated with touch and something being transferred: in this case oil, but also (as it is with laying on of hands), probably something which is intangible and invisible.

G5547 Χριστός Christos; from G5548; *anointed*, i.e. the *Messiah*, an epithet [epithet - an adjective expressing quality or attribute; significant appellation] of Jesus: - Christ.

G5548 χρίω chriō; probably akin to G5530 through the idea of *contact*; to *smear* or *rub* with oil, i.e. (by implication) to *consecrate* to an office or religious service: - anoint.

G5530 χράομαι chraomai; middle voice of a primary verb (perhaps rather from G5495, to *handle*); to *furnish* what is needed; (give an *oracle*, "graze" [touch slightly], *light* upon, etc.), i.e. (by implication) to *employ* or (by extension) to *act towards* one in a given manner: - entreat, use. cf. G5531, G5534.

G5495 χείρ cheir; perhaps from the base of G5494 in the sense of its congener the base of G5490 (through the idea of *hollowness* for grasping); the *hand* (lit. or fig. [*power*]; espec. [by Hebraism] a *means* or *instrument*): - hand

6.0 The Resurrection of the Dead

" ... he which raised up the Lord Jesus shall raise up us also by Jesus, and shall present us with you."
2Cor 4:14

Tour of Duty

NEH 6:1 Now it came to pass when Sanballat, and Tobiah, and Geshem the Arabian, and the rest of our enemies, heard that I had builded the wall, and that there was no breach left therein; (though at that time I had not set up the doors upon the gates;)

NEH 6:2 That Sanballat and Geshem sent unto me, saying, Come, let us meet together in some one of the villages in the plain of Ono. But they thought to do me mischief.

NEH 6:3 And I sent messengers unto them, saying, I am doing a great work, so that I cannot come down: why should the work cease, whilst I leave it, and come down to you?

NEH 6:4 Yet they sent unto me four times after this sort; and I answered them after the same manner.

6.1 Introduction

Please read out loud Ezekiel 37:1-14.

Praise the Lord. Our God will raise the dead. It is through Christ's death and resurrection, that we can trust God to save us, and to give us a good future. We have been given good hope, and consolation through the love given us by God in Christ Jesus.

> ISA 26:19 Thy dead men shall live, together with my dead body shall they arise. Awake and sing, ye that dwell in dust: for thy dew is as the dew of herbs, and the earth shall cast out the dead.

In the following sections, God permitting, we will try to get an overview of the resurrection.

6.2 Eternal Life

> “And this is the will of him that sent me, that everyone which seeth the Son, and believeth on him, may have everlasting life: and I will raise him up at the last day.
>
> … Verily, verily, I say unto you, He that believeth on me hath everlasting life. I am that bread of life.
>
> ... I am the living bread which came down from heaven: if any man eat of this bread, he shall live forever: and the bread that I will give is my flesh, which I will give for the life of the world.
>
> ... Verily, verily, I say unto you, Except ye eat the flesh of the Son of man, and drink his blood, ye have no life in you.
>
> Whoso eateth my flesh, and drinketh my blood, hath eternal life; and I will raise him up at the last day. For my flesh is meat indeed, and my blood is drink indeed. He that eateth my flesh, and drinketh my blood, dwelleth in me, and I in him.
>
> As the living Father hath sent me, and I live by the Father: so he that eateth me, even he shall live by me.
>
> This is that bread which came down from heaven: not as your fathers did eat manna, and are dead: he that eateth of this bread shall live for ever.”
> John 6:40,47-48,51,53-58

We will be resurrected at the last day. Eternal life is not being resurrected.. However, we see above, that faith in Christ leads to both eternal life, and Christ resurrecting us at the last day. It is today that we have eternal life, because we have Jesus living in us.

The bread which Jesus gave was the word of God.

> “Lord, to whom shall we go? (Thou) hast the words of eternal life.” John 6:68

Reading John 5:21-30

In John 5:25-29 the Bible makes reference to two times.

> “The hour is coming, and now is, …” John 5:25

The first reference concerns our Lord Jesus. When we hear his voice for the first time, we are no longer dead, but live (and will live).

> “The hour is coming, and now is, when the dead shall hear the voice of the Son of God: and they that hear shall live.” John 5:25

This first reference is to salvation. It is through hearing God's voice, and trusting him, that we are saved (now is the time we can talk to God).

"For whosoever shall call upon the name of the Lord shall be saved. How then shall they call on him in whom they have not believed? and how shall they believe in him of whom they have not heard? ..."

Rom 10:13-14

"I have heard thee in a time accepted, and in the day of salvation have I succoured thee: behold, now is the accepted time; behold, now is the day of salvation."

2Cor 6:2[276]

"Again, he limiteth a certain day, saying in David, To day, after so long a time; as it is said, To day if ye will hear his voice, harden not your hearts."

Heb 4:7[277]

The next time referred to is the resurrection at the last day[278]. No longer does it say "the hour … is now", but it says simply, the hour is coming.

"Marvel not at this: for the hour is coming, in the which all that are in the graves shall hear his voice, and shall come forth; they that have done good, unto the resurrection of life; and they that have done evil, unto the resurrection of damnation[279]."

John 5:28-29

Everyone whether they are good or evil will be resurrected[280].

"But now is Christ risen from the dead, and become the firstfruits of them that slept. For since by man came death, by man came also the resurrection of the dead. For as in Adam all die, even so in Christ shall all be made alive.[281]"

1Cor 15:20-22

The way in which all will be made alive is likened to the way all men from Adam to the present die.

"But this I confess unto thee, that after the way which they call heresy, so worship I the God of my fathers, believing all things which are written in the law and in the prophets:

And have hope toward God, which they themselves also allow, that there shall be a resurrection (standing up) of the dead, both of the just and unjust."

Acts 24:14-15

---

[276] Isaiah 49:8

[277] Psalm 95:7

[278] In this case, "The hour is coming" does not mean now because the resurrection has not been [2Tim2:18]

[279] G2920 *decision* (subj. or obj., for or against)

[280] Believers now go to be with Jesus, not to be in the grave.

[281] "But every man in his own order: ... " 1Cor 15:23. There is order in the resurrection. Christ first, then later those that believed in Christ and died, then those that believe in Christ and are alive. Death itself shall be incapacitated; it shall be cast into the lake of fire. It is the last of Christ's enemies to be destroyed.
cf. 1Thes 4:13-17; Rev 20:14; 1Cor 15:23-26

6.3 The Resurrection on the Last Day.

Readings Job 14:7-15 and Job 19:23-27

> For I know that my redeemer liveth, and that he shall stand at the latter day upon the earth:
>
> And though after my skin worms destroy this body, yet in my flesh[282] shall I see God:
>
> Whom I shall see for myself, and mine eyes shall behold, and not another[283]; though my reins be consumed[284] within me.
>
> Job 19:25-27

When the pressure comes on, the mind automatically turns to what the future is going to be like. Job remembered that although his body would be destroyed, God would (although not explicitly stated here) resurrect his body, and that in it he would see God.

> "So man lieth down, and riseth not: till the heavens be no more, they shall not awake, nor be raised out of their sleep. O that thou wouldest hide me in the grave, that thou wouldest keep me secret, until thy wrath be past, that thou wouldest appoint me a set time, and remember me!
>
> If a man die, shall he live again? all the days of my appointed time will I wait, till my change come.
>
> Thou shalt call, and I will answer thee: thou wilt have a desire to the work of thine hands."
>
> Job 14:12-15

> "So man lieth down, and riseth not: till the heavens be no more, they shall not awake, nor be raised out of their sleep." Job 14:12

"till the heavens be no more". No comment is made here about whether men rise after the heavens cease to exist. But it hints at it.

> "O that thou wouldest hide me in the grave, that thou wouldest keep me secret, until thy wrath be past, ..."
>
> Job 14:13

> Come, my people, enter thou into thy chambers, and shut thy doors about thee: hide thyself as it were for a little moment, until the indignation be overpast.
>
> Isaiah 26:20

> "... that thou wouldest appoint me a set time, and remember me!"
>
> Job 14:13

---

282 "yet 'out of'/'from' my flesh shall I see God"
H4482; properly a *part* of; hence (prepositionally), *from* or *out of* in many senses

283 i.e. a stranger

284 A prim. root; to *end*, whether intransitively (to *cease, be finished, perish*) or transitively (to *complete, prepare, consume*)

God has appointed a set time for the resurrection. He has not, does not, and will not forget us.

> "If a man die, shall he live again?" Job 14:14

Yes.

> Thou shalt call, and I will answer thee: thou wilt have a desire to the work of thine hands.
>
> Jon 14:15

Who is God going to call, who does he desire? It's the same answer as it has always been, it is us.

We will stand in the body we have now at the end of the days.

> Thy dead men shall live, together with my dead body shall they arise. Awake and sing, ye that dwell in dust: for thy dew is as the dew of herbs, and the earth shall cast out the dead.
>
> Isaiah 26:19

> Some trust in chariots, and some in horses: but we will remember the name of the LORD our God. They are brought down and fallen: but we are risen, and stand upright.
>
> Psalm 20:7-8

We will stand at the resurrection.

> "And he said unto me, O Daniel, a man greatly beloved, understand the words that I speak unto thee, and stand upright: for unto thee am I now sent. ...
>
> Then there came again and touched me one like the appearance of a man, and he strengthened me, And said, O man greatly beloved, fear not: peace be unto thee, ...
>
> ... then said I, O my Lord, what shall be the end of these things? And he said, Go thy way, Daniel: for the words are closed up and sealed till the time of the end. ...
>
> But go thou thy way till the end be: for thou shalt rest, and stand in thy lot at the end of the days."
>
> - From the last few chapters of Daniel[285].

[285] Daniel 10:11,18-19, 12:8-9,13

6.4 Christ's Death

Jesus died, contrary to the hope of his disciples. He was the one who was supposed to save Israel. Nevertheless, Jesus did save Israel. But not from the Romans.

> "Jesus answered, My kingdom is not of this world: if my kingdom were of this world, then would my servants fight, that I should not be delivered to the Jews: but now is my kingdom not from hence."
>
> John 18:36

Jesus was delivered to be crucified.

> "When Jesus therefore had received the vinegar, he said, It is finished: and he bowed his head, and gave up the ghost. The Jews therefore, because it was the preparation, that the bodies should not remain upon the cross on the sabbath day, (for that sabbath day was an high day,) besought Pilate that their legs might be broken, and that they might be taken away. Then came the soldiers, and brake the legs of the first, and of the other which was crucified with him.
>
> But when they came to Jesus, and saw that he was dead already, they brake not his legs:
>
> But one of the soldiers with a spear pierced his side, and forthwith came there out blood and water.
>
> And he that saw it bare record, and his record is true: and he knoweth that he saith true, that ye might believe."
>
> John 19:30-35

I heard one story, whether or not it is true, I do not know. It was that under severe anguish, it is possible for fluid to build up around the heart, and stop the heart from beating. So, perhaps it is true that Christ died of a broken heart. It is remarked that his death was earlier than would normally be expected.

> "And Pilate marvelled if he were already dead: …" Mark 15:44

The soldier was certain that the man was dead. He, I think thrust the spear upward below the rib line, into the heart to make sure that there was no life left in him. I suppose the soldiers would have come along while these three were still on the crosses, and only been able to reach their legs. So the two thieves had their legs broken, and were left a little while to die. Jesus seemed to be already dead, so the soldier thrust upward with his spear piercing Jesus side into his heart, to ensure he was dead. John looked on, and no doubt would have lost all hope in Jesus.

> "… and forthwith came there out blood and water." John 19:34

> "They shall look on him whom they pierced." John 19:37[286]

[286] cf. Zech 12:10

"… for he was cut off out of the land of the living: for the transgression of my people was he stricken. And he made his grave with the wicked, and with the rich in his death; because he had done no violence, neither was any deceit in his mouth. Yet it pleased the Lord to bruise him; he hath put him to grief: … .He [the Lord] shall see of the travail of his soul, and shall be satisfied[287]: ..."

Isaiah 53:8-11

[287] to *sate* i.e. *fill* to satisfaction (lit. or fig.)

6.5 Christ's Resurrection

Reading Luke 24:1-43

> Afterward he appeared unto the eleven as they sat at meat, and upbraided them with their unbelief and hardness of heart, because they believed not them which had seen him after he was risen.
>
> Mark 16:14

I love Jesus, just when you think everything is going wrong, like when Jesus was sleeping in the boat in the storm, God speaks a word, and makes everything all right. The disciples would have been beyond despair at Jesus death. But Jesus came back and rebuked them for their hardness of heart, and their unbelief. I really don't think they would have taken any notice at his rebukes compared with having Jesus back again.

I remember a kid who was making a mask for school and it was her bedtime, and she didn't have any hope of getting it finished, and started crying. The first thing I did was to tell her off for crying. I could help her get it finished in time without any problem whatsoever, but not when she was crying. So after she stopped crying I helped her finish it. She was delighted at the mask, and I was really happy for her that she wasn't sad. I think God treats us like a father. God only rebukes us because he loves us, and he wants the best for us. He doesn't delight in us crying and being stressed out.

It is our God who comforts us.

Sometimes our friends desert us, and there appears to be no future. But remember, it is our God who raises the dead.

> Blessed be God, even the Father of our Lord Jesus Christ, the Father of mercies, and the God of all comfort; Who comforteth us in all our tribulation, that we may be able to comfort them which are in any trouble, by the comfort wherewith we ourselves are comforted of God. For as the sufferings of Christ abound in us, so our consolation also aboundeth by Christ.
>
> And whether we be afflicted, it is for your consolation and salvation, which is effectual in the enduring of the same sufferings which we also suffer: or whether we be comforted, it is for your consolation and salvation.
>
> And our hope of you is stedfast, knowing, that as ye are partakers of the sufferings, so shall ye be also of the consolation.
>
> For we would not, brethren, have you ignorant of our trouble which came to us in Asia, that we were pressed out of measure, above strength, insomuch that we despaired even of life:
>
> But we had the sentence of death in ourselves, that we should not trust in ourselves, *but in God which raiseth the dead*:

Who delivered us from so great a death, and doth deliver: in whom we trust that he will yet deliver us;

2Cor 1:3-10

Hallelujah, the same spirit Christ has dwells in us[288].

"But if the Spirit of him that raised up Jesus from the dead dwell[289] in you, ..."

Rom 8:11

There is always a future with God.

"... when thou hast found it, then there shall be a reward[290], and thy expectation[291] shall not be cut off."

Prov 24:14

Wisdom is hearing God's voice, and doing what he says. I suppose it is also a friendship with God. When we miss the resurrection, we miss the mark.

"Do ye not therefore err, because ye know[292] not the scriptures, neither the power of God?"

Mark 12:24[293]

Not knowing God's power in the resurrection is a cause for error.

"That I may know him, and the power of his resurrection, and the fellowship of his sufferings, ..."

Phil 3:10

Knowing God, or being a friend of God, goes hand in hand with knowing God's power of Christ's resurrection, and also his sufferings. When we limit God to what we can achieve ourselves, we miss the gospel. One of Israel's chief problems was that they never trusted God to save them.

The story of Lazarus without Jesus, and the resurrection, would be very, very sad. Mary and Martha would have lost their dear brother in the prime of his life. This kind of situation happens today. But, hallelujah, today, Jesus is with us, to face the obstacles which stand in our way.

Jesus came to Bethany to raise Lazarus from the dead[294]. Martha didn't believe that Jesus would raise him straight away - she thought it would be later. Martha spoke the truth and Jesus didn't

---

[288] Gal 4:4-6; 1John 2:27; 1Cor 2:12, 3:16, 6:19; John 1:12-13; 7:38, 14:16-17,23; Jer 31:31-33

[289] to *occupy a house* i.e. *reside* (fig. *inhabit, remain, inhere*); by implication to *cohabit:* - dwell

[290] H319 the *last* or *end,* hence the *future;* also *posterity.*
An example of it's use is Jer 31:17 (translated as 'thine end')
"And there is hope in thine end, saith the LORD, that thy children shall come again to their own border."

[291] H8615 lit. a cord (like a rope). Expectation being like a cord which ties you to something you don't see yet (cf. Rom 8:24).
lit. a *cord* (as an *attachment*); fig. *expectancy* (cf. Jer 31:17 footnote 290, where H8615 is translated as 'hope'). Something hoping/longing for. Cf. 'hope' Heb 6:18-19,24-25, 11:1
"Now faith is the (support; 'to stand'-'under') of things hoped for, the (evidence/convicted) of things not seen."

[292] properly to *see* (lit. or fig.)

[293] cf. Mat 22:29

[294] John 11:1-53

correct her for saying that Lazarus would rise again. Martha spoke what she believed - that Lazarus would rise again in the last day. Jesus hearing what she believed added a statement, and asked her whether she believed it. “I am the resurrection and the life: ... ”

> Jesus saith unto her, Thy brother shall rise again.
>
> Martha saith unto him, I know that he shall rise again in the resurrection at the last day.
>
> Jesus said unto her, I am the resurrection, and the life: he that believeth in me, though he were dead, yet shall he live: And whosoever liveth and believeth in me shall never die.
>
> Believest thou this?
>
> She saith unto him, Yea, Lord: I believe that thou art the Christ, the Son of God, which should come into the world.
>
> John 11:23-27

Praise the Lord, with Jesus, there is always hope.

> Knowing that he which raised up the Lord Jesus shall raise up us also by Jesus, and shall present us with you.
>
> For all things are for your sakes, that the abundant grace might through the thanksgiving of many redound to the glory of God.
>
> For which cause we faint not; …
>
> 2Cor 4:14-16

Knowing that God cares about us, and that he will resurrect us keeps us from giving up.

> “I ... brought you unto
>
> ['what does it say? ... not the law, not the land, not the covenant, but ...'[295]]
>
> myself.”
>
> Exod 19:4[296]

The purpose of the cross was to bring us acceptable to God. We have been brought by Jesus to the Father.

God loves us. He chose us.

> “But we are bound to give thanks alway to God for you, brethren beloved of the Lord, because God hath from the beginning chosen you to salvation through sanctification of the Spirit and belief of the truth: ...”
>
> 2Thes 2:13

---

295 Derek Prince, audio recording "Strength through knowing God"

296 "Ye have seen what I did unto the Egyptians, and how I bare you on eagles' wings, and brought you unto myself." Exod 19:4

> “Now our Lord Jesus Christ himself, and God, even our Father, which hath loved us, and hath given us everlasting consolation and good hope through grace, Comfort your hearts, and stablish you in every good word and work.”
>
> 2Thes 2:16-17

Christ and God have loved us. Someone may love someone else, and they may not know for sure. But we know for sure that God loves us. We must hold fast the knowledge that God loves us. It is with God we can stand against the storms which come to hide God's love from our eyes. We stand by faith.

6.6 Christ's Resurrection Body

Call me a fool if you want, but I'm going to ask what kind of body the dead are resurrected with.

Reading 1Cor 15:35-44

> "It is sown in corruption; it is raised in incorruption:
>
> It is sown in dishonour; it is raised in glory: ..."
>
> 1Cor 15:42-43

The scriptures compare the resurrection to a seed germinating. All plants begin as seeds. When a seed first begins to grow, the nutrients inside the seed make the first sprouts. None of the first sprout is created from anything outside the seed (except water and the air). Take Alfalfa sprouts. You get the seeds, put them on a piece of clean wet foam, and put it in the sunlight. What happens? They start to grow. The seed becomes the plant. Yes the seed is not the same as the baby plant just sprouted. It is a transformation of the seed. It is the same with Christ's body, it was transformed, but it was not a completely new body, the body which was formed, came from the body which was crucified on the cross.

> Who shall change our vile body, that it may be fashioned like unto his glorious body, according to the working whereby he is able even to subdue all things unto himself.
>
> Therefore, my brethren dearly beloved and longed for, my joy and crown, so stand fast in the Lord, my dearly beloved.
>
> Phil 3:21 to Phil 4:1

Note that it says change our body, not replace it.

> "And as they thus spake, Jesus himself stood in the midst of them, ... Behold my hands and my feet, that it is I myself: handle me, and see; for a spirit hath not flesh and bones, as ye see me have. And when he had thus spoken, he showed them his hands and his feet. ... And they gave him a piece of a broiled fish, and of an honeycomb. And he took it, and did eat before them."
>
> Luke 24:36-43

Jesus has a body. The disciples did not see a spirit.

The body Jesus has is the same body that was crucified.

> "Then saith he to Thomas, Reach hither thy finger, and behold my hands; and reach hither thy hand, and thrust it into my side: and be not faithless, but believing.
>
> And Thomas answered and said unto him, My Lord and my God.
>
> Jesus saith unto him, Thomas, because thou hast seen me, thou hast believed: blessed are they that have not seen, and yet have believed.
>
> And many other signs truly did Jesus in the presence of his disciples, which are not written in this book:

But these are written, that ye might believe that Jesus is the Christ, the Son of God; and that believing ye might have life through his name."

John 20:27-31

There was no dead body left in the tomb. The body Thomas saw had the marks from the crucifixion.

Christ's body never decomposed. Christ's body was never utterly destroyed. The same state in which it was immediately after it was taken off the cross, was pretty much the worst state it ever got to. God did not build a new body from scratch.

But he, whom God raised again, saw no corruption[297]. Acts 13:37

And as concerning that he raised him up from the dead, now no more (*being about*) *to*[298] return to corruption[299], he said on this wise, I will give you the sure mercies of David.

Acts 13:34

For thou wilt not leave my soul in hell; neither wilt thou suffer thine Holy One to see corruption.

Psalm 16:10

Jesus body was raised up again, not destroyed and replaced.

"And the angel answered and said unto the women, Fear not ye: for I know that ye seek Jesus, which was crucified. He is not here: for he is risen, as he said. Come, see the place where the Lord lay. And go quickly, and tell his disciples that he is risen from the dead; and, behold, he goeth before you into Galilee; there shall ye see him: lo, I have told you."

Mat 28:5-7

This description is similar to one of a person rising up again after sleeping. The reason he wasn't there, was because he got up. It was not because the body was destroyed, and a new one created.

And he saith unto them, Be not affrighted: Ye seek Jesus of Nazareth, which was crucified: he is risen; he is not here: behold the place where they laid him.

Mark 16:6

"... and behold, two men stood by them in shining clothes. And as they themselves became in fear and bowed their faces to the earth, they said to them 'why do you seek the living amid the dead? He is not here, but has risen: remember how he spake unto you when he was yet in Gallilee, …'"

Luke 24:4-6 [a translation]

The women looked for Jesus body. The angel knew this and replied, he is not here, he is risen. The

[297] I suppose this is complete destruction i.e. thorough decay or rottenness

[298] G3195

[299] I suppose this is "returning, or heading in the direction of complete decay".

reason they wouldn't find the body in the tomb is because Jesus was using it. His body was raised again.

> Whom [Jesus of Nazareth] God hath raised up, having loosed the pains of death: because it was not possible that he should be holden of it.
>
> Acts 2:24

Christ will not die any more.

> "Knowing that Christ being raised from the dead dieth no more; death hath no more dominion over him."
>
> Rom 6:9

> "... there ariseth another priest, [i.e. Jesus] Who is made [ordained], not after the law of a carnal commandment, but after the power of an endless life."
>
> Heb 7:16-17

> "And when I saw him [Jesus], I fell at his feet as dead. And he laid his right hand upon me, saying unto me, Fear not; I am the first and the last: I am he that liveth, and was dead; and, behold, I am alive for evermore, Amen; and have the keys of hell and of death."
>
> Rev 1:17-18

Jesus speaking here refers to the death of his body 'and was dead'. Well if his body was dead, what is it now? If he had got himself a new body wouldn't that make him dead and alive?

Jesus only ever had, and only has one body, the same one he grew up in. The same one he worked in his father Joseph's workshop. The same one in which he was crucified.

In the King James version, the word *resurrection* is almost always translated from the word anastasis[300]. It means 'a standing up [again]' for example,

> "... of the hope and *resurrection* (a standing up) of the dead I am called in question."
>
> Acts 23:6

> And as they came down from the mountain, Jesus charged them, saying, Tell the vision to no man, until the Son of man be risen[301] again from the dead.
>
> Mat 17:9

The words "risen again from the dead" refer to the physical body of the Son of man.

> "After these things Jesus shewed himself again to the disciples at the sea of Tiberias; and on this wise shewed he himself.
>
> There were together Simon Peter, and Thomas called Didymus, and Nathanael of Cana in Galilee, and the sons of Zebedee, and two other of his disciples.

[300] G386 *Anastasis;* from G450; a *standing up* again, i.e. (lit.) a *resurrection* from death (individual, gen. or by impl. [its author]), or (fig.) a (moral) *recovery* (of spiritual truth). Translated as:- raised to life again, resurrection, rise from the dead, that should rise, rising again.

[301] G450 to *stand up*

> Simon Peter saith unto them, I go a fishing. They say unto him, We also go with thee. They went forth, and entered into a ship immediately; and that night they caught nothing.
>
> But when the morning was now come, Jesus stood on the shore: but the disciples knew not that it was Jesus."
>
> John 21:1-4

A spirit doesn't stand on something. Jesus has a body.

Jesus resurrected body was not exactly the same as it was before the resurrection. Never the less, there are similarities. The marks of the nails and the scar on his side are on Jesus resurrected body.

> "Except I shall see in his hands the print of the nails, and put my finger into the print of the nails, and thrust my hand into his side, I will not believe.
>
> ...
>
> Then saith he to Thomas, Reach hither thy finger, and behold my hands; and reach hither thy hand, and thrust it into my side: and be not faithless, but believing."
>
> John 20:25,27

Jesus said

> "... handle me, and see; for a spirit hath not flesh and bones, as ye see me have."
>
> Luke 24:39

Our bodies will be like Jesus' body.

> "Beloved, now are we the sons of God, and it doth not yet appear what we shall be: but we know that, when he shall appear, we shall be like him; for we shall see him as he is."
>
> 1John 3:2

> "Behold, I shew you a mystery; ... we shall all be changed, ... For this corruptible must put on incorruption, and this mortal must put on immortality."
>
> 1Cor 15:51-53

We do not know exactly what our bodies will be like. However, the main point is that the resurrected body is formed from the pre-resurrected body. It is not another body, but rather the original changed somewhat.

> "... I will behold thy face in righteousness: I shall be satisfied, when I awake, with thy likeness."
>
> Psalm 17:15

6.7 The Tent Analogy of the Body

An elderly gentleman was once greeted. He replied “John Smith is well, very well thank-you, however my tent appears to be wearing a little thin”.

Praise the Lord. It is good to see a man trusting God.

The body is like a tent. From the old testament, we can see our bodies were formed from the dust of the ground.

> And the LORD God formed man of the dust of the ground, and breathed into his nostrils the breath of life; and man became a living[302] *soul*[303].
>
> Gen 2:7

The meaning of one of the words translated to English as the word ‘body’ sheds some light on the matter.

> "I Daniel was grieved in my spirit in the midst of my *body*, ..."
>
> Dan 7:15

Here the word '*body*' is

> nidneh H5085 A *sheath* (like a sword sheath) fig. the *body* (as the receptacle of the soul).

From this we see that the body is a container. God breathed, and man's body contained His breath, and became a living creature.

> Yea, I think it meet, as long as I am in this (tent), to stir you up by putting you in remembrance; Knowing that shortly I must put off this my (tent[304]), even as our Lord Jesus Christ hath shewed me.
>
> 2Peter 1:13-14

I heard a man preaching, and he was talking about the body being a tent. He then related a story. He said he was asleep, and had a heart attack, he saw his body still lying next to his wife in bed. His comment was something like

> “I knew, that my body was like a tent, but it never seemed quite so real to me until then.”

Our destination is to be with the Father.

> “But the God of all grace, who hath called us unto his eternal glory by Christ Jesus, after that ye have suffered a while, make you perfect, stablish, strengthen, settle you. To him be glory and dominion for ever and ever. Amen.”
>
> 1Pet 5:10-11

---

[302] *alive*

[303] H5315 properly a *breathing* creature

[304] G4638 an *encampment* (derived from, consecutively ...)
G4637 to *tent*, or *encamp* -> G4636 a *hut*, or temporary residence -> G4633 a *tent* or cloth hut.

Our body may die, but we keep on living.

> "And whosoever liveth and believeth in me shall never die."
> John 11:26

When a Christian dies, he departs to be with the Lord.

> And it was about the sixth hour, and there was a darkness over all the earth until the ninth hour.
>
> And the sun was darkened, and the veil of the temple was rent in the midst.
>
> And when Jesus had cried with a loud voice, he said, Father, into thy hands I commend my spirit: and having said thus, he gave up the ghost.
> Luke 23:44-46

This scripture declares that when Jesus died, his spirit departed from his body. Jesus committed his spirit to his Father at his death.

> "Wherefore let them that suffer according to the will of God commit the keeping of their souls to him in well doing, as unto a faithful Creator."
> 1Peter 4:19

We entrust our spirit to the Father always, but like Jesus also when we die.

> "Father, into thy hands I commend my spirit" Luke 23:46

Stephen also entrusted[305] himself to God when he died.

> But he, being full of the Holy Ghost, looked up stedfastly into heaven, and saw the glory of God, and Jesus standing on the right hand of God,
>
> And said, Behold, I see the heavens opened, and the Son of man standing on the right hand of God.
>
> Then they cried out with a loud voice, and stopped their ears, and ran upon him with one accord, And cast him out of the city, and stoned him: and the witnesses laid down their clothes at a young man's feet, whose name was Saul.
>
> And they stoned Stephen [who was], calling upon God, and saying, Lord Jesus, receive my spirit.
>
> And he kneeled down, and cried with a loud voice, Lord, lay not this sin to their charge. And when he had said this, he fell asleep.
> Acts 7:55-60

Stephen asked Jesus to receive his spirit. He was not denied.

> For to me to live is Christ, and to die is gain. But if I live in the flesh, this is the fruit of my labour: yet what I shall choose I wot not.

---

[305] 'entrust', I suppose is similar to giving something or placing something into the care of someone. It is done with expectation that the person will care for that which is entrusted.

> For I am in a strait betwixt two, having a desire to depart, and to be with Christ; which is far better: Nevertheless to abide in the flesh is more needful for you.
>
> And having this confidence, I know that I shall abide and continue with you all for your furtherance and joy of faith; That your rejoicing may be more abundant in Jesus Christ for me by my coming to you again.
>
> Phil 1:21-26

Paul was confident that he would be with the Lord when he departed from his body.

Reading 2Cor 4:13-5:10

> Therefore we are always confident, knowing that, whilst we are at home in the body, we are absent from the Lord: (For we walk by faith, not by sight:)
>
> We are confident, I say, and willing rather to be absent from the body, and to be present with the Lord. Wherefore we labour, that, whether present or absent, we may be accepted of him.
>
> 2Cor 5:6-9

Praise God that we are always confident about life and death. While we are dwelling in our bodies we are absent from the Lord, but when we are absent from our bodies, we shall be present with the Lord. Because we trust we are going to meet the Lord, works result from our faith.

> "Wherefore we labour, ..."

Faith is always practical. I know a man who works patiently, and with content, looking after church maintenance. He trusts God is going to reward him at the resurrection. I am glad to see it because so often it appears that people do things out of obligation, rather than because they want to.

I am reminded of a missionary from Africa, getting back to the States after serving God diligently for forty years. He and his wife flew in to the airport, but there was no one there to greet them. Their family had dispersed. That night in a Hotel, he was crying out to God saying, how could you have forsaken me, and forgotten about all my work that I've done for you, and left me all alone at my home coming? God answered. Don't say that son - You're not home yet.

I know that man is going to get a lot more than he expects when he gets to heaven.

Remember the end of Job that the Lord is very pitiful and of tender mercies. I know God would have provided a good end, even though the missionary probably thought things would be bad.

> Take, my brethren, the prophets, who have spoken in the name of the Lord, for an example of suffering affliction, and of patience.
>
> Behold, we count them happy which endure. Ye have heard of the patience of Job, and have seen the end of the Lord; that the Lord is very pitiful, and of tender mercy.
>
> James 5:10-11

6.8 A New Home

Let not your heart be troubled. Some people say shifting house is one of the most stressful things that can happen in life. Jesus says to trust him, and not to be afraid.

> JOH 14:1 Let not your heart be troubled: ye believe in God, believe also in me.
>
> JOH 14:2 In my Father's house are many mansions: if it were not so, I would have told you. I go to prepare a place for you.
>
> JOH 14:3 And if I go and prepare a place for you, I will come again, and receive you unto myself; that where I am, there ye may be also.
>
> JOH 14:4 And whither I go ye know, and the way ye know.
>
> JOH 14:5 Thomas saith unto him, Lord, we know not whither thou goest; and how can we know the way?
>
> JOH 14:6 Jesus saith unto him, I am the way, the truth, and the life: no man
>
> cometh unto the Father, but by me.
>
> JOH 14:7 If ye had known me, ye should have known my Father also: and from henceforth ye know him, and have seen him.

Jesus said that he was going to leave us and prepare a place for us. He is going to come back and take us away to our new home.

> CO2 5:1 For we know that if our earthly house of this tabernacle were dissolved, we have a building of God, an house not made with hands, eternal in the heavens.

Reading John 16:1-33

Jesus left the disciples for a little while when he died.

> "But now I go my way to him that sent me; and none of you asketh me, Whither goest thou?
>
> But because I have said these things unto you, sorrow hath filled your heart.
>
> Nevertheless I tell you the truth; It is expedient for you that I go away: ..."
> John 16:5-7
>
> “And ye now therefore have sorrow: but I will see you again, and your heart shall rejoice, and your joy no man taketh from you."
> John 16:22

"For the Father himself loveth you, because ye have loved me, and have believed that I came out from God.

I came forth from the Father, and am come into the world: again, I leave the world, and go to the Father."

John 16:27-28

Notice that Jesus doesn't say "I leave the world and go to the green house with the white door on avenue such and such". I think it is like most decisions we make about accommodation. The important thing is often not where we live, but who we live with.

These things I have spoken unto you, that in my ye might have peace. In the world ye shall have tribulation: but be of good cheer; I have overcome the world."

John 16:33

These things were spoken to the disciples, concerning Jesus crucifixion and resurrection, but I think they apply also to us, until we go to be with the Father.

"Father, I will that they also, whom thou hast given me, be with me where I am; ..."

JOH 17:24

If we're with Jesus at the resurrection, we'll be with him forever.

".. and so shall we ever be with the Lord." 1Thes 4:17

"For what is our hope, or joy, or crown of rejoicing? Are not even ye in the presence of our Lord Jesus Christ at his coming?

For ye are our glory and joy."

1Thes 2:19-20

Christ died and rose so that we would always be with him.

"... Who died for us, that, whether we wake or sleep, we should live together with him." 1Thes 5:10

Christ died and rose so that we could say "Whether we live, we live unto the Lord; or whether we die, we die unto the Lord[306]. Either way we are the Lord's." It is because God wants (and loves) us that he died.

"... that he might be Lord[307] both of the dead and living."

Rom 14:9

I think of how you hold a kid really tightly in your arms, and you don't want to let them go. You want them to be yours. It's the same with us and God. He wants us to be his. All his. Not someone else's.

---

[306] cf. Rom 14:8

[307] G2961 to *rule* (from G2962)

G2962 *supreme* in authority, i.e. (as noun) *controller*; by implication Mr. (as a respectful title).

"For I am persuaded, that neither death, nor life, nor angels, nor principalities, nor powers, nor things present, nor things to come, nor height, nor depth, nor any other creature, shall be able to separate us from the love of God, which is in Christ Jesus our Lord."

Rom 8:38-39

6.9 What Happens After the Resurrection?

Praise the Lord, some things do not change. Our God, who has saved us, will rule for ever.

> "... Fear not; I am the first and the last: I am he that liveth, and was dead; and, behold, I am alive forevermore, Amen; and have the keys of hell and of death.
>
> Rev 1:17-18

I think it is impossible to comprehend what heaven will be like, but perhaps we can catch a faint reflection of what it will be like from the following scriptures.

> REV 7:9 After this I beheld, and, lo, a great multitude, which no man could number, of all nations, and kindreds, and people, and tongues, stood before the throne, and before the Lamb, clothed with white robes, and palms in their hands;
>
> ---
>
> REV 7:13 And one of the elders answered, saying unto me, What are these which are arrayed in white robes? and whence came they?
>
> REV 7:14 And I said unto him, Sir, thou knowest. And he said to me, These are they which came out of great tribulation, and have washed their robes, and made them white in the blood of the Lamb.
>
> ---
>
> REV 21:3 And I heard a great voice out of heaven saying, Behold, the tabernacle of God is with men, and he will dwell with them, and they shall be his people, and God himself shall be with them, and be their God.
>
> REV 21:4 And God shall wipe away all tears from their eyes; and there shall be no more death, neither sorrow, nor crying, neither shall there be any more pain: for the former things are passed away.
>
> REV 21:5 And he that sat upon the throne said, Behold, I make all things new. And he said unto me, Write: for these words are true and faithful.
>
> REV 21:6 And he said unto me, It is done. I am Alpha and Omega, the beginning and the end. I will give unto him that is athirst of the fountain of the water of life freely.
>
> REV 21:7 He that overcometh shall inherit all things; and I will be his God, and he shall be my son.
>
> ---
>
> REV 22:5 …and they shall reign for ever and ever.
>
> REV 22:6 And he said unto me, These sayings are faithful and true: and the Lord God of the holy prophets sent his angel to shew unto his servants the things which must shortly be done.

REV 22:7 Behold, I come quickly: blessed is he that keepeth the sayings of the prophecy of this book.

6.10 Christ's Return

> And to wait for his Son from heaven, whom he raised from the dead, even Jesus, (who is rescuing) us from the wrath to come.
>
> 1Thes 1:10

> "For I would that ye knew what great conflict I have for you, and for them at Laodicea, and for as many as have not seen my face in the flesh; That their hearts might be comforted, being knit together in love, and unto all riches of the full assurance of understanding, ..."
>
> Col 2:1-2

Paul was worried about those who he wasn't able to be present with (i.e. us). He wanted us to be comforted, to know God's love for us, and that we would be confident because we understand the facts.

> Now we beseech you, brethren, by the coming of our Lord Jesus Christ, and by our gathering together unto him,
>
> That ye be not soon shaken in mind, or be troubled, neither by spirit, nor by word, nor by letter as from us, as that the day of Christ is at hand.
>
> 2Thes 2:1-2

There are two things which I shall mention here which Jesus emphasised. The first is not to let our hearts be troubled.

> "But when ye shall hear of wars and commotions, be not terrified: for these things must first come to pass; but the end is not by and by."
>
> Luke 21:9

The second is, that men will pretend to be Jesus.

> "And Jesus answering them began to say, Take heed lest any man deceive you: For many shall come in my name, saying, I am Christ; and shall deceive many."
>
> Mark 13:5-6

If you're asking the question "Is it Jesus coming back?" It is not Jesus.

> Wherefore if they shall say unto you, Behold, he is in the desert; go not forth: behold, he is in the secret chambers; believe it not.
>
> For as the lightning cometh out of the east, and shineth even unto the west; so shall also the coming of the Son of Man be."
>
> Mat 24:26-27

Note that every eye shall see him when he returns. Jesus is not hiding in some dark ally giving secret instructions. God won't be hiding the fact that Jesus is the son of God, when Christ returns the second time.

> “But he held his peace, and answered nothing. Again the high priest asked him, and said unto him, Art thou the Christ, the Son of the Blessed?
>
> And Jesus said, I am: and ye shall see the Son of man sitting on the right hand of power, and coming in the clouds of heaven.”
>
> Mark 14:61-62

There will be a trumpet sounding when Christ returns.

> “In a moment, in the twinkling of an eye, at the last trump: for the trumpet shall sound, and the dead shall be raised incorruptible, and we shall be changed.”
>
> 1Cor 15:52

The other common mistake is for some deceiver to say they know when the world is going to end. Jesus calls that man a liar.

> “But of that day and hour knoweth no man, no, not the angels of heaven, but my Father only.”
>
> Mat 24:36

I doubt there’s a man on earth, who understands everything written in the Bible. Some things as Peter says are hard to understand.

> As also in all his [Paul’s] epistles, speaking in them of these things; in which are some things hard to be understood, which they that are unlearned and unstable wrest, as they do also the other scriptures, unto their own destruction.
>
> 2Peter 3:16

God does not want us to be troubled about Christ’s Return. Worry caused by something someone said or was overheard, or a minister preached, or was spoken through another person by a spirit can cause much distress and trouble.

> “… nor by letter as from us, …”. 2Thes 2:2

I kid you not, God inspired these men to write parts of the Bible. Yes, God does not want us to be disturbed, even by those things written in the Bible. Certainly, God takes good care of us, his children.

> “For he doth not afflict willingly[308] nor grieve the children of men.”
>
> Lam 3:33

---

[308] *from his heart*

6.11 Eternity

> For what is our hope, or joy, or crown of rejoicing? Are not even ye in the presence of our Lord Jesus Christ at his coming?
>
> For ye are our glory and joy.
>
> 1Thes 2:19-20

Hallelujah! There is a day coming when we will stand with our friends in heaven before our heavenly Father.

To me friends are the most valuable things you can have. Other things are nice, but they don't rank on the same list as friends. To be able to have our friends with us in heaven. Now that is something to hope for. If we obtain the hope of having our friends in the presence of the Lord at his coming, we are rich because they will be our friends for ever, and we will be together with the Lord. What I would give for this to be true for all my friends. God knows. Praise the Lord.

I suppose we should present our life to God as a living sacrifice. He gave his life for us, so that we could live with him. If we continually present our bodies to God, we can trust him to look after us.

> For the truth's sake, which dwelleth in us, and shall be with us for ever.
>
> 2John 1:2

God will never forsake us.

> "... and, lo, I am with you alway, even unto the end[309] of the (Age[310]). Amen[311]."
>
> Mat 28:20

Consider Elisha. God cared enough to retrieve a borrowed axe[312], how much more will he look after us his sons and daughters? We have a friendship with God, where we can tell him our difficulties, and expect him to do something about them.

We are God's sons and daughters. I remember (more or less) a story a man told about how God gave him a dream. In the dream, there was a road, and along side the road a big sign, and beneath the sign was a little pig.

The man woke up. And said, Lord, don't tell me what the dream is about. I've got this one. Let's see a pig. Well, a pig is an unclean animal. Lord it's something about holiness isn't it? Wait, don't tell me. Cast not your pearls before swine! That's it, maybe I need to preach on wisdom, of how to deal with the precious things you've given us? No? and on he went coming up with more scriptures than I can think of. At the end he said. OK Lord, I give up. What is it? The Lord said, Did you read what it said on the sign? No, I was too busy looking at the little pig. "I went back to

---

[309] from two words: one a preposition denoting union and another denoting completeness: hence "*entire completion*", i.e. *consummation* (of a dispensation). Similar to G5055:- to *end*, i.e. *complete, execute, conclude, discharge* (a debt); which itself is derived from a word meaning 'to set out for a definite point or goal'.

[310] G165 aiōn properly an *age*; by extension *perpetuity* (also past); by implication the *world*. Derived from a word apparently meaning continued duration.

[311] lit. *firm*, [stable] *fig. trustworthy* from H543

[312] 2 Kings 6:1-7

sleep, and God" he said, "graciously gave me the dream again". He looked at the sign, and in big letters was written, "Don't get distracted by little details."

I think this was an excellent illustration. We should not let details obscure the facts: The Lord loves us, and has no plans for us except plans for good. As we present our bodies to God as a living sacrifice, we will see more of his glory.

> "Shew me your Glory, let your presence pass by me, when I am close to you, my spirit can run free. I want to be a child who knows you so intimately ... show me your glory, let your presence pass by me."
>
> - a song

Even as I write this, I find, that there is no way to enter into the Holy of Holies without presenting our bodies, united with Christ, as a living sacrifice. When we enter into God's presence, we have left the natural world behind, in exactly the same way as we will do on the last day.

Reading Ephesians 3:14-19

> "And to know the love of Christ, which (surpasses) knowledge, that ye might be filled with all the fullness of God."
>
> Eph 3:19

The greatest aspiration of any man is like Moses to know God face to face.

> "And the LORD spake unto Moses face to face, as a man speaketh unto his friend."
>
> Exod 33:11

> "And there arose not a prophet since in Israel like unto Moses, whom the LORD knew face to face, ..."
>
> Deut 34:10

To talk with God as a friend is life. There are many other things which claim to give life, but they do not.

> "And this is life eternal, that they might know thee the only true God, and Jesus Christ, whom thou hast sent.
>
> John 17:3

> And this is the promise that he hath promised us, even eternal life.
>
> 1John 2:25

Reading Psalm 121 [The Lord keeps/protects us]

> And when he had spoken these things, while they beheld, he was taken up; and a cloud received him out of their sight. And while they looked stedfastly toward heaven as he went up, behold, two men stood by them in white apparel;

Which also said, Ye men of Galilee, why stand ye gazing up into heaven? this same Jesus, which is taken up from you into heaven, shall so come in like manner as ye have seen him go into heaven.

Acts 1:9-11

7.0 Eternal Judgement

"If thou, Lord, shouldest mark iniquities, O Lord, who shall stand?"
Psalm 130:3

7.1 Introduction

Reading Psalm 11

> "In the Lord I fled for protection. How can you say to my soul, 'wander away to the mountain range like a little bird'? For behold the wicked will tread (string) the bow; they fixed their arrow on the string to shoot with it in darkness[313] at the upright in heart. If the foundations be destroyed, what can the righteous do? The Lord is in his holy temple; the Lord, in heaven is his throne; his eyes see; his [blinking] eyelashes[314] will examine the sons of man. The Lord tries the righteous, but the wicked and him that loves violence his soul hates. He shall rain on the wicked snares[315]; fire and resin[316] and a burning[317] wind is the share of their cup. For just is the Lord, he loves rightness; his countenance doth behold the upright."
>
> Psalm 11[318]

In this Psalm it asks 'what can the righteous do if the foundations are destroyed?'. It then carries on to talk about the eternal judgment. Part of the foundation of the Christian faith is that there is a judgment coming.

Reading Ezekiel Chapter 8

There is a voice which says God has forgotten.

> "Then said he unto me, Son of man, hast thou seen what the ancients of the house of Israel do in the dark, every man in the chambers of his imagery? for they say, The Lord seeth us not; the Lord hath forsaken the earth."
>
> Ezek 8:12

Later in Ezekiel chapter 9, God goes on to explain why the land was filled with blood, and the city full of perversity.

> "Then said he unto me, The iniquity of the house of Israel and Judah is exceeding great, and the land is full of blood, and the city full of perverseness[319]: for they say, The Lord hath forsaken the earth, and the Lord seeth not."
>
> Ezek 9:9

The reason is that in their hearts they say "God's forsaken us. He doesn't take any notice."

The scriptures declare to the contrary.

---

[313] *in dusk* [after sunset] i.e. obscurity

[314] fig. *ray* of light at dawn

[315] a (metallic) *sheet* (as *pounded* thin); also a spring *net* (as spread out like a *lamina*)

[316] H1614 prop. cypress *resin;* by analogy *sulphur* (as equally inflammable): brimstone cf. Gen 19:24

[317] a *glowing*

[318] a translation (not KJV)

[319] H4297 lit. *a stretching,* i.e. *distortion* (fig. *iniquity*) [from H5186 A primitive root; to *stretch* or spread out; by implic. to *bend* away (incl. moral deflection)]

> "... ; he considereth all their works."
>
> Psalms 33:15

God does not forget. God sees. It is evil to say God forgets, that God does not see.

> "For I was envious at the foolish, when I saw the prosperity of the wicked."
>
> Psalm 73:3

I suppose when we forget the judgment, we look at the things happening in this world, and say 'what is the point of righteousness?'

However, we should not give up hope, the righteous will not go unrewarded and the unjust shall not go unpunished.

> But without faith it is impossible to please him: for he that cometh to God must believe that he is, and that he is a rewarder of them that diligently seek him.
>
> Heb 11:6

I believe that God will reward us in this present time, as well as when we reach heaven.

> "... : but godliness is profitable unto all things, having promise of the life that now is, and of that which is to come."
>
> 1Tim 4:8

> "The ungodly are not so: but are like the chaff which the wind drives away. Therefore the ungodly shall not stand in the judgment, nor sinners in the congregation of the righteous.
>
> For the Lord knoweth the way of the righteous: but the way of the ungodly shall perish."
>
> Psalm 1:4-6.

There is no way anyone who does not repent will get away with any little thing, from stealing 5 cents, to lying just once. Those who do not repent will be damned.

> "And it is easier for heaven and earth to pass, than one tittle[320] of the law to fail."
>
> Luke 16:17

Christians have been forgiven their sins.

> "... every tongue that shall rise against thee in judgment thou shalt condemn. This is the heritage of the servants of the Lord, and their righteousness is of me, saith the Lord."
>
> Isaiah 54:17

It is only when we say Jesus took the punishment for my sin, that we can be found guiltless.

[320] the apex (top/peak) of a Hebrew letter cf. Mat 5:18

"For he hath made him to be sin for us, who knew no sin; that we might be made[321] the righteousness of God in him."

2Cor 5:21

By faith in Jesus, we have been forgiven. All those who accuse us of sin, do so unjustly. We have no sin because Jesus has taken it away and paid for it with his life on the cross.

"So Christ was once offered to bear the sins of many; and unto them that look for him shall he appear the second time without sin unto salvation."

Hebrews 9:28

God has already judged us for our sin when we by faith were crucified with Christ.

"Know ye not, that so many of us as were baptised into Jesus Christ were baptised into his death?

Therefore we are buried with him by baptism into death ..."

"... : Knowing this, that our old man is crucified with him, ..."

Rom 6:3-4,6

"Now if we be dead with Christ, we believe that we shall also live with him: ..."

Rom 6:8

When God the judge looks at us, he will see Christ.

"Who shall lay any thing to the charge of Gods elect? It is God that justifieth."

Rom 8:33

"He is near that justifieth me; who will contend with me? let us stand together: who is mine adversary? let him come near to me.

Behold, the Lord God will help me; who is he that shall condemn me?"

Isaiah 50:8-9

It is in this confidence in God that he will justify us, that we can be afraid of no one.

God judges righteously.

Who, when he was reviled, reviled not again; when he suffered, he threatened not; but committed himself to him that judgeth righteously: …

1Pet 2:23

In the day of judgment we will stand and we will see his judgments. I think of my pastor saying many times[322] “When we get to heaven, we are going to say, Yes, Lord. You are right, you have been just, honest, and very merciful.” We won't be saying it because we have to, but because we will see with our eyes, and know in our hearts that it is true.

---

321 'might cause to be'

322 (words to this effect)

"If thou hast anything to say, answer me: speak, for I desire to justify thee."
Job 33:32

Like Elihu, God is out to justify us - his sons and daughters. He wants us to obtain the best rewards possible. He has no interest in men's destruction.

JOH 5:24 Verily, verily, I say unto you, He that heareth my word, and believeth on him that sent me, hath everlasting life, and shall not come into (judgment)[323]; but is passed from death unto life.

Everyone will appear before the judgment seat. We also will stand before the judgment seat of Christ, the same as everyone else. However, because we have been forgiven, we will appear before the judgment seat to receive according to the good that we have done. For us, no judgement will be made between good and evil.

"For we must all appear before the judgment seat of Christ; that every one may receive the things done in his body, according to that he hath done, whether it be good or bad. Knowing therefore the terror of the Lord, we persuade men; ..."
2Cor 5:10

"So then every one of us shall give account of himself to God."
Rom 14:12

"Judge me, O Lord my God, according to thy righteousness; and let them not rejoice over me."
Psalm 35:24

The judgment of our sin had been made previously when we made a covenant with God through Christ for him to take our sin. When we made this covenant, we exchanged Jesus righteousness for our sin.

"To appoint unto them that mourn in Zion, to give unto them an adornment[324] instead of [bestrewn] ashes, liquid oil of cheerfulness instead of mourning, the garment of praise (singing) instead of a feeble spirit; that they might be acclaimed strong [trees] of right, the planting of the Lord, beautifying[325] to him."
Isaiah 61:3 [a translation]

"... much more they which receive abundance of grace and of the gift of righteousness shall reign in life by one [man], Jesus Christ."
Rom 5:17

It is because righteousness is a gift, that no man can boast about his own righteous works.

---

323 G2920 krisis; *decision* (subj. or obj., for or against); by extension a *tribunal* by implication *justice* (specially divine *law*). Usually translated in the KJV as 'judgment'.
324 i.e. something to make beautiful
325 H6286 cf. Isaiah 44:23 'glorified' and Psalm 149:4 'beautify'

"That no flesh should glory in his [God's] presence.

But of him are ye in Christ Jesus, who of God is made unto us wisdom, and righteousness, and sanctification, and redemption:

That, according as it is written, He that glorieth, let him glory in the Lord."
1Cor 1:29-31

The gift of righteousness that God gave us was his son.

We will receive a reward according to those works that have been executed as a result of love and faith in Christ Jesus. God doesn't take pleasure in executing judgment upon people, he would far rather show mercy.

"For the Lord shall rise up as in mount Perazim, he shall be wroth as in the valley of Gibeon, that he may do his work, his strange work; and bring to pass his act, his strange act."
Isaiah 28:21

'These scriptures - and many others like them - reveal that God delights to offer mercy and salvation, but that he is reluctant to administer wrath and judgment.'
- D. Prince.

God has no pleasure in the death of the wicked.

"Have I any pleasure at all[326] that the wicked should die? saith the Lord God: and not [delight] that he should return from his *ways*[327], and live?"
Ezek 18:23

God says to everyone who is sinning.

"Repent, and turn yourselves from all your transgressions; so iniquity shall not be your ruin. Cast away from you all your transgressions, whereby ye have transgressed; and make you a new heart and a new spirit: for why will ye die, O house of Israel?

For I have no pleasure in the death of him that dieth, saith the Lord God: wherefore turn yourselves, and (live)."
Ezek 18:30-32

Reading Isaiah 43:20-24

God reasoning with his people Israel said in effect to them. "I am God, there is no other. And I formed you for myself." Other nations had Gods of which they were proud of. Yet the one true God, Israel grew tired of.

He pleaded with them to turn and come back.

---

[326] or '*Delighting, do I delight ...* ?'

[327] a *road* (as *trodden*); fig. a *course* of life or *mode* of action

"I, even I, am he that blotteth out thy transgressions for mine own sake, and will not remember thy sins.

Put me in remembrance: let us plead together: declare thou, that thou mayest be justified."

Isaiah 43:25-26

"He [the worshipper of a wooden carving] feedeth on ashes: a deceived heart hath turned him aside, that he cannot deliver his soul, nor say, Is there not a lie in my right hand?

Remember these, O Jacob and Israel; for thou art my servant: I have formed thee; thou art my servant: O Israel, thou shalt not be forgotten of me.

I have blotted out, as a thick cloud, thy transgressions, and, as a cloud, thy sins: return unto me; for I have redeemed thee."

Isaiah 44:20-22

7.2 The Dream

I had a dream when I was at college. There were one or two fatal car accidents when I was at school. About that time one car lost steering control and drove off a bridge into a river. In this accident, I think the mother and her two children died. I am not sure whether the dream was about this accident. A description of the dream as best as I remember it follows.

There was a sixteen year old student at my college. He had been in an accident. And he died.

There was a dark room, and a book illuminated. God was seated, looking at the book. The book was open and he was reading about the high school boys life. I don't know how, but he didn't need to turn the pages, because everything was written on the two pages in front of him. Silently, he began to read from the top left. Everything about him, what he'd done wrong when he was eight or nine years old, the friends that he had through third, fourth, and fifth form, what his parents were like, how he grew up and all that he did was recorded. And as he read, God was very sad. The Gospel had been preached to him (it might have been me, or somebody else, I don't know), everything was in order. And God was very sad. He was not interested in anything else. There was no one else he was thinking about. There was no hurry. He was very sad, and there was nothing he could do. As he read down the pages, he wanted to do something, but there was nothing he could do.

I don't know how long this went on for.

Eventually, behind him and to the right, servants began talking quietly, being concerned about the length of time God was taking. At last, one of them came over and touched God on the side of the shoulder. God became slightly aware of what was happening around him. And knew it was time to move on, but he went back to the beginning at the top left, and began reading. He was about halfway through, and while still reading, he slowly began to lift the right hand page. When the page was turned, it would be the last time that he would ever come to God's attention.

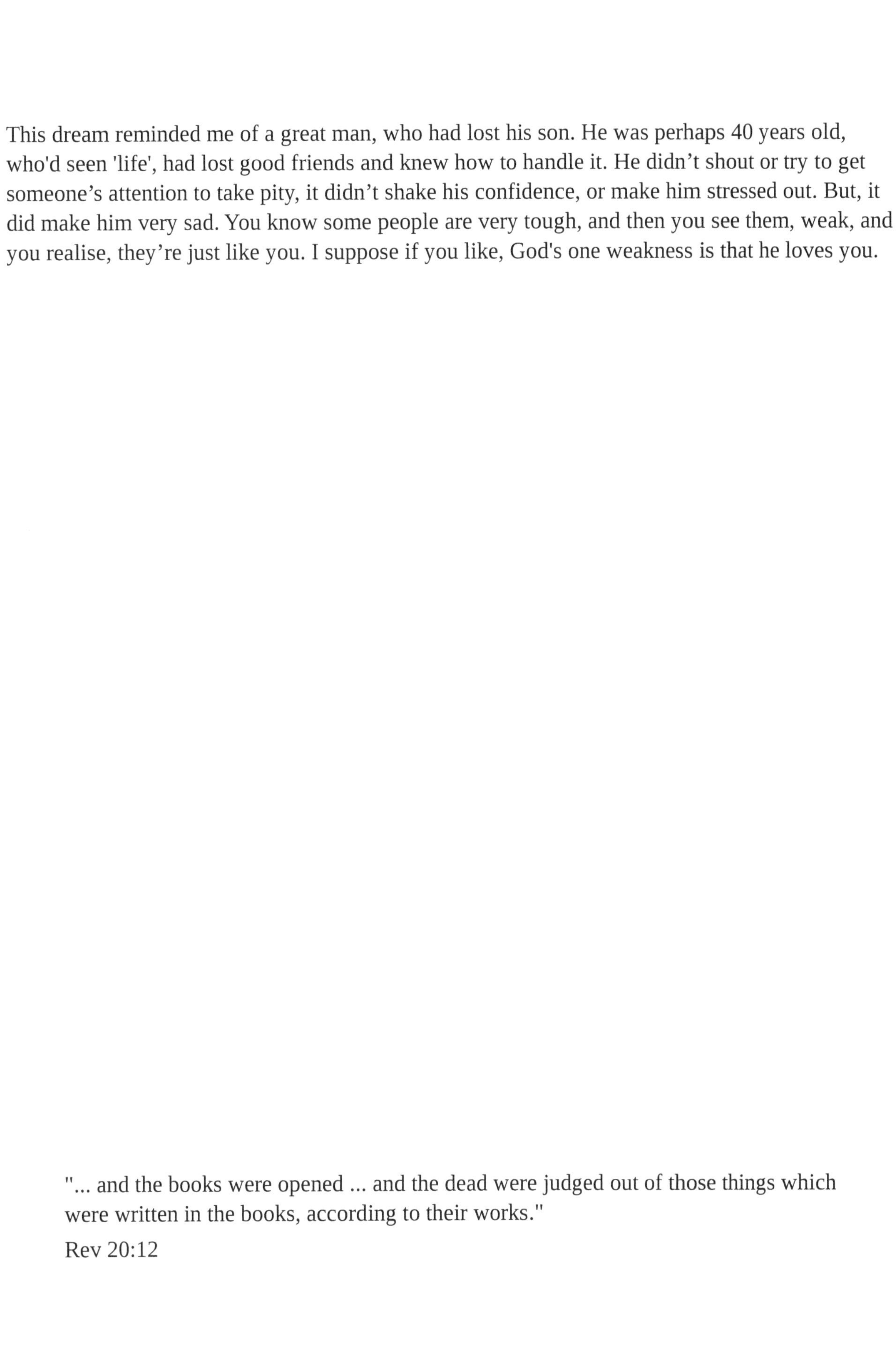

This dream reminded me of a great man, who had lost his son. He was perhaps 40 years old, who'd seen 'life', had lost good friends and knew how to handle it. He didn't shout or try to get someone's attention to take pity, it didn't shake his confidence, or make him stressed out. But, it did make him very sad. You know some people are very tough, and then you see them, weak, and you realise, they're just like you. I suppose if you like, God's one weakness is that he loves you.

"... and the books were opened ... and the dead were judged out of those things which were written in the books, according to their works."
Rev 20:12

7.3 Forgiveness

Reading 1John 3:11-16 ["For this is the message ... that we should love one another."]

> We know that we have passed from death unto life, because we love the brethren. He that loveth not his brother abideth in death. Whosoever hateth his brother is a murderer: and ye know that no murderer hath eternal life abiding in him.
> 1John 3:14-15

> If a man say, I love God, and hateth his brother, he is a liar: for he that loveth not his brother whom he hath seen, how can he love God whom he hath not seen? And this commandment have we from him, That he who loveth God love his brother also.
> 1John 4:20-21

It is good to love one another.

> "Beloved, let us love one another: for love is of God; and every one that loveth is born of God, and knoweth God." 1John 4:7

It is a cold, hard heart which does not love.

> " ... (we bless) God, even the Father; and therewith curse we men, which are made after the similitude of God. Out of the same mouth proceedeth blessing and cursing. My brethren, these things ought not so to be."
> James 3:9-10

A heart which is soft, will love the Lord, the same heart will love his 'brother'. The heart is the same.

> "... the darkness is past, and the true light now shineth. He that saith he is in the light, and hateth his brother, is in darkness[328] even until [just] now.
>
> ... , and walketh in darkness, ... "
> 1John 2:8-11

Remember " ... if we walk in the light, ... the blood ... cleanseth us from all sin."[329]

There is no forgiveness if you hate your brother.

> "There is one lawgiver, who is able to save and to destroy: ..."
> James 4:12

> Grudge not one against another, brethren, lest ye be condemned: behold, the judge standeth before the door.
> James 5:9

---

[328] G4653 *dimness, obscurity* (lit. or fig.) [related to *shadiness*, i.e. occlusion from direct light]

[329] 1John 1:7

Remember Paul saying to Philemon[330] concerning Onesimus,

> Not now as a servant, but above a servant, a brother beloved, specially to me, … , receive him as myself. If he hath wronged thee, or oweth thee ought, put that on mine account; I Paul have written it with mine own hand, I will repay it: albeit I do not say to thee how thou owest unto me even thine own self besides.
>
> Philemon 1:16-19

I think Jesus would say of our brethren, if he or she owes you anything, put it on my account. I will repay it.

Reading Mat 18:21-35 [Parable of an unforgiving servant[331]]

Ten thousand talents are worth ~$160 million dollars[332]. A hundred pence is worth ~$200 dollars.

If one considers dictatorships in the middle east, one concludes he would certainly be executed. It is astonishing that the king forgave this man.

> "The servant therefore fell down, and worshipped him, saying, Lord, have patience with me, and I will pay thee all."

This man had no chance of paying all this money, and the King knew it.

> "Then the lord of that servant was moved with compassion, and loosed him, and forgave him the debt."

Do you ever wonder at what God does. I think of the scripture "Behold therefore the goodness and severity of God"[333] Still I remember the words of the song amazing grace.

> "Twas grace that taught my heart to fear, and grace my fears relieved."

The destruction of this servant was more to do with his callous heart, than with a lack of God's mercy. We always have a chance to repent from holding grudges against our fellowservants while we are alive. I have never found God negligent in reminding people to forgive one another. If there is a problem with unforgiveness and one comes to talk to God, whether it be in church on Sunday or on the way to hospital in an ambulance, God will make it known.

---

[330] one of the books in the new testament: Philemon (just before Hebrews)

[331] Certain numbers were used as figurative representations and not actual quantities. Seven times means completely. So I suppose Seventy times seven means completely complete. cf. Psalm 12:6 and Gen 4:24 "truly Lamech seventy seven." I heard Seventy represents God's administration in the world. Hence perhaps seventy times seven indicates God's kingdom in terms of forgiveness being worked out completely in the world. Anyway, 'Seventy times seven' is commonly accepted to mean 'infinity' (ref. Mat 18:21-22, Luke 17:3-4).

[332] One silver Roman penny was a days wages (Mat 20:2). One hundred pence would be about 100 days wages. One penny was 3.9 grams i.e. almost exactly an eighth of a troy ounce. One troy ounce is worth about 8 days work. One talent is roughly 1000 troy ounces. Therefore 10,000 talents would be worth ~80 million days work. If wages are $2 US per day, then the debts are $200 and $160 million US dollars.
Another method:- If price per silver troy ounce is $16 US per ounce ($16.50 per troy ounce March 2018) 10,000 talents are 160 million dollars and 100 pennies are 12.5 troy ounces or $200. A Talent is assumed to be 1000 troy ounces [i.e. approximating an assumed Roman talent, weighing 1,038 troy ounces (32.3kg)]. Incidentally, one troy ounce = 1.097 British or American ounces = 31.10 grams.

[333] Rom 11:22

"So likewise shall my heavenly Father do also unto <u>you</u>, if ye from your hearts forgive not every one his brother their trespasses."

Mat 18:35

7.4 Faithfulness

> For if we sin wilfully[334] after that we have received the knowledge (/recognition) of the truth, there remaineth no more sacrifice for sins,
>
> But a certain fearful looking for of judgment and fiery indignation, which shall devour the adversaries.
>
> He that despised[335] Moses' law died without mercy under two or three witnesses:
>
> Of how much sorer punishment, suppose ye, shall he be thought worthy, who hath trodden under foot the Son of God, and hath counted the blood of the covenant, wherewith he was sanctified, an unholy thing, and hath (insulted)[336] the spirit of grace?
>
> For we know him that hath said, Vengeance belongeth unto me, I will recompense, saith the Lord. And again, The Lord shall judge his people.
>
> It is a fearful thing to fall into the hands of the living God.
>
> Heb 10:26-31

We made a covenant with God. When we stand before God on the day of judgment, he will judge us as either faithful or unfaithful in our covenant with him.

> "There is one lawgiver, who is able to save and to destroy: ..."
>
> James 4:12

If we sin, God gives space for us to repent.

> "Notwithstanding I have a few things against thee, because thou sufferest that woman Jezebel, which calleth herself a prophetess, to teach and to seduce my servants to commit fornication, and to eat things sacrificed unto idols.
>
> And I gave her space to repent of her fornication; and she repented not.
>
> Behold, I will cast her into a bed, and them that commit adultery with her into great tribulation, except they repent of their deeds.
>
> And I will kill her children with death; and all the churches shall know that I am he which searcheth the reins and hearts: ..."
>
> Rev 2:20-23

It is possible for a man to reject God after having made a covenant with him.

> "... he was sanctified, ..." Heb 10:29

The man was sanctified, but no longer is sanctified. This sanctification was through faith.

---

[334] G1596 *voluntarily.*

[335] cf. Num 15:30-36 [man gathering sticks]

[336] G1796 (from G1722 and G5195) to *insult*

G1722 primary preposition denoting fixed *position* (in place, time or state) and (by implic. *instrumentality* (medially or constructively), i.e. a relation of *rest* (intermed. between G1519 and G1537); *in, at,* (up-) *on, by,* etc.

G5195 to *exercise violence,* i.e. *abuse*

"... sanctified by faith that is in me." Acts 26:18

In the old testament, there was a man[335] that was sentenced to death for gathering sticks on the Sabbath. I think this is the man that is referred to in Hebrews[337] as despising Moses law. The punishment of the "wilful sin" in Hebrews[338] was compared with the punishment for despising the law of Moses. Is not this comparison made because in both cases, the significant aspect of the crime was to despise the authority that they were under?

Wilful (i.e. voluntary) sin is in my view pardonable by God[339]. But this particular wilful sin in Hebrews falls under a different category.

I believe that so long as one has not voluntarily sinned with the intention of by that sin rejecting the covenant made with God through Jesus, we have the opportunity to repent.

> "If we confess our sins, he is faithful and just to forgive us our sins, and to cleanse us from all unrighteousness."
>
> 1John 1:9

There is a sin not unto death, and there is a sin unto death.

> "There is a sin unto death: I do not say that he shall pray for it. All unrighteousness is sin: and there is a sin not unto death."
>
> 1John 5:16-17

Here death refers to 1John 5:12

> "He that hath the Son hath life; and he that hath not the Son of God hath not life."
> 1John 5:12

I believe that a man may choose to reject Christ, and the result of this action is some sin against God. This sin is a sin unto death.

In the scripture earlier, we saw that there was a space to repent. During this space, there is a possibility to repent; after this space there is not.

In summary so far, we have looked at how a man can choose to reject God, and that that decision is permanent. We can refuse to obey God for (usually I think) long periods of time during which we have opportunity to repent. But at some stage that opportunity will be removed[340].

> "Brethren, if any of you do err from the truth, and one convert him;
>
> Let him know, that he which converteth the sinner from the error of his way, shall save a soul from death, and shall hide a multitude of sins."
>
> James 5:19-20

---

[337] i.e. in Hebrews 10:28

[338] i.e. in Hebrews 10:26

[339] Some things like smoking, for example, remain unmentioned by God, and unrecognised by a new Christian for many months. Under these cases, the blood of Jesus cleanses from this unknown sin. There are other times where we sin intentionally and God will forgive us of those when we repent.

[340] I think God gives no guarantee to warn us that the time allocated to repent is up.

Repentance is not something done only once when we first believe. Continual repentance is part of the foundation of our Faith. Jesus will constantly remind us when we sin. God calls us to repent now, not just before the time he gives us to repent is up. We think our sin is only for a moment, but it so easily turns into days, and weeks, and years.

> "O come, let us worship and bow down: let us kneel before the Lord our maker.
>
> For he is our God; and we are the people of his pasture, and the sheep of his hand.
> Today if ye will hear his voice,
>
> Harden not your heart, ..."
> Psalm 95:6-8

If we continue to honestly pray the Lords prayer

> "And forgive us our sins; for we also forgive every one that is indebted to us."
> Luke 11:4

and do something (no matter how small and insignificant it seems) to resist temptation, we have no fear of eternal Judgment.

Let us consider the phrase 'the knowledge of the truth'. The person in verse 29 of Hebrews chapter ten had 'received the knowledge of the truth'. This man or woman knew Jesus (the truth)[341]. Verse 26 refers to sinning wilfully (voluntarily). The writer explains *wilfully/voluntarily sinning after knowing the truth* in verse 29. The person described in verse 29 clearly sees, and recognises exactly what he is doing. He counts Jesus blood as unholy. And insults the spirit of grace.

One wonders how a clear recognition of the truth goes with such evil and darkness, at the eternal death of the relationship between a man and his maker. But I suppose that God in his mercy holds back confusion and the authorities of darkness for one last chance that his son may go to heaven.

At the end of the day, I don't think its merely a matter of good and evil, or right and wrong. Its a matter of do you love me? That is the question God asks. Do you love me? If the answer is no, we will sin and evil will take away our soul. If the answer is Yes, there will be suffering, and sadness and cares and worries which will assail us, but in the midst of the storm, we will have someone in our boat who will never fail us, who will never leave us, who no one else knows how much time he spends looking at us, and watching us, and loving us, and caring for us, and taking time to plan things for us, and looking out for us, and seeing if there's anything he can do to help us, for our God is the one who made us who loves us with all his heart, he is the faithful husband, and we are his bride.

If we deny him by our actions, if we murder, if we steal, if we lie, if we commit adultery, how can we say we know Christ, that we have faith in him? What we have is words, it is not faith. Yet God is still out to save us though we may have, as Christians committed such things.

---

[341] cf. 1Tim 2:4; 2Tim 2:25; 2Tim 3:7; Tit 1:1

Remember Paul's comment.

> "And lest, when I come again, my God will humble me among you, and that I shall bewail many which have sinned already, and have not repented of the uncleanness and fornication and lasciviousness which they have committed."
> 2Cor 12:21

Paul did not lament those Christians who had sinned and repented, because they were no longer sinning and had been forgiven. You know one of the reasons I think David was great in God's eyes, was because unlike all the other kings who erred, he turned his whole heart and soul back to God, and not away when he had sinned.

With God we always have a chance to start over again. We may sin, and God will go to extreme efforts to get us to come back. We may still choose to sin against God and never return to God, to never say sorry.

> "But when the righteous turneth away from his righteousness, and committeth iniquity, and doeth according to all the abominations that the wicked man doeth, shall he live? All his righteousness that he hath done shall not be mentioned: in his *trespass* that he hath *trespassed*, and in his sin that he hath sinned, in them shall he die."
> Ezek 18:24

The words *trespassed* and *trespass* used here are the root word *maw-al' G4603* and its derivative G*4604 mah'-al*. They are translated as *treacherously and treachery*.

H4603 *maw-al* a prim. root; prop. to *cover* up; used only fig. to *act covertly*[342], i.e. *treacherously*.

H4604 *mah-al treachery*, i.e. sin. [from H4603[343]]

Oxford English Dictionary meaning is violating faith or betraying trust, perfidious (breach of faith), not to be relied upon, deceptive. Also translated as betrayal.

I think this covering up is not a general covering up of things so that people can't see, but someone who knows God - a righteous man, trying to deceive God. There is more to this than sin, it is an unfaithful hard heart, who leaves walking humbly with his God, and doing justly, and loving mercy to turn away to wickedness, arrogancy, injustice, and cruelty. Betrayal and unfaithfulness, are not words one can use about an enemy. They are words used to describe someone who was once your friend.

---

[342] secret or disguised

[343] Strong's Forty-third printing in 1984 references H4603, and not H4608

7.5 Rewards

7.5.1 The Knowledge of God

> Judas saith unto him, not Iscariot, Lord, how is it that thou wilt manifest thyself unto us, and not unto the world?
>
> Jesus answered and said unto him, If a man love me, he will keep my words: and my Father will love him, and we will come unto him, and make our abode with him.
>
> He that loveth me not keepeth not my sayings: and the word which ye hear is not mine, but the Father's which sent me.
>
> John 14:22-24

> "But without faith it is impossible to please him [God]: for he that cometh to God must believe that he is, and that he is a rewarder of them that diligently seek him."
>
> Heb 11:6

When we pray, we come to God.

> "Draw nigh to God, and he will draw nigh to you."
>
> James 4:8[344]

Sometimes it seems that God does not draw night to us when we pray. Appearances are frequently deceiving. We must continually trust God's word.

> "Draw nigh to God, and he will draw nigh to you."
>
> James 4:8

If we make an effort to seek God. He will see it, and come to us. Don't believe appearances, if we have drawn nigh by calling out to God through Christ, then we can be certain he has drawn nigh to us. Perseverance pays dividends.

Reading Luke 11:1-13 [The Lords Prayer, The man without bread, A son asking their Father]

> For every one that asketh receiveth; and he that seeketh findeth; and to him that knocketh it shall be opened.
>
> Luke 11:10

The preceding reading contained a story about someone who was not going to give anything to the man asking him, even though he was his friend. I think God uses this illustration to emphasise the importance of being persistent. If this man in bed could be persuaded to get up and give as many loaves as required, how much more should we expect our heavenly Father to give us what we need when we ask him patiently, without faltering or giving up hope that we will receive what he has promised to us.

---

[344] cf. Deut 4:29; 2Chr 15:4

Now faith is the (*assurance*)[345] of *things hoped for*[346], the *evidence*[347] (reproof) of *things*[348] not seen.

For by it the elders obtained a good report.

Heb 11:1-2

Faith that God will give us things is a prerequisite for knowing God. If you say I trust God, but God will do nothing, what you have is a lie.

"They that observe[349] lying[350] vanities[351] forsake[352] their own mercy[353]."

Jonah 2:8

We can ask God, and expect him to answer us.

"And ye shall seek me, and find me, when ye shall search for me with all of your heart. And I will be found of you, saith the LORD: and I will turn away your captivity, ..."

Jeremiah 29:13-14

I have been to prayer meetings where those in charge have endlessly talked on, and on. It's hard to say even a word of praise or thanks to God, because of their list of things to pray about.

"Forasmuch as this people draw near me with their mouth, and with their lips do honour me, but have removed their heart far from me, and their fear toward me is taught by the precept of men: ..."

Isaiah 29:13

When we pray, how often do we pray about things we think God is interested in, but not the things which are closest to our heart? Is not God interested in the heart? An earnest prayer to God about something small, where our heart is, is more important to God than hours talking about things we do not care about.

"For where your treasure is, there will your heart be also."

Luke 12:34

God usually wants us to talk about what is important to us.

---

345 G5287 a *setting under* (*support*); [from a compound of G5259 {under} and G2476 {to stand}]

346 G1680 to *expect* or *confide*

347 *proof, conviction*

348 G4229 pragma; [From G4238]; a *deed*, by implication an *affair*; by extension an *object* (material):- business, matter, thing, work.

G4238 prasso; a prim. verb; "to practise", i.e. *perform repeatedly* or *habitually*

349 H8104 prop. to *hedge* about (as with thorns), i.e. *guard*; generally to *protect, attend to,* etc.

350 H7723 from the same as H7722 in the sense of *desolating*; *evil* (as *destructive*), lit. (*ruin*) or mor. (espec. *guile*); fig. *idolatry* (as false, subj.), *uselessness* (as deceptive, obj.; also adv. in *vain*):- false(-ly), lie, lying, vain, vanity.

H7722 from an unused root meaning to *rush* over; a *tempest*; by impl. *devastation*:- desolate (-ion), destroy, destruction, storm, wasteness.

351 H1892 *emptiness* or *vanity*, fig. something *transitory* and *unsatisfactory.* [from H1891]

H1891 a prim. root; to *be vain* in act, word, or expectation; spec. to *lead astray*:- be (become, make) vain.

352 H5800 a prim. root; to *loosen*, i.e. *relinquish, permit,* etc.

353 H2617 *kindness*; from {H2616 prop. perh. to *bow* (the neck only in courtesy to an equal), i.e. to be *kind*}

I remember a wealthy Australian businessman who had not long ago become a Christian. After he became a Christian, God said, give all your business to me. So he submitted himself to God, and said, it is yours, do with it as you will. Apparently, his business doubled in value in the space of a few months. He was a little bit miffed that God could run it better than he could. We can not say what God will do, when we present our lives to him. It may mean that God will take all our money from us, or he may give us great wealth.

I heard of another man, who owned a chain of hotels on some islands in the pacific. God woke him up one night, and said to him. Sell your hotel chain today. He argued, Lord, the chain is doing well. But in the morning, he came to his broker and said. Sell my hotel chain. The broker said, but the business is doing well, it is foolish to sell now. The business man replied, Sell my hotel chain today, or I will find another broker who will. So the broker sold the hotel chain. Sometime soon after, there was an earthquake, and the hotels on the islands were destroyed, or badly damaged.

Reading Luke 12:13-34 [The rich man and the barns]

Reading 1Timothy 6:6-21 [But Godliness with contentment ...]

There is nothing intrinsically wrong with having riches in this world. However, I agree with the statement of an accountant I met.

> "Money makes a good servant, but a bad master."[354]

7.5.2 Earning Treasure

Reading Matthew 4:24-5:12 ["Blessed are the ..."]

> For whosoever shall give you a cup of water to drink in my name, because ye belong to Christ, verily I say unto you, he shall not lose his reward.
>
> Mark 9:41

> For verily I say unto you, Till heaven and earth pass, one jot or one tittle shall in no wise pass from the law, till all be fulfilled.
>
> Matthew 5:18

Every detail will be accounted for: no reward will go missing and no judgement will be left unexecuted.

> "... God is not unrighteous to forget your work and labour of love, which ye have shewed toward his name, in that ye have ministered to the saints, and do minister."
>
> Heb 6:10

[354] not a quote from the Bible.

"Blessed are ye, when men shall revile you, and persecute you, and shall say all manner of evil against you falsely, for my sake.

Rejoice, and be exceeding[ly][355] glad: for great is your reward in heaven: for so persecuted they the prophets which were before you."

Mat 5:11-12

Note that it doesn't say "great *will be* your reward in heaven".

"great **is** your reward in heaven"

As we work now, there are in heaven riches being placed into our 'bank account'.

"That they [them that are rich in this world] do good, that they be rich in good works, ready to distribute, willing to communicate; Laying up in store for themselves a good foundation against the time to come, that they may lay hold on eternal life."

2Tim 6:18-19

"Blessed is the man that endureth temptation: for when he is tried[356], he shall receive the crown of life, which the Lord hath promised to them that love him."

James 1:12

Love does not fail under pressure.

"Charity (Love) never faileth: ..." 1Cor 13:8

If we display through our actions our love for God, we will pass through them, and be found faithful. If we love God, and in a time of temptation sin, we repent and turn to God, and he will forgive us, and we will be found faithful. I believe the main thing that will enable us to come through temptations is love for God. If we continue to love God, we will obtain eternal life.

"... the crown of life, which the Lord hath promised to them that love him."

I suppose if we are to be rewarded, we must do some work. What does God want us to do? There are a many scriptures that specify what God's will is for all of us. Of course each person is different, and some of what God's will is for one person to do, will not be the same as that for another, or even any other man.

---

[355] G21 properly to *jump for joy*, i.e. *exult*.
[from 'much' + (G242 to *jump*, fig. to *gush*:-leap, spring up.)]

[356] G1384 properly *acceptable* (*current* after assayal), i.e. *approved*. [from G1380]
G1380 A prolonged form of a prim. verb "doko" (used only as an alternate in certain tenses; cf. the base of G1166); of the same meaning; to *think*; by implic. to *seem* (truthfully or uncertainly). Translated in KJV as:- be accounted, (of own) pleas(-ure), be of reputation, seem (good), suppose, think, trow.
G1166 a prol. form of an obsol. prim. of the same meaning; to *show* (lit. or fig.).

Comment	Reference
Serve others as though we were serving God i.e. doing God's will from our heart.	Acts 13:36 Eph 6:6
That we should be sanctified, and abstain from fornication	1Thes 4:3
Not oppress our brother	1Thes 4:6 Neh 5:1-19
Love thy brother	1Thes 4:9
Be fond of being settled. And do ones own routine work. And be engaged in the things we are responsible for.	1Thes 4:11
With well doing, silence the ignorance of foolish men	1Pet 2:15
Have patience, and receive the promise of eternal heirship.	Heb 10:36 2Pet 3:9 1Tim 2:4
In everything give thanks	1Thes 5:18

Reading 1Peter 3:10-18

But and if ye suffer (the will of God can be for suffering) for righteousness sake by others speaking evil of you as though we were evil doers. God says to sanctify the Lord in your heart, and be ready to give reason of the hope in you. Having a good conscience that they may be ashamed who falsely accuse you.

We have work to do, and one day it will be made clear what we have done and we will be rewarded.

> "Whom [Christ] we preach, warning every man, and teaching every man in all wisdom; that we may present every man perfect in Christ Jesus: Whereunto I also labour, striving according to his working, which worketh in me mightily."
>
> Col 1:28-29

To which end did Paul labour? To be presented perfect in Christ Jesus before God. Its not only us who wants to see us do well and receive a good reward. Our heavenly Father cares for us, and he is for us.

One day we will see Jesus in the sky and perhaps we will depart to be with the Lord on the hospital bed[357]. No matter what happens our confidence is in the Lord.

> "Therefore we are always confident, knowing that, whilst we are at home in the body, we are absent from the Lord: ..."
>
> 2Cor 5:6

[357] This sentence is intentionally worded this way.

> But thanks be to God, (who) giveth us the victory through our Lord Jesus Christ.
>
> Therefore, my beloved brethren, be ye steadfast, unmoveable, always abounding in the work of [who?] the Lord, forasmuch as ye know that your labour is not in vain in the Lord.
>
> 1Cor 15:57-58

Hallelujah. God gives us eternal life through Jesus Christ our Lord. We will be resurrected. God will reward us on the day when Christ returns.

7.6 Christ's Judgement

> "But we see Jesus, ... crowned with glory and honour; that he by the grace of God should taste death for every man." Heb 2:9

> Then said Jesus unto Peter, Put up thy sword into the sheath: the cup which my Father hath given me, shall I not drink it?
>
> John 18:11

> "And in the evening he cometh with the twelve. And as they sat and did eat, ...
>
> ...
>
> And he took the cup, and when he had given thanks, he gave it to them: and they all drank of it.
>
> And he said unto them, this is my blood of the new testament, which is shed for many."
>
> Mark 14:17-24[358]

We worry, that Christ will condemned us, but forget that he set his face towards Jerusalem and Calvary for our sakes[359].

> "Who is he that condemneth? It is Christ that died, ..."
>
> Rom 8:34

Tell me the old, old story of Jesus and his love, ... for I forget so soon[360].

---

[358] cf. Matthew 26:27-28, "which is shed for many for the remission of sins." and Luke 22:19-20 "And he took bread, and gave thanks, and brake it, and gave unto them, saying, This is my body which is given for you: … , This cup is the new testament in my blood, which is (*poured forth*) for you."

[359] cf. Luke 9:51; Mark 10:33-34,47-49

[360] - a song, 'Tell me the old, old story', by Kate Hankey

7.7 Case Studies

In the following case studies, we may consider examples of God's judgment. God's judgment is usually delayed until the last day. For this reason people often think that God does not pay attention to us[361].

> "Knowing this first, that there shall come in the last days scoffers, walking after their own lusts, And saying, Where is the promise of his coming? for since the fathers fell asleep, all things continue as they were from the beginning of the creation. …
>
> But, beloved, be not ignorant of this one thing, ...
>
> The Lord is not slack concerning his promise, as some men count slackness; but is longsuffering to us-ward, not willing that any should perish, but that all should come to repentance."
>
> 2Peter 3:3-4,8-9

It is through God's mercy that he delays judgment, because he is not inclined to destroy anyone. God gives everyone time to say sorry and to turn away from sin.

> "As it is written, There is none righteous, no, not one: There is none that understandeth, there is none that seeketh after God."
>
> Rom 3:10-11

> "For all have sinned, and come short of the glory of God;"
>
> Rom 3:23

While God loves judgment to be done swiftly, he exercises restraint for our sakes.

> "For the Son of man is not come to destroy men's lives, but to save them. And they went to another village."
>
> Luke 9:56

[361] cf. Ezekiel chapters 8-9 "The LORD seeth us not; the LORD hath forsaken the earth."

7.7.1 Jonah

Reading Jonah

> "They that observe lying vanities forsake their own mercy. But I will sacrifice unto thee with the voice of thanksgiving; I will pay that that I have vowed. Salvation is of the LORD."
>
> - the prophet Jonah (Jonah 2:8-9)
>
> "And God said to Jonah, Doest thou well to be angry for the gourd? And he said, I do well to be angry, even unto death. Then said the LORD, Thou hast had pity on the gourd, for the which thou hast not laboured, neither madest it grow; which came up in a night, and perished in a night:
>
> And should not I spare Nineveh, that great city, wherein are more then sixscore thousand persons that cannot discern between their right hand and their left hand; and also much cattle?"
>
> Jonah 4:9-11

7.7.2 Lazarus

Reading Luke 12:15-21 [Rich man and the barns]

Reading Luke 16:19-31 [Lazarus[362] the beggar and the Rich man]

> "And he said, Nay, father Abraham: but if one went unto them from the dead, they will repent.
>
> And he said unto him, If they hear not Moses and the prophets, neither will they be persuaded, though one rose from the dead."
>
> Luke 16:30-31

Perhaps God did hear the rich man's request and grant it, for one is raised from the dead.

I listened to a sermon on this, which was very good. The point was made that the story Jesus told was not a parable. It was an account of what actually took place before Christ's resurrection. Lazarus is an actual person. We may note a few things about the rich man. We see he was tormented. He could still speak, communicate, feel and retained all of his mental faculties. Not only so but we also see that he still cared about his family namely his five brothers. It can not be said he was only self-centred.

Hell is a place. Before Christ's resurrection, everyone who died went to hell. When Christ died, he took those people in the good part of hell. He took (captured[363]) those captives in Hell, and brought them with him into the presence of the Father, and of the Holy angels.

> "When he ascended up on high, he led captivity captive, and gave gifts unto men. (Now that he ascended, what is it but that he also descended first into the lower parts of the earth? He that descended is the same also that ascended up far above all heavens, ..."
>
> Eph 4:8-10

Hell does still exist, but it only contains those who did not put their trust and hope in God. People who do not believe in Jesus will still go to hell. People who believe in Christ, depart to be with the Lord. Consider Steven, who was martyred. He said, "Lord Jesus, receive my spirit"[364]. Also consider Paul's statement "having a desire to depart, and to be with Christ"[365].

Hell (and those in it) will, along with death, eventually be cast into the lake of burning fire.

Reading Rev 20:11-15 [Hell being cast into lake of fire]

---

[362] Lazarus could perhaps be translated as "The Mighty is my protector."

[363] Jesus captured from the enemy in a military operation their captives. Thus effectively the captives were freed. Our God is not only the God of peace (Rom 16:20), he is also the Lord of Hosts (mass of people or an army). "The LORD is a man of war: the LORD is his name" Exod 15:3

[364] Acts 7:59

[365] Phil 1:23

There is no such thing as "purgatory". Those who have sin whether it is small or great will be punished eternally. Men can not repay their own debt.

Reading Psalm 49

> "None of them can by any means redeem his brother, nor give to God a ransom for him: (For the redemption of their soul is precious, and it ceaseth[366] [i.e. would be lacking or insufficient] forever:) …"
>
> Psalm 49:7-8

Fortunately the psalmist continues

> "But God will redeem my soul ..." Psalm 49:15

Hallelujah, true salvation only comes from God.

> "And as it is appointed unto men once to die, but after this the judgment: ..."
>
> Heb 9:27

> For we must all appear before the judgment seat of Christ; that every one may receive the things done in his body, according to that he hath done, whether it be good or bad.
>
> 2Cor 5:10

We will focus a little more accurately on the detail of this, but for the moment let us concentrate on the phrase

> "… that everyone may receive the things done in his body, ..."

For justice to be carried out for every person, we must all appear before the judgment seat of Christ. The judgment only concerns those things which have occurred during a man's lifetime. The judgment will be of those things done here, in this present time. The decisions we make now will hold for eternity. They will not be mitigated by any occurrence after death. For this reason it is pointless to pray for the physically dead. Those in the presence of the Lord have reached the goal of the high calling which God has called us.

> "in thy presence is fullness of joy", "where the Spirit of the Lord is, there is liberty.", "I shall be satisfied, when I awake, with thy likeness.", "we shall be like him; for we shall see him ..."[367]

For those who have rejected the word of the Lord and have (physically) died, no prayer will save them from judgment.

---

366 H2308 a prim. root, prop. to *be flabby*, i.e. (by implic.) *desist*; (fig.) *be lacking* or *idle*

367 Psalm 16:11; 2Cor 3:17; Psalm 17:15; 1John 3:2

Finally the one who my soul hates has had an eternal decree sentenced upon him which God shall execute. It shall not be altered. Our adversary the devil will be punished and crushed permanently in the day of judgment.

> 'And the devil [Satan] that deceived them was cast into the lake of fire and brimstone, ... and shall be tormented day and night for ever and ever.'
> Rev 20:10

7.7.3 The Passover

"And thou shalt say unto Pharaoh, Thus saith the Lord, Israel is my son, even my firstborn: And I say unto thee, Let my son go, that he may serve me: and if thou refuse to let him go, behold, I will slay thy son, even thy firstborn."

Exod 4:22-23

Reading Exodus 11 and 12

And it came to pass, when Jesus had finished all these sayings, he said unto his disciples,

Ye know that after two days is the feast of the passover, and the son of man is betrayed to be crucified."

Matthew 26:1-2

"For even Christ our passover is sacrificed for us: ..."

1Cor 5:7

"Your lamb shall be without blemish, a male of the first year: ye shall take it out from the sheep, or from the goats:

And ye shall keep it up until the fourteenth day of the same month: and the whole assembly of the congregation of Israel shall kill it *in the evening*[368].

And they shall take of the blood, and strike it on the two side posts and on the upper door post of the houses, wherein they shall eat it."

Exod 12:5-7

It is Christ's death, which protects us from the equivalent of the angel which destroyed all the first born sons of Egypt.

"Thus saith the Lord, About midnight will I go out into the midst of Egypt: ..."

Exod 11:4

"... : it is the Lord's passover. For I will pass through the land of Egypt this night, and will smite all the firstborn in the land of Egypt, both man and beast; and against all the gods of Egypt I will execute judgment: I am the Lord.

And the blood shall be to you for a token upon the houses where ye are: and when I see the blood, I will pass over you, and the plague shall not be upon you to destroy you, when I smite the land of Egypt."

Exod 12:11-13

Jesus gives us a just reason for God to passover our sins.

[368] at dusk (i.e. *darker stage of twilight*)

"For God so loved the world, that he gave his only begotten Son, that whosoever believeth in him should not perish, but have everlasting life."

John 3:16

7.7.4 The Parable of the Sheep and the Goats

Reading Matthew 25:31-46 [The Parable of the Sheep and the Goats]

I have heard that the sheep and goats in the middle east are similar in appearance, although they are fundamentally different animals. The sheep were separated from the goats.

Consider first the sheep. The sheep are blessed for all their good works towards the King, not one bad thing is mentioned against them.

Now we know

> "There is none righteous, no, not one: ... , there is none that seeketh after God. ... , they are together become unprofitable; there is none that doeth good, no, not one."
> Rom 3:10

> "Now we know that what things soever the law saith, it saith to them who are under the law: that every mouth may be stopped, and all the world may become guilty[369] before God. Therefore by the deeds of the law there shall no flesh be justified in his sight: for by the law is the knowledge of sin."
> Rom 3:19-20

Why then is not mention made of their sin? It is because these men, women and children, are justified through faith in Christ Jesus.

> "But now the righteousness of God without[370] the law is manifested[371], being witnessed by the law and the prophets; Even the righteousness of God which is by faith of Jesus Christ unto all and upon all them that believe: for there is no difference: For all have sinned, and come short of the glory of God; Being justified[372] freely by his [God's] grace through the redemption[373] that is in Christ Jesus: Whom God hath set forth[374] to be a propitiation[375] through faith in his blood, to (display[376]) his [God's] righteousness for the remission of sins that are past, through the forbearance of God; …
> Rom 3:21-25

---

[369] G5267 *under sentence*, i.e. (by implic.) *condemned*

[370] G5565 at a space i.e. separately or apart (from G5561 room, i.e. space or territory)

[371] G5319 to *render apparent* (lit. or fig.). From G5318
G5318 From G5316; *shining*, i.e. *apparent* (lit. or fig.); neut. (as adv.) *publicly, externally*
G5316 Prolong. for the base of G5457 (see footnote 142); to *lighten* (*shine*), i.e. *show* (trans. or intr., lit. or fig.)

[372] G1344 to *render* (i.e. *show* or *regard* as) *just* or *innocent.* From G1342.
G1342 *Equitable* (in character or act); by implic. *innocent, holy* (absol. or relatively)

[373] G629 (the act) *ransom* in full, i.e. (fig.) *riddance*, or (spec.) Chr. *salvation*. (From a compound of G575 ["*off*", i.e. *away* (from something near)] & G3083 [something to *loosen* with, i.e. a redemption *price* (fig. *atonement*)]).

[374] G4388 middle voice from G4253 ["*fore*", i.e. *in front of, prior to*] and G5087 [*to place*, prop. in passive or horizontal posture]; to *place before*, i.e. (for oneself) to *exhibit*; (to oneself) to *propose* (*determine*)

[375] G2435 a neut. of a der. of 2433; an *expiatory* (place or thing), i.e. (concr.) an atoning *victim*, or (spec.) the *lid* of the ark (in the Temple). Translated in KJV as:- mercyseat, propitiation.

[376] G1732 *indication* (abstr.)

God exhibited Jesus as the payment that displayed his righteousness and forbearance in remitting sins that are passed. I suppose in doing so he also showed his love for us.

> "Herein is love, not that we loved God, but that he loved us, and sent his Son to be the propitiation for our sins."
>
> 1John 4:10

Because Jesus death paid for our sins, God was able to do something, and still be a just Judge.

> "To (show[376], now[377] at this set time[378]) his [God's] righteousness: that he [God[379]] might be just, and the justifier of him which believeth in Jesus."
>
> Rom 3:26

That was to justify those who believe in Jesus.

The goats on the other hand, are cursed for their lack of works. Not one good work is mentioned on their behalf. Why is there no mention of any good thing which the goats did? Surely they did something good in their whole life?

> "For if Abraham were justified by works, he hath whereof to glory; but not before God. ... Now to him that worketh is the reward not reckoned of grace, but of debt. But to him that worketh not, but believeth ..."
>
> Romans 4:2,4-5

Perhaps if they had not owed God a debt, God would have assessed them for rewards. But they were found owing God a debt. They were required to prove their righteousness, and in works they were found lacking.

> "For by grace are ye saved through faith; and that not of yourselves: it is the gift of God: Not of works, lest (anyone) should boast."
>
> Eph 2:8-9

> "But after that the kindness[380] and love[381] of God our Saviour toward man appeared, Not by works of righteousness which we have done, but according to his mercy[382] he saved us, ..."
>
> Titus 3:4-5

---

[377] G3568

[378] G2540

[379] "It is God that justifieth" Rom 8:33

[380] G5544 *usefulness*, i.e. moral *excellence* (in character or demeanour) [from G5543]

[381] G5363 fondness of mankind, i.e. benevolence ("philanthropy") [from same as G5364]

[382] G1656 compassion

7.7.5 The Man Dying On the Roadside

Reading Mark 10:17-22[383] [rich young ruler]

There was another occasion when Jesus was talking about commandments and eternal life. It is recorded in John 15:1-17

> "If ye keep my commandments, ye shall abide in my love; even as I have kept my Father's commandments, and abide in his love. These things have I spoken unto you, that my joy might remain in you, and that your joy might be full. This is my commandment, That ye love one another, as I have loved you.
>
> Greater love hath no man than this, that a man lay down his life for his friends. Ye are my friends, if ye do whatsoever I command you. Henceforth I call you not servants; for the servant knoweth not what his lord doeth: but I have called you friends; for all things that I have heard of my Father I have made known unto you."
>
> John 15:10-15

One often has to clear away the wood and hay to discover the foundation of repentance and faith, before building can start. We must have solid rock to build on.

> "... not laying again the foundation of repentance from dead works, and of faith towards God, ..."
>
> Heb 6:1

Our friendship with God began when we repented from our sin and trusted in Jesus to save us. At the cross Jesus died for us, and our sins were paid. Sin also loses its grip on us at the cross. When we out of love for God present our bodies as a living sacrifice, we are free to follow Jesus. It is by going through the cross of Christ and crucifying the flesh with its desires that we stand in righteousness and holiness in our Lords presence[384].

> "He that loveth his life shall lose it; ..." John 12:25
>
> "... : and he that loseth his life for my sake shall find it." Mat 10:39
>
> And he said to them all, If any man will come after me, let him deny himself, and take up his cross daily, and follow me.
>
> Luke 9:23

The scripture says

> "... ; and what doth the Lord require of thee, but to do justly, and to love mercy, and to walk humbly with thy God?"
>
> Micah 6:8

---

383 cf. Mat 19:16; Luke 18:20

384 Gal 5:24 "And they that are Christ's have (impaled) ..."

Yet, we have just seen Jesus expects us to give up our life. They don't seem like equal requests. I believe the only way we can do justly, love mercy and walk humbly in love with our God, is to present our life to him.

> "... : my soul thirsteth for thee, my flesh longeth for thee in a dry[385] and thirsty[386] land, where no water is;
>
> To see thy power and thy glory, so as I have seen thee in the sanctuary.
>
> Because thy lovingkindness is better than life, my lips shall praise thee."
>
> Psalm 63:1-3

A friendship with God is better than this life.

> "... : if a man would give all the substance of his house for love, it would utterly be contemned."
>
> Song of Solomon 8:7

It says

> "Ye are my friends, if ye do whatsoever I command you." John 15:14

This is an astonishing statement. If we said that to one of our friends, I'm not sure how much longer the friendship would last. But before we rush off to get a new friend, let us examine what Christ commands.

> "This is my commandment, That ye love one another, as I have loved you."
>
> John 15:12

If we can't trust God with our life, and lay it down, there will always be something else which we will be busy with that comes first, and will take away from our friendship with God.

> "Hereby perceive we the love of God, because he laid down his life for us: and we ought to lay down our lives for the brethren.
>
> But whoso hath this world's good, and seeth his brother have need, and shutteth up his bowels of compassion from him, how dwelleth the love of God in him?"
>
> 1John 3:16-17

I suppose it is only in the complete knowledge of the love God has for us[387], revealed by the Spirit, that we can cheerfully give up our lives for those we love.

> "Wherefore let them that suffer according to the will of God commit the keeping of their souls to him in well doing, as unto a faithful creator."
>
> 1Peter 4:19

---

[385] H6723 from an unused root meaning to *parch*; *aridity*; concretely a *desert*.

[386] H5889 (from H5888 to languish) *languid*. Translated in KJV as:- faint, thirsty, weary.

[387] Eph 3:14-21 "... ; And to know the love of Christ, ..."

Reading Luke[388] 10:25-37

The lawyer came to Jesus and asked about what he needed to do to inherit eternal life. Jesus asked him what was written in the law, and how he read it.

> "And he [the lawyer] answering said, Thou shalt love the Lord thy God with all thy heart, and with all thy soul, and with all thy strength, and with all thy mind; and thy neighbour as thyself.
>
> And he said unto him, Thou hast answered right: this do, and thou shalt live.
>
> But he, willing[389] to justify[372] himself, said unto Jesus, And who is my neighbour?"
> Luke 10:27-29

Jesus then recounts a true story. Jesus asks him, which of the three was neighbour (became near) to the man that was attacked by robbers and left almost dead?

And he replied, "He that showed mercy on him".

[388] cf. Mark 12:28-34, Mat 22:35-40

[389] G2309 to *determine* (as an act. *option* from subj. impulse), i.e. *choose* or *prefer* (lit. or fig.); by impl. to *wish, i.e. be inclined* to

7.7.6 The Parable of the Sower

Reading Matthew 13:3-23 [parable of the Sower[390]]

The seed is the word of God.

> Luke 8:11

The ground is a man's heart.

> "that which was sown in his heart." Mat 13:9

There are two types of ground. One which bears fruit, and the other which does not bear fruit.

The hard ground by the roadside rejects the word of God and so does not bear fruit[391].

> "Those by the wayside are they that hear; then cometh the devil[392], and taketh away the word out of their hearts, lest they should believe and be saved[393]."
> Luke 8:12

The stony ground believes (or endures) for a brief time, and then because they are offended, they move away. They "for a while believe".

> "They on the rock are they, which, when they hear, receive the word with joy; and these have no root, which for a while believe, and in time of temptation fall away[394]."
> Luke 8:13[395]

> And the cares of this world, and the deceitfulness of riches, and the lusts[396] of other things entering in, choke the word, and it becometh unfruitful.
> Mark 4:19

---

[390] parable also in: Matthew 13:3-23; Mark 4:1-20

[391] This hardness is probably due to sinful practices. Sinful practices harden the hearts of both believers and unbelievers alike. "lest any of you be hardened through the deceitfulness of sin." Heb 3:13. God can still save, but the ground will need to be broken up. God has the tools to do it.

[392] G1228 διάβολος, diabolos; a *traducer* (slanderer, a person who utters a false report to injure or defame); spec. Satan (cf. H7854). From G1225.

G1225 (fig.) 'to *traduce'* [from 'through' and 'to throw (in various applications, more or less violent or intense; denotes a deliberate hurl)'] translated (KJV) as 'accuse'.

H7854 śâṭân; an *opponent;* espec. (with the article prefixed) Satan, the arch enemy of good. From H7853.

H7853 śâṭan; A prim. root; to *attack*, (fig.) *accuse*

[393] "in order that they not 'have faith in'/entrust and be rescued/protected."

[394] G868 to *remove,* i.e. (actively) *instigate* to revolt; usually (reflex.) to *desist, desert, etc.* From [To stand] and ["off" or away (from something near)]

[395] Mat 13:21; Mark 4:17

[396] G1939 ἐπιθυμία epithumia ep-ee-thoo-mee'-ah

From G1937; a longing (especially for what is forbidden): - concupiscence, desire, lust (after).

G1937 ἐπιθυμέω epithumeō ep-ee-thoo-meh'-o

From G1909 and G2372; to set the *heart upon,* i.e. *long* for (rightfully or otherwise): - covet, desire, would fain, lust (after).

The thorns I believe are other things that distract, such as wealth, or physical pleasure. Love for these things must not be permitted to grow. Love for these things will take the place in our hearts for God. We can unwittingly spend our time and effort on things which are worthless and even harmful to us. These things grieve the Holy Spirit[397].

> "*For what* shall it profit a man, if he shall gain the whole world, and lose his own soul?"
>
> Mark 8:36; Matthew 16:26

If we have some idol we can not control. Ask God to save. Ask for forgiveness. Endeavour to do what is right and wait for God's salvation. If you are willing to commit yourself into God's hands, and say you're sorry. God will not turn you away, no matter how many times you fall.

> And that which fell among thorns are they, which, when they have heard, go forth, and are choked with cares and riches and pleasures of this life, and bring no fruit to perfection[398].
>
> Luke 8:14

> For out of the heart proceed evil thoughts, murders, adulteries, fornications, thefts, false witness, blasphemies: ....
>
> Matthew 15:19[399]

Don't look at the idol, or the obstacles. Look at God who gives the weak strength. Who makes the desperate, safe and sound.

Never Give up[400]. God is our Father. He cares about us and what makes us sad or troubled and our grief.

> For ye know the grace of our Lord Jesus Christ, that, though he was rich, yet for your sakes he became poor, that ye through his poverty might be rich.
>
> 2Cor 8:9

> The Lord recompense thy work, and a full reward be given thee of the Lord God of Israel, under whose wings thou art come to trust.
>
> Ruth 2:12

If we are under grace, it is the grace of someone. It is under the grace of God, that exists by Jesus Christ, we are set free from sin.

---

397 Eph 4:29-32 'Let no corrupt (putrid G4550) communication (topic) ...'
G4550 (from G4595); *rotten*, i.e. *worthless* (lit. or morally). G4550 indicates degeneracy from original virtue.
G4595 appar. a prim. verb; to *putrefy*, i.e. (fig.) *perish*.

398 "and it gave no (absolute negative) fruit"
G5052 τελεσφορέω telesphoreō tel-es-for-eh'-o
From a compound of G5056 and G5342; to *be a bearer to completion* (maturity), i.e. to *ripen* fruit (fig.): - bring fruit to perfection.

399 cf. Mark 7:21.
also cf. Gal 5:19-22 "Now the works of the flesh are ... But the fruit of the spirit is ..."

400 Luke 18:1-8 "[its necessary] always [at all times/circumstances] to pray, and not to faint [weak, tired (in heart?)]".

> “Neither yield ye your members as instruments of unrighteousness unto sin: but yield yourselves unto God[401], as those that are alive from the dead, and your members as instruments of righteousness unto God.
>
> For sin shall not have dominion over you: for ye are not under the law, but under grace.”
>
> Rom 6:14

We are commanded to be under obedience to our husband Jesus Christ the Lord[402].

> "… ; and him that cometh to me I will in no wise cast out." John 6:37

> “And this is the will of him that sent me, that every one which seeth the Son, and believeth on him, may have everlasting life: and I will raise him up at the last day.”
>
> John 6:40

God wants us to have everlasting life, and to be raised up at the last day. If we come to God and say sorry, he will forgive us and accept us. If we reject the agreement we made with God through Christ. If we reject the Word, the Spirit, Christ and God himself, then there is no forgiveness of sins.

> If I forget thee, O Jerusalem, let my right hand forget her cunning. If I do not remember thee, let my tongue cleave to the roof of my mouth; if I prefer not Jerusalem above my chief joy.
>
> Psalm 137:5-6

Reading Hebrews 2:9-18

> If we confess our sins, he is faithful and just to forgive us our sins, and to cleanse us from all unrighteousness.
>
> 1John 1:9

It takes time to learn obedience. There can be times where we need to repent daily, or even hourly.

> “Our Father ... Give us this day our daily bread. And forgive us …”[403]

We can become like Christ. But to begin with, we need to turn to him for help, and forgiveness of sin.

> I have surely heard Ephraim bemoaning himself thus; Thou hast chastised me, and I was chastised, as a bullock unaccustomed to the yoke: turn thou me, and I shall be turned; for thou art the Lord my God. Surely after that I was turned, I repented; and after that I was instructed, I smote upon my thigh: I was ashamed, yea, even confounded, because I did bear the reproach of my youth.

---

[401] cf. Rom 12:1 "I beseech you therefore, brethren, by the mercies of God, that ye present your bodies a living sacrifice, ..." and Heb 4:16 "Let us therefore come boldly unto the throne of grace, that we may obtain mercy, and find grace to help in time of need."

[402] "...; that ye should be married to another [i.e. were married to "the law of Moses"], even to him who is raised from the dead [Jesus], that we should bring forth fruit unto God." Rom 7:4

[403] reference Mat 6:9-13, Luke 11:2-4

Is Ephraim my dear son? is he a pleasant[404] child? for since I spake against him, I do earnestly remember him still: therefore my bowels are troubled for him; I will surely have mercy upon him, saith the Lord.

Set thee up waymarks, make thee high heaps: set thine heart toward the highway, even the way which thou wentest: turn again, O virgin of Israel, turn again to these thy cities.

Jer 31:18-21

Repentance is part of the road that Jesus leads toward the ground becoming good, and clear of thorns. We can break up the fallow ground, and take away the thorns with God's help through Jesus Christ.

But that on the good ground are they, which in an honest and good heart, having heard the word, keep it, and bring forth fruit with patience[405].

Luke 8:15

I think the two things God will look for is faith and love. If he bases his judgment on our words and our works, he can determine if there is faith and love. The reason for this is that works can not be separated from faith and love.

There were two categories of ground: fruitful ground, and unfruitful ground. There are only two types of ground (or the hearts of men): that which has faith, and that which does not.

For whatsoever is born of God overcometh the world: and this is the victory that overcometh the world, even our faith. Who is he that overcometh the world, but he that believeth that Jesus is the Son of God?

1John 5:4-5

It is through the seed of faith and love which comes from God, that we begin to grow up to be like our heavenly father.

“For thus saith the Lord to the men of Judah and Jerusalem, Break up your fallow ground, and sow not among thorns.

...: lest my fury come forth like fire, and burn that none can quench it, because of the evil of your doings.”

Jer 4:3-4

I believe sin, if it is not dealt with, can grow and destroy our friendship with God. Left undealt with, eventually, it will completely overcrowd our heart so that we have no place for God. A man then rejects Christ, because his love for other things is more important than the space in his heart he gave to God. When a man chooses to break the covenant he made with God through Christ, he ceases to bring forth the fruit that results from love for, and trust in God.

---

[404] enjoyment, a delight

[405] G5281 ὑπομονή hupomonē hoop-om-on-ay' From G5278; cheerful (or hopeful) *endurance*, *constancy*: - enduring, patience, patient continuance (waiting).

G5278 ὑπομένω hupomenō hoop-om-en'-o
From G5259 and G3306; to *stay under* (*behind*), i.e. *remain*; fig. to *undergo*, i.e. *bear* (trials), *have fortitude*, *persevere*: - abide, endure, (take) patient (-ly), suffer, tarry behind.

God looks at the works, and he can see that there is no longer any faith and love, that that man has rejected him. When it comes to our relationship with God, we fear that God will not forgive us. The main danger is that we choose other things above God, and leave him.

> “If we suffer, we shall also reign with him: if we deny him, he also will deny us: If we believe not, yet he abideth faithful: …”
>
> 2Tim 2:12-13

God abides faithful, even if we are unfaithful. It is not God who ends it. I think it can be us who choose to reject God. God does not leave us, unless we tell him to go.

In each of the cases of the bad ground, the ground rejected the word of God. In each of the cases, if the ground had said sorry to God, and forsaken it's sin, God would have forgiven them, and the ground would have brought forth fruit unto God.

I personally believe God will make it clear to a man that he is about to make the decision to reject him.

I remember rowing down a stream when I was quite young, and there was a boat trapped in a slow whirl of water near a bend in the river. Dad said, quick, try rowing as hard as you can over to the other side away from there. I was, I suppose, even a little on the other side of the river already. I said its OK, we are nowhere near there. Sure enough, we ended up where the other boat was. And it took Dad a lot of effort to get us out of there.

There is no excuse for sinning. Sin must be dealt with immediately. When we find ourselves in sin, we need to fear God, and repent quickly. To have God as a friend is better than anything else put in the balance beside him.

7.7.7 Hypocrites

Reading Matthew 25:14-30

The servant who did nothing. I think said he believed, but really did not. He actually did not do anything good out of love[406].

Remember the sheep and the goats[407] and how Christ never accused the sheep of doing anything wrong. He did much evil, but was forgiven through Christ. However upon special review he was rejected because there was no faithfulness found in him. He almost got in through faith, in saying he was a Christian, but when his works were examined closely, he was found to be an unbeliever, because there was no fruit which comes from the word of God planted in his heart. There was no love, there was no righteousness, there were no kind acts toward his neighbour. The garden of his heart was completely barren. He justly was appointed his portion with the hypocrites and the unbelievers, because he was a hypocrite and did not believe in Jesus Christ.

The word faithful in Greek, as it is in English comes from the word faith (trust). A man who has faith or confidence in God trusts God. This faith will always work out of his heart. It will show compassion on his fellow servants. It will be a friend to those in trouble.

I hope I do not do Bruce Uren injustice by quoting him here. He said

> "A man is not saved by works, but without works no man shall be saved."
>
> -Bruce Uren

If there is faith, there will be works. If there are no works, then it can be sure that there is no faith.

He will be looking for the works that are present when a man trusts in God. Many good works will always result from a man's faith and love for God. In the end it is God who saves through his word. We are the sons and daughters of God by faith in Jesus Christ, and we have evidence of the faith and love in our hearts for God.

Remember the commendation of the servants "thou good and faithful servant." A faithful servant is one who has faith. Not one who does things perfectly.

---

[406] Love is the reason faith acts. "...; but faith which worketh by love." Gal 5:6

[407] section 7.7.4 The Parable of the Sheep and the Goats, page 176

7.7.8 The Steward placed in Charge of the Household.

Reading Matthew 24:45-51 and Luke 12:41-48

The interesting thing is this “Faith” and Action were done by a man called "a faithful and wise steward" who God had appointed a ruler to care for the church.

> “But[408] and if[409] that evil servant …” Mat 24:48

Even faithful men can turn away and reject God.

His punishment was to be "cut in sunder[410], and his portion appointed with the unbelievers."

Faith:

> "My lord delayeth his coming; ..."
> Mat 24:48; Luke 12:45

Actions:

> "... begin to beat the menservants and maidens, and to eat and drink, and to be drunken;"
> Luke 12:45

His “faith” stood against God's words.

> "Surely I come quickly."
> -Jesus (Rev 22:20)

and also

> "... thou shalt love thy neighbour as thyself: ..." Lev 19:18

> “He that loveth not his brother abideth in death.” 1John 3:14

> “Inasmuch as ye have done it unto one of the least of these my brethren, ye have done it unto me.”
> Mat 25:40

These things don’t happen over night. You don’t go to sleep one night, and wake up and find you’re an axe murderer. It takes time for people to change, and it is the little decisions along life’s journey which build a man's character.

> “Moreover it is required in stewards, that a man be found faithful.”
> 1Cor 4:2

---

[408] Gr. 1161 δέ; A prim. particle (adversative or continuative); *but, and,* etc.

[409] Gr. 1437 ἐάν*;* a conditional particle often used in association with other particles to indicate indefiniteness or uncertainty.

[410] Gr. 1371 dichotomeō

The judgment of whether a man has broken the covenant he made with Christ is for God to make. We may break the law, but the law is no longer our master. In this case we see God decided that this servant had broken the covenant he made with God through Christ Jesus our Lord.

One definition of an hypocrite is “an actor under an assumed character.”[411]

The Greek word for unbeliever means “not trustworthy”[412].

The condemned servant was both a hypocrite and an unbeliever (compare verses Mat 24:51 and Luke 12:46). i.e.:

> “an actor under an assumed character who is not trustworthy”

Jesus was very strict about some topics. As far as I recall there were two main groups of people he warned severely concerning hypocrisy. One was the Pharisees, who were then the spiritual oversight. The other his friends the twelve disciples.

> “Take heed, beware of the leaven of the Pharisees, ...”
> Mark 8:15; Luk 12:1; cf. Mat 16:12

Paul[413] says

> “Know ye not that a little leaven leaveneth the whole lump?”
> 1Cor 5:6; Gal 5:9

A little bit of leaven makes the whole lump of dough to rise when the temperature is turned up.

Paul then continues “For even Christ our passover is sacrificed for us: ...”

If we want God to passover our sins, we do well to eat unleavened bread. It doesn’t take much covering up of sin for a person to be a total hypocrite. I think it is better to have the attitude of the publican[414].

> “God be merciful to me a sinner.” Luke 18:13

The valuable righteousness comes from God.

> “..., that I may win Christ, And be found in him, not having mine own righteousness, which is of the law, but that which is through the faith of Christ, ...”
> Phil 3:8-9

It is best to keep an empty list of sins with God by quickly asking for his forgiveness.

> He that covereth his sins shall not prosper: but whoso confesseth and forsaketh[439] them shall have mercy.
> Prov 28:13

---

[411] G5273
[412] *unbelievers* Gr. 571
[413] Paul and Sosthenes 1Cor 1:1
[414] G5057 tax collector

Another definition of hypocrite is 'someone who conceals or disguises something so that a decision ("distinguishing") will be made subject to false pretences'. Normally the action of "distinguishing" is used to separate two different things. The servant who began to beat the menservants and maidens tried to deceive God so that He (God) couldn't separate good from evil. His[415] punishment was that he was cut in two.

There follows the account of two other servants that didn't do what their master commanded. I believe these servants are in the same category as the servant who did nothing with the talent (Mat 25:24) and the servant who did nothing with the pound (Luke 19:20). They were not found faithful and were punished, but not as badly as the servant put in charge of the household.

> My brethren, be not many masters[416], knowing that we shall receive the greater condemnation (judgment).
>
> James 3:1

James carries on to say

> "For in many ways we all stumble. If anyone in word does not stumble, he is a mature[417] man, able to bridle also the whole body."
>
> James 3:2-3 [a translation]

Evidently Church leaders stumble in many ways. James placed himself in this category. He was not an ungodly man, and had to his honour a whole book recorded by him (through the Holy Ghost) in the Bible. James is now with Christ at the right hand of the Father.

What can we conclude? A church leader may stumble in many ways, but shall (God permitting) still be forgiven and go to heaven. However, if a person is judged to be unfaithful to Christ, then his judgment will be according to how much has been entrusted to him. The servant placed over the household, was cut in sunder. The servant who had received his masters instructions, was punished with many stripes. The servant who hadn't received the masters instructions, was punished with few stripes.

---

[415] i.e. the servants

[416] instructors, teachers

[417] G5046 From G5056; *complete* (in various applications of labor, growth, mental and moral character, etc.);
G5056 From a primary word τέλλω tellō (to *set out* for a definite point or *goal*); properly the point aimed at as a *limit*, i.e. (by impl.) the *conclusion* of an act or state (*termination* [lit. fig. or indef.], *result* [immed., ultimate or prophetic], *purpose*);

7.7.9 The Parable of the Talents

Reading Matthew 25:14-30 Parable of Talents allocated according to ability.

Reading Luke 19:11-27 Parable of Talents allocated equally to each servant.

It is evident that in the Kingdom of God we are under authority. And that servants have responsibilities and work to accomplish. The Lord is merciful and gracious, and has here granted us to know a little of how his judgments will be executed.

Reading Matthew 21:28-32 [A certain man had two sons; ...]

Reading Malachi 3:13-18

> "And they shall be mine, saith the Lord of hosts, in that day when I make up my jewels; and I will spare them, as a man spareth his own son that serveth him."
> Malachi 3:17

> Jesus answered them, Verily, verily, I say unto you, Whosoever committeth sin is the servant of sin. And the servant abideth not in the house forever: but the Son abideth ever. If the Son therefore shall make you free, ye shall be free indeed. I know that ye are Abraham's seed; but ye seek to kill me, because my word hath no place in you. I speak that which I have seen with my Father: and ye do that which ye have seen with your father.
> John 8:34-38

I think we must present our bodies to God as a living sacrifice. If we are to be free from sin, we need to present our bodies as slaves to God, so that sin does not rule over us. This does not mean we are not sons, or friends of God.

If we submit ourselves to God, he will give us freedom to do almost anything we want. Most of the time he leaves it up to us to decide what to do. He will provide for everything we need. Our Father has some works for us to do, but they are not arduous.

> "Come unto me, all ye that labour and are heavy laden, and I will give you rest. Take my yoke upon you, and learn of me; for I am meek and lowly in heart: and ye shall find rest (to) your souls. For my yoke is easy, and my burden is light."
> Mat 11:28-30

God will spare us in the day that he allocates his treasures as rewards for faithfulness and righteousness. God is our Father, and because of this the fruit of righteousness that comes from obeying God grows.

Reading James 2:21-26 [Was not Abraham our father justified by works, ...]

Reading Hebrews 12:9-11 [Further more we have had fathers of our flesh ...]

Obedience comes from faith (i.e. trust). There are some bad Fathers whose children don't obey them because they know that their Father doesn't care. We love our Father and trust him because he cares for us.

For this case study, we will only consider those servants who worked trading with the money given to them. Let us consider the parables in turn.

In Matthew the master of the servants knew that some servants were better than others at trading. So he gave the most money to those servants. I am not sure how many servants he had, never the less, three servants are mentioned in particular. Of these, one of his servants was allocated 5 talents, another two talents and another one talent.

We will consider the first two servants. Each servant doubled the amount given to them. They were each given the same commendation.

> "Well done, thou good and faithful servant: thou hast been faithful over a few things, I will make thee ruler over many things: enter thou into the joy of thy lord."
>
> Mat 25:21 (cf. v23)

Now let us turn to Luke. In Luke no mention is made of the servants abilities. The master allocated the money equally. Ten of his servants received one pound each. Again three servants are mentioned in particular.

We will consider the first two servants.

The first servant multiplied his pound by 10. His Lord said:

> "Well, thou good servant: because thou hast been faithful in a very little, have thou authority over ten cities."
>
> Luke 19:17

The second servant multiplied his pound by 5. His Lord said:

> "Be thou also over five cities." Luke 19:19

Now let us look at both parables together.

The Son of Man allocated the money in both cases. I think the method he used was the same, so that although not mentioned in the second parable, the ten servants were allocated a pound each because they were equally skilled in trading.

> "For unto whomsoever much is given, of him shall be much required: and to whom men have committed much, of him they will ask the more."
>
> Luke 12:48

The Lord allocated the same amount to each servant. This means he expected the same return from each servant. This may explain why he didn't have anything particularly good to say to the servant who multiplied his pound by 5. He was hoping for 10.

In the parable in Matthew, the two servants obtained different amounts by trading (2 talents and 5 talents), yet they received the same reward. The servants in the second parable all had the same ability, but some worked harder than the others. Their effort directly reflected in how much money they made. They were rewarded according to their works, but if we consider these parables together, it is apparent that God seeks to reward according to what is in the heart.

No matter what ability a man has, or how much God has given him, the rewards will basically be for how diligent and faithful a man is to God.

With regards to us as individuals personally getting a reward, I would say that God seems to say by these parables 'Don't worry about how good you are at doing things. Also don't worry about how little you may have compared to others. Just do what you can.'

We are more than servants to God, otherwise he would not have bothered to tell us what he will do. If we were only servants, he could have said "I am just, and the rewards that I give to you will be fair, and that is enough for you to know."

> "Ye are my friends, if ye do whatsoever I command you.
>
> Henceforth I call you not servants; for the servant knoweth not what his lord doeth: but I have called you friends; for all things that I have heard of my Father I have made known unto you."
> John 15:14-15

Faithfulness is important. There is a reward for keeping faith and love over time. There is value to time spent remaining faithful to God from a heart of love. Righteousness has rewards now, and in eternity.

One concludes that the reward is not based only on how much profit one makes. It depends also on what God has given one to achieve it. We see many people today making huge profits for God's kingdom. But, what we don't see is how much God gave them in the first place. We don't know whether God made them a brilliant sportsman or woman. We don't know whether they were blessed with parents who knew a lot about the word of God. We don't know whether they grew up in a place where they were taught social skills which later helped them to display God's love and faithfulness. There are many people who do small things for the kingdom of God which people don't recognise. They may be small works, but they have diligently put their weight and effort behind seeing them through to the end. They have used every last ounce of the abilities God has given them to achieve those results.

> "... God is not unrighteous to forget your work and labour of love, ..."
> Heb 6:10

At the end, they will receive as much reward as anyone will.

Like many things God does[418], the rewards are impressive. Getting one pound (perhaps five hundred dollars) and ruling over one city aren't equal. One would have to say the ruler was not really looking for the money. He was looking for faithfulness.

---

[418] Psalm 40:5 "Many, O Lord my God, are thy wonderful works which thou hast done, ..."
Psalm 72:18 "Blessed be the Lord God, the God of Israel, who only doeth wondrous things."

The meaning of the word 'occupy' in Luke 19:13 is:

G4231 pragmatĕuŏmai (from G4229)

to *busy oneself* with, i.e. to *trade*

G4229 pragma (from G4238)

a *deed;* by implication an *affair*; by extension an *object* (material):- business, matter, thing, work.

G4238 prassō

a primary verb; to "*practise*', i.e. *perform repeatedly* or *habitually* (thus differing from G4160, which properly refers to a *single* act); by implication to *execute*, *accomplish,* etc.; specially to *collect* (dues), *fare* (personally):-commit, deeds, do, exact, keep, require, use arts.

7.7.10 The House tested by Fire

Reading 1Cor 3:5-15

Paul uses two analogies in the reading. One is of a plant growing. The other a house. Both are about believers.

> " ... ye are God's husbandry, ye are God's building."
>
> 1Cor 3:9

The seed which is placed in the ground and covered up represents God's word coming into a man's heart when he decides to believe in Jesus. The house foundation also represents faith in Christ. A good concrete foundation will prevent a house collapsing when the storms during a man's life come.

> "For other foundation can no man lay than that *is laid*[419], which is Jesus Christ."
>
> 1Cor 3:11

The discussion of how much a man is rewarded is directed to those who have laid the foundation by choosing to trust the record God gave of Jesus Christ. Without this starting point for building a house, all of a man's work will be lost.

> "If anyone's work be burned[420], he will suffer loss; but he himself will be saved, <u>yet so as through fire</u>."
>
> 1Cor 3:15 [a translation]

We see that this judgment is of a man's works, but not of the man himself. Derek Prince makes the following comment.

> "When it comes to the assessment of believers' works, these are placed by Paul in one or other of two categories. On the one hand, there are: gold, silver, precious stones. On the other hand, there are: wood, hay, straw.
>
> The basis on which these two categories are separated from each other is the ability to stand the test of fire. The items in the first category - gold, silver, precious stones - will be able to pass through the fire without being consumed,. The items in the second category - wood, hay, straw - will be consumed in the fire.
>
> One thought immediately emerges from contrasting these two categories: quality is of infinitely greater importance to God, than quantity. Gold, silver, precious stones are all things that are normally found in small quantities, but are nevertheless of great value. Wood, hay, straw are all things that take up much space and are obtainable in large quantities, but are of relatively little value."
>
> *Derek Prince*[421]

---

[419] [already] lying (flat)

[420] G2618 (From G2596 and G2545) to *burn down* (to the ground), i.e. *consume wholly:* - burn (up, utterly)

[421] see Appendix 'A. Recommended Reading and References'

In the analogy of the house, we see the need of a solid foundation. But then our attention is drawn to the materials used to build it. Say one man builds a wooden house. The other makes it of stone. The two men start work at 7am, and work until sundown for three months, and then finish their houses. After the two houses are built, they look similar in appearance, have roughly the same bedrooms, interior decorations and so forth.

When you've worked hard and look back at what you've accomplished, you don't usually regret the effort you put into it. Here Paul warns about the materials to use, so that the house remains intact even under adverse circumstances.

We read, both of the houses are tested by fire. It says,

> "…: for the day shall declare it,..." 1Cor 3:13

This could mean at the end of the days when the natural things pass away.

> "But the day of the Lord … in the which the heavens shall pass away … the earth also and the works that are therein shall be burned up."
>
> 2Peter 3:10

But perhaps it could mean throughout a man's life. Some men say around fifty or so for example, are kind, always have a good word and something to encourage. The things they have gone through have made it clear what kind of person they are. They are not about to change in a hurry. Perhaps it is as difficulties and temptations arise, it will be made evident if our actions are constructed out of love and trust in God. I believe works that result from faith and love will abide the test of fire.

> "... God is not unrighteous to forget your work and labour of love, …"
>
> Heb 6:10

> "Remembering without ceasing your work of faith, and labour of love, and patience of hope in our Lord Jesus Christ, in the sight of God and our Father;"
>
> 1Thes 1:3

> "Moreover … in keeping of them [the judgments[422] of the Lord] there is great reward."
>
> Psalm 19:11

The reason we keep God's commandments[423] is because we love him. We will receive a reward for these works.

[422] H4941 prop. a *verdict* (favourable or unfavourable) pronounced judicially, espec. a *sentence* or formal decree (human or {particularly} divine *law*, individual or collectively) [...]; abstr. *justice* [...].
From [H8199 - a primitive root; to *judge*, i.e. pronounce *sentence* (for or against)]

[423] Psalm 19:8 '*commandment*' is H4687 (From H6680) a *command*, whether human or divine (collectively the *Law*)

> “If any man's work abide which he hath built thereupon, he shall receive a reward.”
> 1Cor 3:14

There are three things that will abide the fire: faith, hope and love. Love (for God and those around us) is the greatest of these three. It is out of love for his wife, that a man will be faithful to her, and disdain any thought of impurity[424]. It is out of love for God, that we obey his voice.

> “I delight[425] to do thy will, O my God: yea, thy law is within my heart.”
> Psalm 40:8

Most of the time, it is not a heaviness to obey God. Love makes light work of our chores.

> "..., though now for a season, if need be, ye are in heaviness through manifold temptations: That the trial of your faith, being much more precious than of gold that perisheth, though it be tried with fire, might be found unto praise and honour and glory at the appearing of Jesus Christ: ..."
> 1Peter 1:6-7

Faith is compared with gold. Gold may be tested to see its purity. When gold is heated by fire in a furnace, any impurity will float to the surface because it weighs less than gold. Gold does not burn and it is not damaged no matter how many times it is melted. The trial or testing of our faith is done by temptations in the same way gold is tested by the fire of the furnace melting it and bringing the rubbish to the surface. In very pure gold, there is no rubbish, and I guess the gold is bright and shiny on its surface when it is melted. I think of the scripture

> “They (my fears) looked unto him (the Lord), and were lightened[426] [made bright]: and their faces were not ashamed[427].”
> Psalm 34:5

When we pass through the fire, we learn not to be afraid, because we know by experience that God stands beside us holding our hand. Did God ever leave? No. But after the trials, we now have a trust in him, to know that no matter what faces us, it is no match for our heavenly Father.

> “Yea, though I walk through the valley of the shadow of death, I will fear no evil: for thou art with me; …”
> Psalm 23:4

We will never find any better reason for not being afraid, than knowing God has forgiven us, that he stands with us and is on our side. We may shout "God is for me!"[428]

> "Behold, the Lord God will help me; who is he that shall condemn me?”
> Isaiah 50:9

---

[424] paraphrased from a sermon by Smith Wigglesworth

[425] “Pictures one bending down toward the object of one’s delight” -Translator Jay P. Green.
H2654 A prim. root; properly to *incline* to; by implication (lit. but rarely) to *bend*; fig. to *be pleased* with, *desire.*

[426] H5102 A prim. root; to *sparkle*, i.e. (fig.) be *cheerful*; hence (from the *sheen* of a running stream) to *flow*, i.e. (fig.) *assemble*

[427] H2659 A prim. root (perh. rather the same as H2658 through the idea of *detection*): to *blush*; figuratively to *be ashamed, disappointed*; causatively to *shame, reproach.*

[428] cf. Rom 8:28-39 "And we know that all things work together for good ..."

"The Lord is for me, I will not fear; what can man do to me? The LORD taketh my part with them that help me: therefore shall I look upon those hating me."
Psalm 118:7-8 [a translation]

It says that temptations cause us to be in heaviness. We know gold is heavier than the scum (dross). God is looking for the thing that is heavy when it is in the fire. We are the gold God is looking for[429].

"For thus saith the Lord of Hosts; After the glory (weight[430]) hath he [the Lord] sent me [the angel] unto the nations which spoiled you: for he that toucheth you toucheth the apple[431] of his eye."
Zech 2:8; cf. Deut 32:9-11

"For the eyes of the Lord run to and fro throughout the whole earth, to show himself strong in the behalf of them whose heart is perfect[432] toward[433] him.
2Chr 16:9

He has no interest in the sin, it is worthless. But we are priceless to God.

God paid the most expensive price ever paid, for us.

"They that trust in their wealth, and boast themselves in the multitude of their riches;

None of them can by any means redeem his brother, nor give to God a ransom for him: ..."
Psalm 49:6-7

God paid excessive amounts for us.

For I am the Lord thy God, the Holy One of Israel, thy Saviour: I gave Egypt for thy ransom, Ethiopia and Seba for thee.
Isaiah 43:3

He doesn't want us to be poverty stricken. So he gives us instruction on how to become rich.

"Wherefore do ye spend money for that which is not bread? and your labour for that which satisfieth not? hearken diligently unto me, and eat ye that which is good, and let your soul delight itself in fatness.

---

429 It is a man who trusts in God. Is God looking for the man or the faith? He wants us, to win our trust and love. See later this section "Since thou was precious (heavy) in my sight ..." Isaiah 43:4

430 H3519 From H3513 ("to *be heavy*"); properly *weight*; but only fig. in a good sense, *splendor* or *copiousness*: - glorious (-ly), glory, honour (-able).

431 The pupil of the eye, i.e. the thing which everything one sees comes through. Participle of verb meaning something *hollowed* (as a *gate*).

432 H8003 From H7999; *complete* (lit. or fig.); especially *friendly*.
H7999 A primitive root; to *be safe* (in mind, body or estate); fig. to *be* (causatively *make*) *completed*; by implication to *be friendly*; by extension to *reciprocate* (in various applications)

433 H413 a prim. particle, properly denoting motion *towards*, but occasionally used of a quiescent position, i.e. *near*, *with* or *among*; often in general, "*to*".

Incline your ear, and come unto me: hear, and your soul shall live; and I will make an everlasting covenant with you, even the sure mercies of David."

Isaiah 55:2-3

Reading Heb 12:1-6 [... run with patience the race …, My son, ...]

There will be a reward for winning the race. Part way through the race, one can think, I'm going to be too tired, perhaps I can't make it. We need to not give up, and aim with God to take first place.

"But though he [the Lord] cause grief, yet will he have compassion according to the multitude of his mercies.

For he doth not afflict (from his heart) nor grieve the children of men. To crush under his feet all the prisoners of the earth, To turn aside the right of a man before the face of the most High, To subvert a man in his cause, the Lord approveth[434] not."

Lam 3:32-26

Obedience is learnt, and it comes through suffering.

"Though he (Christ) were a son, yet learned he obedience by the things which he suffered; ..."

Heb 5:8

If bad things happen to us, it doesn't mean that we are not good people through faith in Christ[435]. If we stay with God, obeying God, and thus enduring temptations, we will see more of God, than those who turn aside. God will purify our hearts, as we stay and walk talking with him. A pure heart will bring forth praise, and honour and glory to God in the midst of temptations, and also when we stand before God when our Lord appears.

We are at an advantage over unbelievers, God gives us a chance through temptation, to go through some fire before judgment and see our weaknesses and sins. Each time we are tempted, we can gain experience and trust in God. My pastor reminded us, remember Shadrach, Meshach and Abednego? Did the fire harm them? No. They went into the fire bound in ropes, the only thing the fire served to do, was to burn the ropes, and set them free. And they got to meet Jesus.

"Then Nebuchadnezzar the king was astonished, and rose up in haste, and spake, and said unto his counsellors, Did not we cast three men bound into the midst of the fire? They answered and said unto the king, True, O king. He answered and said, Lo, I see four men loose, walking in the midst of the fire, and they have no hurt; and the form of the fourth is like the Son of God."

Dan 3:24-25

---

[434] H7200 a prim. root; to *see* (lit. or fig.)

[435] Although Christ says none is good save one, that is God. I believe by faith in Christ, we are made one with God. Jesus also says a good man out of the treasure of his heart brings out good things. In another place speaking of Barnabus it says:

"For he was a good man, and full of the Holy Ghost and of faith …" Acts 11:24

We are like the gold, when the fire comes, it does nothing to harm the gold, rather, under the control of the smith, the fire helps to separate the gold from the dross. God doesn't want us to be harmed in the slightest.

> "When thou passest through the waters, I will be with thee; and through the rivers, they shall not overflow thee: when thou walkest through the fire, thou shalt not be burned; neither shall the flame kindle upon thee.
>
> For I am the Lord thy God, the Holy One of Israel, thy Saviour: I gave Egypt for thy ransom, Ethiopia and Seba for thee.
>
> Since thou wast precious (heavy[436]) in my sight, thou hast been honourable, and I have loved thee: therefore will I give men for thee, and people for thy life.
>
> Fear not: for I am with thee: I will bring thy seed from the east, and gather thee from the west; ..."
> Isaiah 43:2-5

> "When thou passest ... , I will be with thee; ..."

The material which is tested by fire is our trust in God. Perhaps it is also a test of our love for God as well. A person who loves someone, will be faithful (or trustworthy) to them.

> "... faith which worketh by love." Gal 5:6

Without love there is no motivation for faith to act. Without love and faith for God[437] being the reason for the works, we will receive no reward for them. They will be burnt up.

> "everything I do, I do it for you."
> - a song.

Reading 1Cor 13 [The greatest of these is Love]

Without love, there is no lasting profit in anything.

> "And though I bestow all my goods to feed the poor, and though I give my body to be burned, and have not charity (love), it profiteth me nothing."
> 1Cor 13:3

> "Many waters can not quench love, neither can the floods drown it: if a man would give all the substance of his house for love, it would utterly be contemned."
> Song of Solomon 8:7

But Hallelujah, we have someone we love, and someone who loves us.

---

[436] H3365 yaw-kar'
A prim. root; properly appar. to *be heavy*, that is, (fig.) *valuable*; causat. to *make rare*

[437] faith and love are always towards something or someone

> "I [the Lord thy God] will never leave[438] thee, nor forsake[439] thee."
> Heb 13:5[440]

God is with us and will not fail us or leave us, because he loves us. He always did love us, and he always will.

[438] here 'leave' is KJV translation of G447 to *let up*, i.e. (lit.) *slacken*, or (fig.) *desert, desist* from. (From G303 {A primary preposition and adverb; properly *up*}and ἵημι hiēmi {to *send*});
Equivalent Hebrew word used in Deut 31:6 & Joshua 1:5 (translated as 'fail') is
H7503 *to slacken* [from H7495 *to mend* (by stitching)].

[439] here 'forsake' is KJV translation of G1459 *To leave behind in* some place. The equivalent Hebrew word used in Deut 31:6 & Joshua 1:5 is H5800 to *loosen* i.e. *relinquish, permit* etc.

[440] Deut 31:6; Joshua 1:5

> "Be strong and of a good courage, fear not, nor be afraid of them: for the Lord thy God, he it is that doth go with thee; he will not fail thee, nor forsake thee."
> Deut 31:6 [Moses speaking unto all Israel]
> "… I will be with thee: I [The Lord thy God] will not fail thee, nor forsake thee. Be strong and of a good courage: …"
> Joshua 1:5-6 [The Lord speaking to Joshua]

7.7.11 Things that destroy

Reading 2Peter chapter 2

> "... But these, as unreasoning physical/instinctive animals, having been born for capture[441] and destruction[442] [slaughter], that in which they are ignorant, they speak evil; in the corruption/ruin[442] of themselves they shall utterly perish/wither;
>
> being about to receive the reward of injustice, deeming indulgence[443] in the day time as pleasure, revelling[444] in spots[445] and blemishes; in their delusions [cheating themselves through deceit] faring well with you.
>
> Having eyes full of an adulteress, and not desisting[446] from sin; alluring unstable souls, an heart they have busied with covetous[447] practices; children of curse:
>
> forsaking a straight way, they erred, following the way of Balaam the son of Bosor, who loved the wages of injustice."
> 2Peter 2v.12-15 [a translation]

Chapter two talks about people who have forsaken Jesus. I shall try to outline the chapter as best as I can. In verses one to three, it begins talking about false teachers. There were false prophets in the days Israel first inherited the promised land. These prophets were commanded under the law to be executed. Today, it appears the task of leading people away from Christ falls mainly to teachers[448].

Toward the end of the chapter (about verse 12 onwards), the writer talks of a group of people who shall be destroyed in the day of judgment. "They speak great swelling words of vanity." "They promise them liberty." They beguile unstable[449] souls. If they are not officially church leaders, they are persuasive, articulate people in the midst of the church. "faring [participating]... with you."

---

[441] or 'to be taken' KJV

[442] G5356 *decay*, i.e. *ruin* (spontaneous or inflicted, lit. or fig.) From G5351.
G5351 probably strengthened form of 'phthio' (to pine, or waste): properly *to shrivel* or *whither*, i.e. *to spoil* (by any process) or (gen.) *to ruin* (especially fig. by moral influences, to deprave).

[443] Greek 5172 *effeminacy*, i.e. *luxury* or *debauchery*. [From Greek θρύπτω to *break* up or [fig.] *enfeeble*, espec. the mind and body by indulgence.]

[444] Greek 1792 *to revel in; from G1722 and G5171*
G1722 a prim. prep. denoting (fixed) *position* (in place, time or state), and (by impl.) *instrumentality* (medially or constructively), i.e. a relation of *rest* (intermediate between G1519 and G1537); "*in*," *at*, (up-)*on*, *by*, etc.
G5171 to *indulge in luxury* [from G5172]

[445] G4695 from G4696; *to stain* or *soil* (lit. or fig.)
G4696 of uncertain derivation; *a stain* or *blemish*, i.e. (fig.) *defect*, *disgrace*.

[446] G180 *unrefraining* [from G1 (as a negative particle) and a derivative of G2664]
G2664 to *settle down*, i.e. (lit.) to *colonize*, or (fig.) to (*cause to*) *desist*. Translated in KJV as:- cease, (give) rest (-rain). From G2596 "down" and G3973.
G3973 to *stop* (transitive or intrans.), i.e. *restrain*, *quit*, *desist*, *come to an end*. Translated in KJV as:- cease, leave, refrain.

[447] G4124 *avarice*, i.e. (by implic.) *fraudulency*, *extortion*. From G4123.
G4123 *holding* (*desiring*) *more*, i.e. *eager for gain* (*avaricious*, hence a *defrauder*). From G4119 & G2192.
G4119 *more* in quantity, number, or quality; also (in plural) the *major portion*.

They may look like part of the church, but they are not. It says they forsook the right way, and have gone astray, following a path taken by a prophet employed (i.e. paid) to curse Israel. Thus it appears once they were saved through faith. Their characteristic is that they speak about the natural (i.e. physical) body, to capture peoples attention.

> "For when they speak great swelling words of (emptiness), they allure[450] through the (longing[451]) of the flesh, ..."
> 2Peter 2:18

In verses 20 to 22 we see the result of what happens to someone who is enslaved by the "philosophy" of these teachers.

> "For if after they have escaped the pollutions[452] of the world through the knowledge[453] of the Lord and Saviour Jesus Christ, they are again entangled therein, and overcome (defeated)[454], the latter end is worse with them than the beginning."
> 2Peter 2:20

We catch a glimpse of God's judgment.

> "..., to whom the *mist* of *darkness* is reserved[455] for ever."
> 2Pet 2:17

darkness

Gr. 4655 *shadiness*, i.e. *obscurity* (lit. or fig.) [from the base of Gr. 4639]

Gr. 4639 apparently a primary word; "shade" or a shadow (lit. or fig. [darkness of *error* or an *adumbration* (sketched/represented in outline; faintly indicated)]).

mist

Gr. 2217 *gloom* (as shrouding like a *cloud*)

G2192 a prim. verb *to hold*. (used in very various applic., lit. or fig. direct or remote; such as *possession*, *ability*, *contiguity*, *relation* or *condition*).

[448] cf. Mat 7:15-20, Acts 20:29-30, Acts 15:1-29, 1Tim 1:3-4, 4:3, 6:5, 2Tim 2:18 & Rev 2:14

[449] G793 astēriktos From G1 (as a negative particle) and a presumed derivation of G4741; *unfixed*, i.e. (fig.) *vacillating:* - unstable.

G4741 stērizō to *set fast*, i.e. (lit.) to *turn resolutely* in a certain direction, or (fig.) to *confirm:* - fix, (e-) stablish, stedfastly set, strengthen. From a presumed derivative (like G4731) of G2476 {to *stand*}

G4731 stĕrĕōs From G2476; *stiff*, that is, *solid*, *stable* (lit. or fig.): - stedfast, strong, sure.

[450] G1185 [from the base of G1388]; to *entrap*, i.e. (fig.) *delude*.

G1388 [from an obs. prim. dello (prob. mean. to decoy; comp. G1185)]; a *trick* (*bait*), i.e. (fig.) *wile*.

[451] G1939 from G1937; a *longing* (espec. for what is forbidden): - concupiscence, desire, lust (after)

G1937 to set the *heart upon*, i.e. *long* for (rightfully or otherwise).

[452] G3393 foulness

[453] G1922 *recognition* i.e. (by impl.) full *discernment*, *acknowledgment*. From G1921.

G1921 from 1909 and 1097; to *know upon* some mark, i.e. *recognise*; by impl. to *become fully acquainted with*, to *acknowledge*.

G1909 a prim. prep. prop. mean. *superimposition* (of time, place, order, etc.), as a relation of *distribution* [with the gen.], i.e. *over*, *upon*, *etc.*; of *rest* (with the dat.) *at*, *on*, etc.; of *direction* (with the acc.) *towards*, *upon*, *etc.* In compounds it retains essentially the same import, *at*, *upon*, etc. (lit. or fig.).

G1097 a prolonged form of a prim. verb "to know"

7.7.12 Today Jesus gives Rest

> And the LORD said unto Samuel, Hearken unto the voice of the people in all that they say unto thee: for they have not rejected thee, but they have rejected me, that I should not reign over them.
>
> According to all the works which they have done since the day that I brought them up out of Egypt even unto this day, wherewith they have forsaken me, and served other gods, so do they also unto thee.
>
> 1Sam 8:7-8

Reading Numbers chapter 14

On our own, we are not very reliable, or faithful. When God looked for a wife so to speak, he chose someone from the wrong side of the tracks. With Israel, we see the grief he endured. In the following discussion, those who entered not by faith, or were prevented, were those who wilfully refused to listen to the truth.

In Hebrews, it is written

> "as the Holy Ghost saith, To day if ye will hear[456] his voice, ..."
>
> Heb 3:7

In Psalm 95 the same speaker continues.

> "Harden not your heart, as in the provocation[457], and as in the day of temptation[458] in the wilderness: when your fathers tempted me, proved me, and saw my work. Forty years long was I grieved with this generation, and said, It is a people that do err[459] in their heart, and they have not known my ways[84]: ..."
>
> Psalm 95:8-10
>
> "And the Lord said, ... Because all those men which have seen my glory, and my miracles, ... , and have tempted me now these ten times, and have not hearkened to my voice; ..."
>
> Num 14:20-22

From the beginning, throughout their time in the wilderness, they were unfaithful to God, and refused to listen.

---

[454] G2274 From the same as G2276; to *make worse*, i.e. *vanquish* (lit. or fig.); by implic. to *rate lower:* - be inferior, overcome.

[455] G5083 to *guard* (from *loss* or *injury*, properly by keeping *the eye* upon)

[456] I think "will hear" signifies a choice, rather than a question of ability,
cf. Mat 18:15 "...: if he shall hear thee, ..."

[457] H4808 merîybâh *quarrel* (from H7378) ; cf. Exod 17:7 Meribah

[458] H4531 massâh *testing*; cf. Exod 17:7

[459] H8582 A primitive root; to *vacillate*, i.e. *reel* or *stray* (lit. or fig.); also causatively of both: - (cause to) wander, (cause to) go astray, seduce, (cause to, make to) err, (make to) stagger, deceive, pant, be out of the way, dissemble.
cf. Isaiah 29:24 "They also that *erred* in spirit shall come to understanding, ..."
Isaiah 53:6 "All we like sheep have gone *astray*; ..."

> "Hear, O Israel; the Lord our God is one Lord: and thou shalt love the Lord thy God with all thy heart, and with all thy soul, and with all thy mind, and with all thy strength: ..."
>
> Mark 12:29-30

> "..., because they obeyed not the voice of the Lord: ..."
>
> Joshua 5:6

Literally the word translated as 'obey' means "to hear intelligently". It often has the implication of attention, and obedience[460]. If someone hears, and refuses to act, they are refusing to listen.

> How oft did they provoke him in the wilderness, and grieve him in the desert!
>
> Ps 78:40

The word provoke comes from a word meaning "to embitter"[461]. In the new testament, the equivalent word for provoke[462] is derived from a word meaning "to embitter alongside" (fig. to exasperate). The word 'grieve' in this verse means literally "to carve"[463]. From the context it is to carve the heart.

> I the Lord have said, I will surely do it unto all this evil congregation, that are gathered together against me: in this wilderness they shall be consumed, and there they shall die.
>
> Num 14:35

He swore that they would not enter into his rest[464], because they entered not by faith. They were not accepted by God because they refused to accept his words. He was continually wearied[465] with their iniquities.

> "Behold, I am pressed under you, as a cart is pressed that is full of sheaves."
>
> Amos 2:13

But he also still loved them, even though Israel was unfaithful.

> "And they lay themselves down upon clothes laid to pledge[466] by every altar, and they drink the wine of the condemned[467] in the house of their god. Yet destroyed I the Amorite before them, whose height was like the height of the cedars, and he was strong as the oaks; yet I destroyed his fruit from above, and his roots from beneath. Also I brought you up ..."
>
> Amos 2:8-10

---

[460] H8085 A primitive root; to *hear* intelligently (often with implication of attention, obedience, etc.; causatively to *tell*, etc.)

[461] H4784 mârâh A primitive root; to *be* (causatively *make*) *bitter* (or unpleasant); (fig.) to *rebel* (or resist; causatively to *provoke*)

[462] Heb 3:8,15 'provocation' G3894 *irritation* {from G3893 to *embitter alongside*}

[463] H6087 A primitive root; properly to *carve*, that is, *fabricate* or *fashion*; hence (in a bad sense) to *worry*, *pain* or *anger*

[464] cf. Hebrews chapters 3 & 4

[465] cf. Isaiah 1:14-16 "I am weary ..."

[466] Exod 22:6

[467] perhaps means 'wine which was *confiscated*'

They may have even thought the things God allowed, such as dry surroundings, and little food, were a sign of God's unfaithfulness.

> And thou shalt remember all the way which the Lord thy God led thee these forty years in the wilderness, to humble thee, and to prove thee, to know what was in thine heart, whether thou wouldest keep his commandments, or (not).
>
> And he humbled thee, and suffered thee to hunger, and fed thee with manna, which thou knewest not, neither did thy fathers know; that he might make thee know that man doth not live by bread only, but by every word that proceedeth out of the mouth of the Lord doth man live.
>
> ... Thou shalt also consider in thine heart, that, as a man chasteneth his son, so the Lord thy God chasteneth thee[468].
>
> Deut 8:2-3,5

But the unpleasant things he allowed so that they would learn to trust him and realise that he was, for them, providing everything they needed. He wanted them to know what is seen is not as important as what is unseen, even faith-fullness and love which originally come from God and his word.

He was desperately looking for any sign that they would listen and trust him. He couldn't really contain himself, and gave them things they did not deserve.

> And I have led you forty years in the wilderness: your clothes are not waxen old upon you, and thy shoe is not waxen old upon thy foot.
>
> Deut 29:5

> Nevertheless they did flatter him with their mouth, and they lied unto him with their tongues. For their heart was not right with him, neither were they steadfast in his covenant. But he, being full of compassion, forgave their iniquity, and destroyed them not: yea, many a time turned he his anger away, and did not stir up all his wrath.
>
> Ps 78:36-38

But though they had seen so many miracles, and everyday they received bread, and their clothes and shoes didn't get old, they never understood that he loved them.

---

[468] Heb 12:6 "For whom the Lord loveth he chasteneth, ..."

But to Israel he saith, All day long I have stretched forth my hands unto a (disbelieving[469]) and (disputing[470]) people.

Rom 10:21

Reading 1Cor 10:1-13

Israel made a covenant with God.

"Moreover, brethren, I would not that ye should be ignorant, how that all our fathers were under the cloud, and all passed through the sea; And were all baptized into Moses in the cloud and in the sea; And did all eat ...; And ... drink ... of that spiritual (rock) that followed them: and that (rock) was Christ."

1Cor 10:1-4

When we first believe, we choose not to be callous and hard hearted, but to hear what God says, to repent from our sin and say sorry. At that time, we are crucified with Christ and cease from our old works. The Holy Spirit then begins to work in our heart. Baptism represents a choice to become a friend of God, to be resurrected to life. This choice (not the ceremony of water baptism) is necessary for the pardon of sins.

“For we which have believed do enter into rest, ...”

Heb 4:3

It is by faith combined with works that we continue to walk with God in the rest we obtained when we first believed in Jesus[471].

Wherefore we (dearly esteem/desire)[472], that, whether present or absent, we may be *accepted of*[473] (fully agreeable to) him.

2Cor 5:9

---

[469] G544 (from G545) to *disbelieve* (wilfully and perversely):- not believe, disobedient, obey not, unbelieving.

G545 From G1 (as a negative particle) and G3982; *unpersuadable*, i.e. *contumacious*

G3982 G3982 πείθω peithō *pi'-tho*

A primary verb; to *convince* (by argument, true or false); by analogy to *pacify* or *conciliate* (by other fair means); reflexively or passively to *assent* (to evidence or authority), to *rely* (by inward certainty): - agree, assure, believe, have confidence, be (wax) content, make friend, obey, persuade, trust, yield.

[470] G483 to *dispute, refuse;* From G473 {“anti; opposite”} and G3004 (to “lay” forth, i.e. relate [in words]);

G473 ἀντί anti *an-tee'*

A primary particle; *opposite*, that is, *instead* or *because* of (rarely *in addition* to): - for, in the room of. Often used in composition to denote *contrast, requital, substitution, correspondence*, etc.

G3004 λέγω legō *leg'-o*

A primary verb; properly to “lay” forth, i.e. (fig.) *relate* (in words [usually of systematic or set *discourse*; whereas G2036 and G5346 generally refer to an *individual* expression or speech respectively; while G4483 is properly to *break silence* merely, and G2980 means an *extended* or random harangue]); by implication to *mean.*

[471] James 2:21-26 "... by works a man is justified, and not by faith only."

[472] G5389 Middle voice from a compound of G5384 and G5092; to be *fond of honor*, i.e. *emulous* (*eager* or *earnest* to do something.) In KJV, 'labour' is usually a translation of words meaning to 'toil' i.e. to 'work with considerable effort'.

G5384 φίλος philos *fee'-los* Properly *dear*, that is, a *friend*; actively *fond*, that is, *friendly* (still as a noun, an *associate, neighbor*, etc.): - friend.

"Take heed, brethren, lest there be in any of you an evil heart of unbelief, in departing from the living God. But exhort one another daily, while it is called To day; lest any of you be hardened through the deceitfulness of sin.

For we are made partakers of Christ, if we hold the beginning of our confidence stedfast unto the end;"

Heb 3:12-14

"There remaineth therefore a rest to the people of God. For he that is entered into his rest, he also hath ceased from his own works, as God did from his. Let us labour[474] therefore to enter[475] into that rest, lest any man fall after the same example of unbelief."

Heb 4:11

This labour means to "use speed", or to "hasten getting something done". I suppose it takes work, but it is not the toil that we had before when we served under the law.

Initially we make an agreement with God to love and obey him. Throughout life we have many opportunities to show out of love[476] through the choices we make, that we are faithful and obedient. We may fail God on occasion, but as long as we repent and say sorry, God is faithful and promises to forgive us[477].

It carries on to say,

"Seeing then that we have a great high priest, ... , Jesus the Son of God, let us hold fast our profession." Heb 4:14

What do we profess? I think it is that we have made an agreement with God through Jesus. If we hold fast the profession of our faith, we enter into rest.

"For we have not an high priest which can not be touched with the feeling of our infirmities; but was in all points tempted like as we are, yet without sin.

Let us therefore come boldly unto the throne of grace, that we may obtain mercy, and find grace to help in time of need."

Heb 4:15-16

In view of all this, we have been given a much better opportunity than those men in the wilderness to obtain mercy. God invites us without merit on our part, to come boldly to his throne, to ask for forgiveness, mercy and help when we are in trouble. He loves us. From the beginning God wanted to give us a home: safety, comfort and love. The greatest of all things, he offers to us, is himself. Even the opportunity to talk with him, and to be his friend.

G5092 τιμή timē *tee-may'* From G5099; a *value*, that is, *money* paid, or (concretely and collectively) *valuables*; by analogy *esteem* (especially of the highest degree), or the *dignity* itself: - honour, precious, price, sum.

473 G2101 From G2095 and G701; *fully agreeable:* - acceptable (-ted), wellpleasing

474 G4704 to *use speed* i.e. to *make effort, be prompt* or *earnest*. Usually translated in KJV as either 'diligent' or 'endeavour'.

475 I think 'entering' occurs throughout a man's life, beginning when he first believes in Christ.

476 through faith

477 1John 1:9 "If we confess our sins, ..."

"To day if ye will hear his voice, Harden[478] not your hearts[479], ..."
Heb 3:7-8; Psalm 95:7-8

[478] G4645 From G4642; to *indurate*, i.e. (fig.) *render stubborn*
H7185 קָשָׁה qâshâh *kaw-shaw'*
A primitive root; properly to *be dense*, i.e. tough or *severe* (in various applications): - be cruel, be fiercer, make grievous, be ([ask a], be in, have, seem, would) hard (-en, [labour], -ly, thing), be sore, (be, make) stiff (-en, [-necked]).

[479] G2588 kardia Prolonged from a primary κάρ kar (Latin *cor*, "heart"); the *heart*, i.e. (fig.) the *thoughts* or *feelings* (*mind*); also (by analogy) the *middle:* - (+ broken-) heart (-ed).
H3824 לֵבָב lêbâb *lay-bawb'*
From H3823; the *heart* (as the most interior organ); used also like H3820.
H3820 לֵב lêb *labe*
A form of H3824; the *heart*; also used (fig.) very widely for the feelings, the will and even the intellect; likewise for the *centre* of anything: - + care for, comfortably, consent, X considered, courag [-eous], friend [-ly], ([broken-], [hard-], [merry-], [stiff-], [stout-], double) heart ([-ed]), X heed, X I, kindly, midst, mind (-ed), X regard ([-ed)], X themselves, X unawares, understanding, X well, willingly, wisdom.

7.7.13 The sermon from the boat

Reading Luke 5:1-11

Jesus had a problem with finding a good location to preach. So he got in a boat and asked Simon if he'd put the boat out a bit from the shore. He then sat down in the boat and began to teach.

> "And he sat down, and taught the people out of the ship. Now when he had left speaking, he said unto Simon, ..."
>
> Luke 5:3-4

Often I have gone to a service where Jesus has certainly been speaking. And I feel like the author here. Lord you've got my boat and I've come here at your request and you've done all this speaking and you seem to have forgotten about me. Sure the sermon was great, and the people were no doubt blessed.

I'm glad that even from God's perspective sometimes the sermons not so important as the person who he's sitting next to in the boat. And that’s me and you. In chapter 5 in Luke how much time on this occasion is spent on discussion of the sermon Jesus spoke? None. How much time was spent talking about what happened after the sermon was finished, and what Jesus said to Peter, and his reactions to what happened and also those of James and John? About 8 verses.

Sometimes the practical things of our friendship with our Lord at the moment, are more important than the sermon spoken on the boat, or the judgment which is coming up in the future. If God is with us now, and pays attention to us now, will he not also pay attention through loving kindness and mercy when we stand before him at the judgment on the day we are resurrected?

God’s character does not change. Praise the Lord.

7.8 Faith and Salvation

Reading John 6:1-69 [the bread - the words of eternal life]

> 28 Then said they unto him, What shall we do, that we might work the works of God?
>
> 29 Jesus answered and said unto them, This is the work of God, that ye believe on him whom he hath sent.
>
> John 6:28-29

The foundation for doing God's work, is a work of God. It is that a man believes. By faith we die to the law and become a servant of Christ. As we serve him, we will be set free from sin.

Reading John 8:19-59 [the truth and sin]

> “If ye continue in my word, then are ye my disciples indeed; And ye shall know the truth, and the truth shall make you free.
>
> ... Whosoever committeth sin is the servant of sin.
>
> ...
>
> If the Son therefore shall make you free, ye shall be free indeed.”
>
> John 8:31-32,34,36

It is by continuing in the words Jesus has said, and by following his commandments, that Christ will gradually set us free from sin. Remember God left some of the enemies to test Israel, and so that they could learn how to fight.

> “Now these are the nations (that) the Lord left, ... ; Only that the generations of the children of Israel might know, to teach them war, at the least such as before knew nothing thereof; ...”
>
> Judges 3:1-2

We have a major victory over Satan when we first come to believe in Christ. Many of our enemies that were oppressing us run away in terror at this time.

If we continue to follow God, these other enemies that remain will become subject to us, and be destroyed. We will see God's victory over them. But it does require patience and persistence to see God's will done, and his kingdom to come to reign in our hearts.

Still, for the present, if we hold faith and a good conscience, those sins which are unknown to us will be covered by the blood of Christ.

> “... if we walk in the light, as he is in the light, we have fellowship one with another, and the blood of Jesus Christ his (son cleanses) us from all sin.”
>
> 1John 1:7

The light here is the light we have available for us to discern good and evil, to tell the difference between right and wrong. Perhaps like when Adam and Eve did not know they lacked clothes, and

God did not punish them for their lack of clothing, he doesn't punish us for the things we unknowingly do wrong.

> Who can understand his errors? cleanse thou me from secret faults.
>
> Psalm 19:12

In my first few years talking with God, God dealt with many idols in my heart bringing them to my attention one at a time. He taught me how love is the greatest of all things.

If we out of love are subject to Christ, God will help keep us from sin.

> "... : he [The Lord] is a buckler to them that walk uprightly."
>
> Prov 2:7

Christians are a new creation[480], having a new nature being born from above[481]. They are being changed from glory to glory, as by the Spirit of the Lord[482]. God will save them from evil works[483]. Man looks on the outward appearance[484], and notes their faults. God looks on the heart, and justifies the ungodly through faith[485].

> Blessed are they that do his commandments, that they may have right to the tree of life, and may enter in through the gates into the city.
>
> Rev 22:14

It is only through faith that a man may be saved. Christians do God's commandments, maybe not perfectly, but there are works which result from faith and trust in God. These works are sufficient evidence of faith in Christ.

> For the promise, that he should be the heir of the world, was not to Abraham, or to his seed, through the law, but through the righteousness of faith."
>
> Rom 4:13

Derek Prince makes a relevant argument concerning faith. If God has forgiven us, then we are guiltless because Jesus has taken away our sins.

> If we confess our sins, he is faithful and just to forgive us our sins, and to cleanse us from all unrighteousness.
>
> 1John 1:9

---

[480] "Therefore if any man be in Christ, he is a new creature: old things are passed away; behold, all things are become new." 2Cor 5:17

[481] "We know that whosoever is born of God sinneth not; but he that is begotten of God keepeth himself, and that wicked one toucheth him not." 1John 5:18

[482] "But we all, with open face beholding as in a glass the glory of the Lord, are changed into the same image from glory to glory, even as by the Spirit of the Lord." 2Cor 3:18

[483] "And the Lord shall deliver me from every evil work, and will preserve me unto his heavenly kingdom: to whom be glory for ever and ever. Amen." 2Tim 4:18

[484] "But the LORD said unto Samuel, Look not on his countenance, or on the height of his stature; because I have refused him: for the LORD seeth not as man seeth; for man looketh on the outward appearance, but the LORD looketh on the heart." 1Sam 16:7

[485] "But to him that worketh not, but believeth on him that justifieth the ungodly, his faith is counted for righteousness." Rom 4:5

> "These passages [which include 1John 1:7-9] teach that if a believer in Christ sins, and thereafter repents and confesses his sin, the efficacy of Christ's atonement is such that the record of his sin is erased and he himself is cleansed from all unrighteousness.
>
> This is the logical reason why the true believer in Christ need not fear that the result of judgment for him will be condemnation. God's provision both to cleanse the sinner himself and to erase the record of his sins means that there will be no record of sin remaining, upon which any just judgment of condemnation could be based."
>
> *Derek Prince*

My little children, these things I write to you, that you sin not. And if anyone sins, we have an advocate with[486] the Father, Jesus Christ the righteous. And He Himself is the propitiation[487] for our sins, and not for ours only but also for the whole world.

1John 2:1-2 [a translation]

---

[486] or *toward*

[487] G2434 *atonement*, i.e. (concretely) an *expiator:* - propitiation.

The Concise Oxford dictionary (1933):

Atone - (As v.t., archaic) reconcile (enemies), compose (quarrel); Hence atonement n. [AT+ONE, = set at one, unite]

7.9 Eternity

The Old Testament books had prophecies of Jesus, his death and his resurrection.

> For unto us a child is born, unto us a son is given: and the government shall be upon his shoulder: and his name shall be called Wonderful, Counsellor, The mighty God, The everlasting Father, The Prince of Peace.
>
> Of the increase of his government and peace there shall be no end, upon the throne of David, and upon his kingdom, to order it, and to establish it with judgment and with justice from henceforth even for ever. The zeal of the LORD of hosts will perform this.
>
> Isaiah 9:6-7

God Almighty will always have new and better things in store for us, even in eternity.

> “That in the ages to come he might show the exceeding riches of his grace in his kindness toward [or upon] us through Christ Jesus.”
>
> Eph 2:7

The blessings God has given and will give us on earth, aren’t a billionth of what God wants to show us. God has to have eternity, and even then its going to be hard for him to pack in enough to show us the riches given to us through Jesus death on the cross.

Two definitions of eternity[488] may be found by taking the definitions of the respective Greek and Hebrew words that are translated to English as “for ever”:

The Old Testament

> The destination/terminus, a bright glittering object in the distance travelled towards on a bright sunny day, which one can't see clearly because it is hidden by reason of distance[489].

The New Testament

> Perpetual age, period of time which is for ever or always[490].

God wants us to have peace and confidence in our hearts through Jesus our Lord.

> "... : for at the time appointed the end shall be."
>
> Dan 8:19

God has everything under control. He has appointed the time when the end shall be. It will not happen by accident. We sometimes think of Jesus reign, and wonder if we will be forgotten. But God never forgets us.

Reading Isaiah 54:6-10 [but my kindness shall not depart from thee]

---

[488] paraphrased from James Strong’s Hebrew and Greek dictionary

[489] cf. H5769 עוֹלָם עֹלָם ʽôlâm ʽôlâm

[490] cf. G165 αἰών aiōn

> "But Zion said, The LORD hath forsaken me, and my Lord hath forgotten me.
>
> Can a woman forget her sucking child, that she should not have compassion on the son of her womb? yea, they may forget, yet will I not forget thee.
>
> Behold, I have graven thee upon the palms of my hands; ..."
> Isaiah 49:14-16

Remember Thomas and what Jesus said unto him.

> The other disciples therefore said unto him, We have seen the Lord. But he said unto them, Except I shall see in his hands the print of the nails, and put my finger into the print of the nails, and thrust my hand into his side, I will not believe.
>
> And after eight days again his disciples were within, and Thomas with them: then came Jesus, the doors being shut, and stood in the midst, and said, Peace be unto you.
>
> Then saith he to Thomas, Reach hither thy finger, and behold my hands; and reach hither thy hand, and thrust it into my side: and be not faithless, but believing.
> John 20:25-27

God does not forget us. The scars of the nails in his hands always remind him of us. Praise the Lord, he's going to watch over us, and see that we stand in righteousness with him in glory, at the Last day. There will be a multitude of people. There will be much business on that final day. But remember, its our Dad, who is the most important person on that day. He will sit as the Judge, he will be the one to deal with all the complicated things we don't understand. And be sure he is going to keep us safe. We're precious. There will be many on that day. But God is our Father. And he has time for me. It will be busy, I think like on a wedding day, many people being worried, others talking. Some rushing to put the last minute things right. But God I think will give us a pat on the shoulder, and a wink, and say don't worry son, I'm going to be busy for a bit, but I'll be back after its over. Hallelujah! God loves us.

I stand trusting you will forgive me through our Lord Jesus Christ[491].

> "For the scripture saith, Whosoever believeth on him shall not be ashamed[492].
>
> For there is no difference between the Jew and the Greek: for the same Lord over all is rich unto all that call upon him.
>
> For whosoever shall call upon the name of the Lord shall be saved[493]."
> Rom 10:11-13; cf. Joel 2:26-32[494]

---

[491] 1John 1:9

[492] cf. Isaiah 28:16, 50:7; Rom 9:33; Isaiah 8:14

[493] cf. Acts 2:16-21

[494] Joel says "... : and *my people* shall never be ashamed."

7.10 The blessing of Abraham

At the beginning God promised Abraham that he would have a son.

Reading Genesis 17:1-7

> "As for me, behold, my covenant is with thee, and thou shalt be a father of many nations. ... And I will establish my covenant between me and thee and thy seed after thee ..." Gen 17:4,7
>
> "And in thy seed shall all the nations of the earth be blessed; because thou hast obeyed my voice." Gen 22:18
>
> "Seeing that Abraham shall surely become a great and mighty nation, and all the nations of the earth shall be blessed in him?" Gen 18:18.

The promise to Abraham to have a son was also a promise of mercy and to receive remission of sins. This promise was not only to Abraham, but also to his children that came after him.

> "..., he will have compassion upon us; he will subdue our iniquities; and thou wilt cast all their sins into the depths of the sea. Thou wilt perform the truth to Jacob, and the mercy to Abraham, which thou hast sworn unto our fathers from the days of old."
>
> Micah 7:19-20

Abraham believed God would bless all the nations of the earth through his seed.

> "He saith not, And to seeds, as of many; but as of one, And to thy seed, which is Christ." Gal 3:16
>
> "And the scripture, foreseeing that God would justify the heathen through faith, preached before[495] the gospel unto Abraham, saying, In thee shall all nations be blessed."
>
> Gal 3:8[496]

The story of the children of Israel coming out of slavery in Egypt and making a covenant with God to be their king is an illustration of a man turning from serving under sin to make a covenant with God. It was through death with Christ at the cross, that sin lost its grip upon us, even as the army of the Egyptians assaying to cross the red sea were drowned.

> Moreover, brethren, I would not that ye should be ignorant, how that all our fathers were under the cloud, and all passed through the sea; And were all baptized unto Moses in the cloud and in the sea; And did all eat the same spiritual meat; And did all drink the same spiritual drink: for they drank of that spiritual Rock that followed them: and that Rock was Christ.
>
> 1Cor 10:1-4

[495] in advance

[496] cf. Acts 3:25; Gen 22:18

“By faith they passed through the Red sea as by dry land: ...”
Heb 11:29

Through faith we were baptised into one body.

“For by one Spirit are we all baptized into one body, whether we be Jews or Gentiles, whether we be bond or free; ....” 1Cor 12:13[497]

By faith in Christ all the nations of the earth are blessed with the righteousness that is a gift from above.

"For they are not all Israel, which are of Israel: Neither, because they are the seed of Abraham, are they all children: but, In Isaac shall thy seed be called. That is, They which are the children of the flesh, these are not the children of God: but the children of the promise are counted for the seed."
Rom 9:6-7[498]

“For the promise, that he should be the heir of the world, was not to Abraham, or to his seed, through the law, but through the righteousness of faith.”
Rom 4:13

By faith, we have inherited the blessing of righteousness[499], and the promise of the spirit of adoption given to Abraham, Isaac and Jacob.

“Yet now hear, O Jacob my servant; and Israel, whom I have chosen:

Thus saith the Lord that made thee, and formed thee from the womb, which will help thee; Fear not, O Jacob, my servant; and thou, Jesurun, whom I have chosen. For I will pour water upon him that is thirsty, and floods upon the dry ground: I will pour my spirit upon thy seed, and my blessing upon thine offspring: ...”
Isaiah 44:1-3

God has anointed us with his Holy Spirit and called us his sons and daughters. Through Christ's death and resurrection, we have received the Holy Spirit and are united together with God, being born into one family. Now that we are sons, we cry 'Daddy'[500], and God hears us.

“For ye have not received the spirit of bondage again to fear; but ye have received the Spirit of adoption, whereby we cry, Abba, Father.

---

[497] It is Christ who has reconciled both Jews and Gentiles to God by Jesus Christ.
“For he is our peace, (having made/making [in the past]) both [Jew and Gentile] one, and hath broken down the middle wall of partition between us; Having abolished in his flesh the enmity, even the law of commandments contained in ordinances; for to make in himself of twain one new man, so making peace; And that he might reconcile both unto God in one body by the cross, having slain the enmity thereby: ...”
Eph 2:14-16; cf. Rom 4:16 & Rom 15:8-9

[498] Num 6:22-27 cf. Mat 23:37 and Rom 11:1&11 “A remnant according to the election of grace.”

[499] “Blessed is he whose transgression is forgiven, whose sin is covered. Blessed is the man unto whom the Lord imputeth not iniquity, and in whose spirit there is no guile (H7423 *remissness*, *treachery* -from G7411 'to *hurl*').” Psalm 32:1-2; cf. Rom 4:7-8 “... whose iniquities are forgiven, and whose sins are covered.”

[500] A baby doesn't know right from wrong. It can't hold a glass of water to drink, it doesn't know how to say “please” or “thankyou”, yet the Father and Mother of the child are as pleased as anything when the little one is born into the world. God's love toward us doesn't change as we grow up. He loves us the same as at the beginning. Rom 8:28-39 “And we know that all things work together for good ... ”. God wants the best for us.

The Spirit itself beareth witness with our spirit, that we are the children of God: And if children, then heirs; heirs of God, and joint-heirs with Christ; ..."
Rom 8:15-17[501]

"Know ye therefore that they which are of faith, the same are the children of Abraham." Gal 3:7

We are born into the same family as David, Naomi, Ruth, Moses, Abraham, Phillip, Rhoda, Cornelius, Lydia, Onesimus[502] and all the saints[503] through faith in Jesus Christ our Lord. We have one God, our Father who is the ruler over all.

Reading Hebrews 12:18-24

We stand on holy ground in the congregation of saints. Hallelujah.

"For ye are ... come ... (to) the general assembly and church of the firstborn, which are written in heaven, and to God the Judge of all, and to the spirits of just men made perfect, and to Jesus the mediator of the new covenant, and to the blood of sprinkling, ..."
Hebrews 12:18-24[504]

"... : for by faith [in God] ye stand." 2Cor 1:24

We can come and talk with God in his presence.

"Having therefore, brethren, boldness to enter into the holiest by the blood of Jesus, ... , through the veil, that is to say, his flesh; ... ; Let us draw (nigh) with a true heart ..."
Heb 10:19-22

"O come, let us worship and bow down: let us kneel before the Lord our maker. For he is our God; and we are the people of his pasture, and the sheep of his hand."
Psalm 95:6

In God's presence he commands the blessing, and we look around and find that our Father has finished the battle for us and given us victory over all our enemies.

"Now thanks be unto God, (who) always causeth us to triumph in Christ, and maketh manifest the savour of his knowledge by us in every place."
2Cor 2:14

"Let thy priests be clothed with righteousness; and let thy saints shout for joy."
Psalm 132:9

---

501 cf. Gal 4:6-7 "And because ye are sons, ..."

502 [Phillip] Acts 8:26, [Cornelius] Acts 10:1, [Lydia] Acts 16:14, [Onesimus] Philemon 1:1-25

503 Those who believe in Christ have been sanctified, and are saints.

504 "Only take heed to thyself ... lest thou forget ... specially the day that thou stoodest before the Lord thy God in Horeb ..." Deut 4:9-12

Praise the Lord that the price for our sins was paid with the blood of Jesus Christ. The Lord God Almighty reigns. Hallelujah, for God is the judge of all.

> "The Lord of hosts is with us; the God of Jacob is (a refuge for us). Selah."
> Psalm 46:11

Reading Psalm133[505] & Psalm149[506]

God loves us. We were once judged with Christ, we can not be tried again for our crimes. God has taken away every sin. In confident cheerfulness and good will towards us, God has taken us by the hand[507] and looks after us.

> "Who shall lay anything to the charge of Gods elect? It is God (who) justifieth."
> Rom 8:33

> "... : holiness becometh thine house, O Lord, for ever."
> Psalm 93:5

Praise the Lord. Hallelujah.

> "Rejoice in the Lord, O ye righteous: for praise is comely for the upright."
> Psalm 33:1

Reading Psalms 147 & 148

Let us conclude with the blessing[508] God gave to the children of Israel not by the law, but by his son Jesus, the son of Abraham, Isaac and Jacob.

The Lord bless you, and keep you. The Lord make his face to shine upon you, and be gracious unto you. The Lord lift up his countenance upon you, and give you peace.

> "For ye are all the children of God by[509] faith in Christ Jesus." Gal 3:26

Here I Stand.

---

505 "Behold, how good and how pleasant it is for brethren to dwell together in unity!" Psalm 133

506 "For the Lord taketh pleasure in his people: he will beautify the meek with salvation." Psalm149

507 "Not according to the covenant ... in the day that I took them by the hand ..." Jer 31:32

508 Num 6:22-27

509 or 'through' G1223 διά

8.0 Appendices

A. Recommended Reading and References

[1] The Cross and the Switchblade, by David Wilkerson

Pyramid Books (1962), ISBN 978-0515023367

[2] Run Baby Run, by Nicky Cruz

Pyramid/Logos International (1974), ISBN 978-0515020663

[3] Ever Increasing Faith, by Smith Wigglesworth, Editor Wayne E. Warner

Gospel Publishing House, ISBN 0-88243-494-2

[4] Faith that Prevails, by Smith Wigglesworth

Gospel Publishing House, ISBN 0-88243-711-9

[5] The Interlinear Bible, by Jay P Green

Hendrickson Publishers, 2nd Edition (1986), ISBN 0-913573-25-6

[6] Strong's Exhaustive Concordance of the Bible (and Dictionaries of the Greek and Hebrew Words), by James Strong

Abingdon Press, 1st Edition, Forty-third printing, ISBN 0-687-40030-9

[7] Foundation Series, by Derek Prince

Derek Prince Ministries, Revised Three Volume Edition (1986), ISBN 1-85240-006-4

B. Notation

Greek and Hebrew definitions are adapted from the Hebrew and Greek dictionary that accompanies *Strong's Exhaustive Concordance of the Bible*[510]. An example of an entry in Strong's dictionary is

> H216 אוֹר ôr *ore*
>
> From H215; *illumination* or (concretely) *luminary* (in every sense, including *lightning, happiness,* etc.): - bright, clear, + day, light (-ning), morning, sun.

For each word there is a reference number e.g. H216. Often more than one English word is used on different occasions as a translation of a single word in the original language. These words are shown after the “:” in the dictionary e.g.

"אוֹר" is translated in various places as:

> bright, clear, + day, light (-ning), morning, sun.

for example,

> “And God said let there be *light* ...” Gen 1:3

> “Also ... he scattereth his *bright* cloud ...” Job 37:11

> "And he read therein before the street that was before the water gate from the *morning* until midday, ..." Neh 8:3

The King James version (KJV) was, in general, used as the basis for discussion. Where other translations are used, they are noted in the text. To improve clarity, some quotes of the KJV have words added to them within brackets. Square brackets indicate that the words are added to explain the context e.g.

> “So when they [Jesus and the disciples] had dined ...” John 21:15

Round brackets indicate a different translation has been used. The translation may be [A] added in addition to the KJV translation, or [B] may replace the KJV translation e.g.

> [A] "By the word of the Lord were the heavens (skies) made; and all their host by the breath (wind) of his mouth." Psalm 33:6
>
> or
>
> [B] "By the word of the Lord were the (skies) made; and all their host by the (wind) of his mouth." Psalm 33:6

For comparison the original is

> "By the word of the Lord were the heavens made; and all the host of them by the breath of his mouth." Psalm 33:6

---

[510] by James Strong, first published in 1894.

C. Quotes

God speaks. Ask Aaron when he complained about Moses whether God spoke. Ask Paul whether God spoke to him on the way to Damascus. Ask Peter whether the Spirit said to go down and meet the men sent by Cornelius. Ask Adam whether God spoke to him after he had sinned. Ask Noah whether God told him to build an ark. Ask Moses whether God told him to take his shoes off at the burning bush. Ask Elijah about when he came out of the cave and heard a small still voice. Ask Samuel who called him three times. Ask Samson if God answered his prayer to be avenged of his eyes.

Ask God.

A man spoke concerning the Word of God:

“Never compare this book with other books. Comparisons are dangerous. Never think or never say that this book contains the word of God. It is the word of God. It is supernatural in origin, eternal in duration, inexpressible in value, infinite in scope, regenerative in power, infallible in authority, universal in interest, personal in application, inspired in totality.

Read it through, write it down, pray it in, work it out, and then pass it on.”

Going through the motions doesn't please you,
a flawless performance is nothing to you.
I learned God-worship when my pride was shattered.
Heart-shattered lives ready for love don't for a moment escape God's notice.

Psalm 51:16-17[511]

[511] a paraphrased translation of the Bible, "The Message" by Eugene Peterson.

A preacher 65 years of age was talking to his son in law, also a preacher. The two were discussing their profession. The younger man said I am young and you're going to slow down, and I'm going to catch you up. The older gentleman said, Son, come and sit down, I've got something to say to you. They sat down, and He said I'm not going to be slowing down. I'm like a jumbo aeroplane. I don't slow down as I reach the end of the runway.

- from a sermon delivered by Reinhard Bonnke

1. Is it true, certain and reliable?

2. Does it show God's love for us?

3. Does it turn our hearts to God?

4. Is it peaceable, gentle, and easy to be entreated?

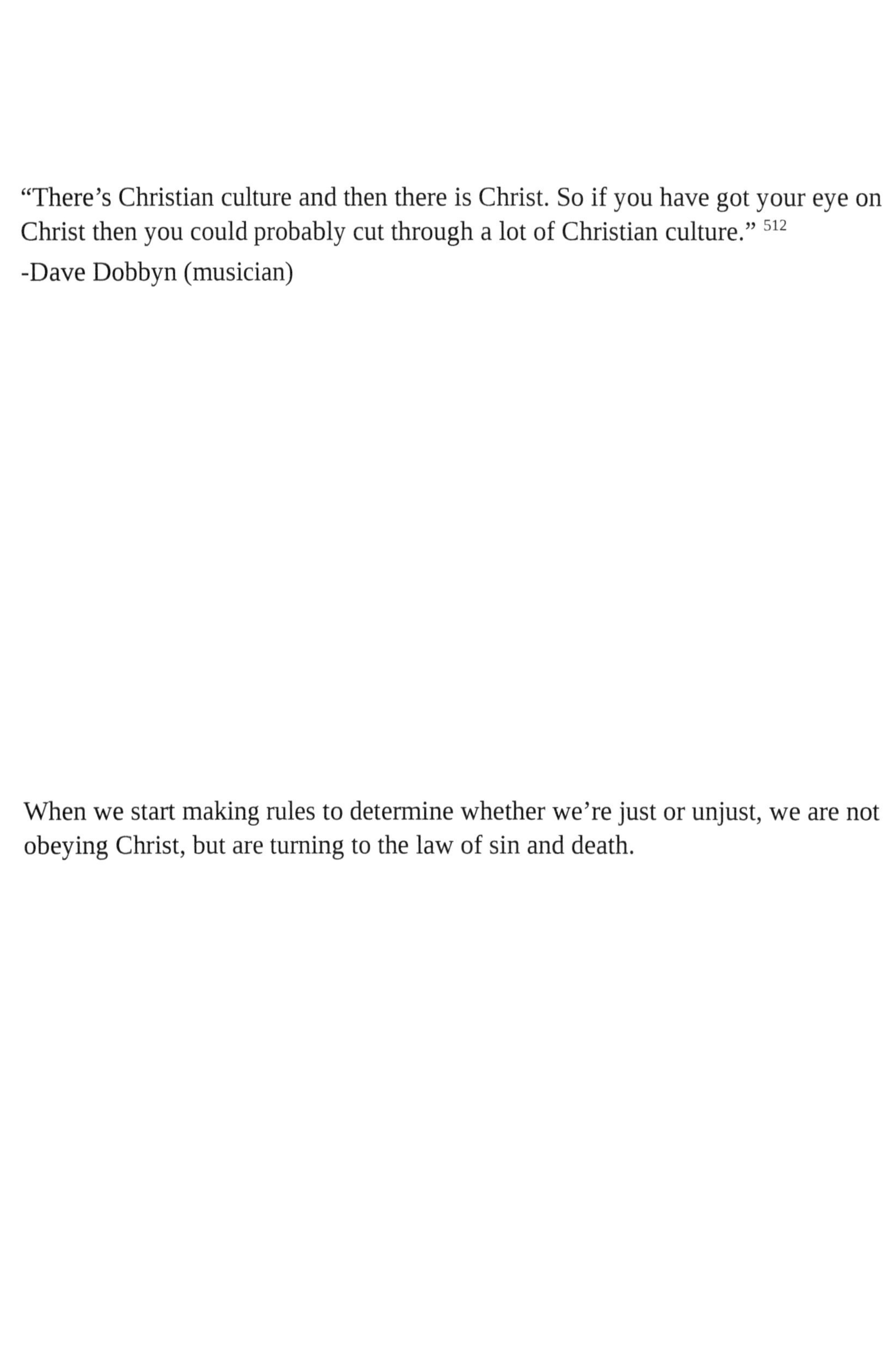

"There's Christian culture and then there is Christ. So if you have got your eye on Christ then you could probably cut through a lot of Christian culture." [512]

-Dave Dobbyn (musician)

When we start making rules to determine whether we're just or unjust, we are not obeying Christ, but are turning to the law of sin and death.

[512] 'The Press' newspaper, 30th June 2005, Christchurch, New Zealand cf. Mat 23:4 & Gal 2:20-21

Stubbed Your Toe

Did you ever pass a youngster, who had been an' stubbed his toe,
And was sitting by the road side, just crying soft an' low?
A holding of his rusty foot so hard and brown and bare,
An trying to keep back from his eyes the tears that's gathering there.

You hear him sorter sobbin' like, and a snifflin' of his nose,
You stoop an' pat him on the head and try to ease his woes,
You treat him sorter kind like, and the first thing you know
He's up and off a smilin', clean forgot he stubbed his toe.

Along the road of human life, you'll find a fellow goin' slow,
And like as not he's some poor cuss, that's been an' stubbed his toe,
He was makin' swimmin' headway, until he bumped into a stone,
And his friends kept hurryin' on, and they left him here alone.

He ain't sobbing, he ain't snifflin, he's too old for sobs and cries,
But he's grievin' just as earnest, if it only comes in sighs,
And it does a lot of good sometimes to go a little slow,
And speak a word of kindness, to the guy that's stubbed his toe.

You can't tell yourself, and there ain't no way to know,
When it's going to come your turn to slip and stub your toe,
To-day you're bright an' happy, in the World's sunlight and glow,
And to-morrow you're a freezin' and a trudgin' thru the snow.

The time you think you've got the World the tightest in your grip
Is the very time you'll find, you're the likeliest to slip,
And it's mighty comfortin', sometimes, I know,
To have a fellow stop, and help you, when you've been and stubbed your toe.

Author unknown

Amor cuesta demasiado,
pero vale mas de lo que se pierde.
Tres palabras tan fáciles,
son mas de lo que se puede ganar
en toda una vida de esfuerzo.
Yo te amo.

Love costs too much,
but its worth more than what you lose.
Three words so easy,
are more than what you can gain in
all of a lifetimes effort.
I love you.

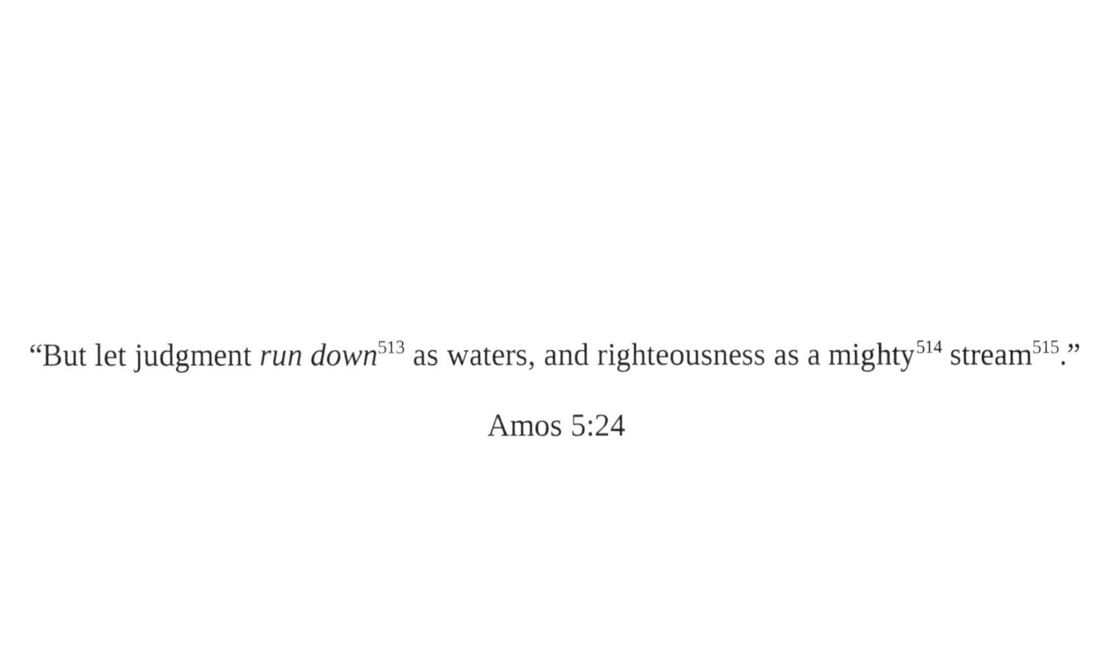

"But let judgment *run down*[513] as waters, and righteousness as a mighty[514] stream[515]."

Amos 5:24

[513] H1556 a primitive root; to *roll* (lit. or fig.)

[514] H386 From an unused root (meaning to *continue*); *permanence*; hence (concretely) *permanent*; specifically a *chieftain:* - hard, mighty, rough, strength, strong.

[515] H5158 From H5157 in its original sense ['to descend'?]; a *stream*, especially a winter *torrent*; (by implication) a (narrow) *valley* (in which a brook runs); also a *shaft* (of a mine): - brook, flood, river, stream, valley.

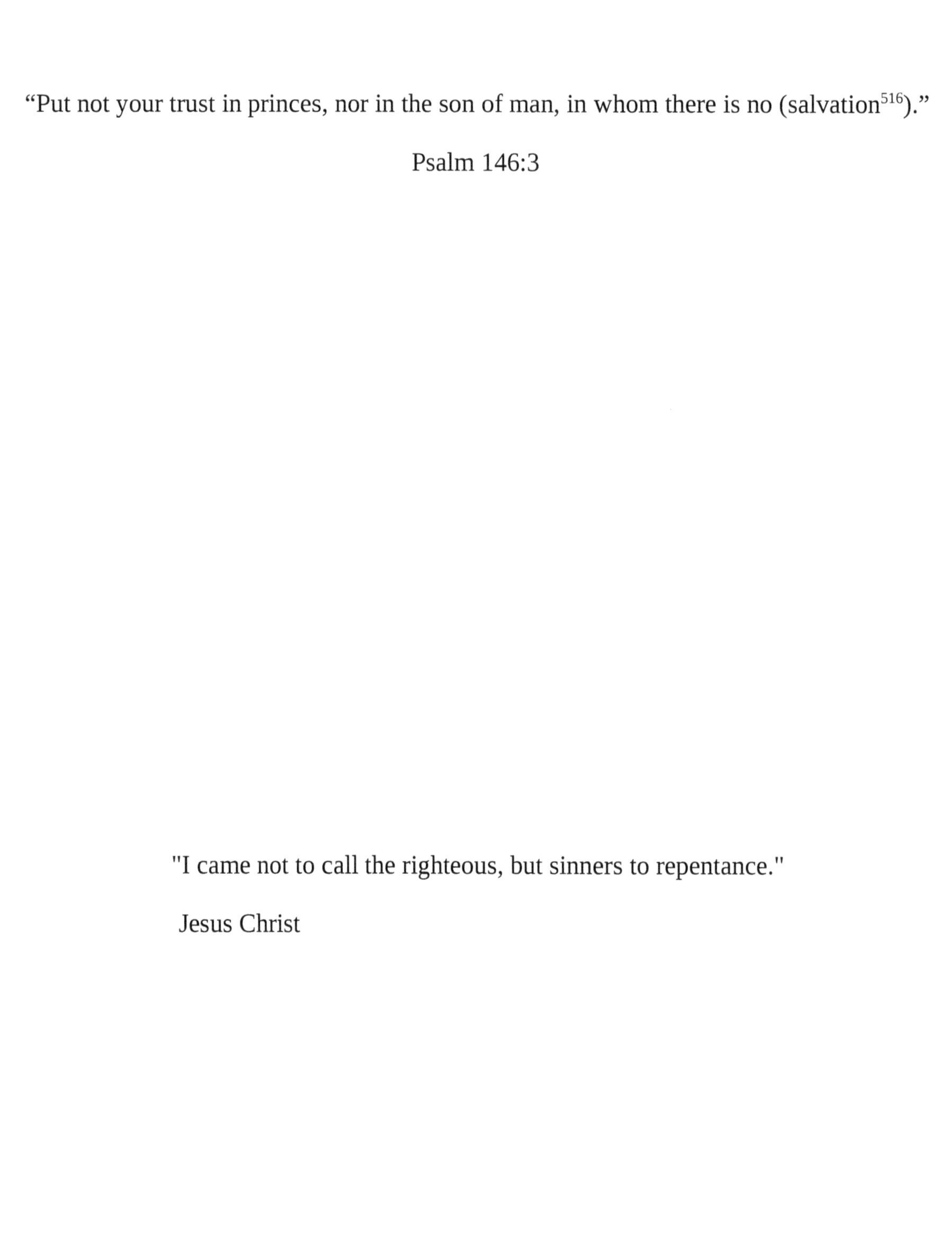

"Put not your trust in princes, nor in the son of man, in whom there is no (salvation[516])."

Psalm 146:3

"I came not to call the righteous, but sinners to repentance."

Jesus Christ

[516] H8668 *rescue* (lit. or fig., personal, national or spiritual).
From H7768 {prop. to be free; but used only causatively and reflexively to yell/halloo (attract attention) for help} in the sense of H3467 {to *be open*, *wide* or *free*, i.e. (by implic.) to be *safe*}

"And we know that the Son of God is come, and hath given us an understanding, that we may know him that is true, and we are in him that is true, even in his Son Jesus Christ. This is the true God, and eternal life."

1John 5:20; cf. John 17:3

"... : he that followeth me shall not walk in darkness, ..."

Jesus

"A little storm, and then a rainbow appears."

A Maori proverb

There is no situation in which one can not be ungrateful.

And the end of all real faith always is rejoicing.

Smith Wigglesworth[517]

[517] Faith that Prevails, section 'Present time Blessings'. See Appendix A page 228.

“...; who [Jesus] for the joy (cheerfulness) that was set before him endured the cross, despising the shame, ...”

An Invitation

Will you come and be my bride? Open doors let me inside?
Are you always faithful, true?
My word says I love you.

I have loved you always with an everlasting love.
My desire towards you is to fill you with my love.
I have prepared a place for you.
An everlasting home.
Where joy and peace and friendship mean you'll never be alone.

Above all pleasures and rewards of my great love;
is the knowledge of your saviour who is King of love.
Don't say I am unworthy of my Lord the King of Kings.
He died for your transforming and he wants to hear you sing.

Will you say yes to Jesus?

He says yes to you.

Whosoever comes to me will find my word is true.

Say no to fear and uncertainty, say goodbye to your sin.

Say yes to God your Saviour

And he truly will come in.

by Patricia Clow

D. A Question About Marriage and the Resurrection

LUK 20:27 Then came to him certain of the Sadducees, which deny that there is any resurrection; and they asked him,

LUK 20:28 Saying, Master, Moses wrote unto us, If any man's brother die, having a wife, and he die without children, that his brother should take his wife, and raise up seed unto his brother.

LUK 20:29 There were therefore seven brethren: and the first took a wife, and died without children.

LUK 20:30 And the second took her to wife, and he died childless.

LUK 20:31 And the third took her; and in like manner the seven also: and they left no children, and died.

LUK 20:32 Last of all the woman died also.

LUK 20:33 Therefore in the resurrection whose wife of them is she? for seven had her to wife.

MAR 12:24 And Jesus answering said unto them, Do ye not therefore err, because ye know not the scriptures, neither the power of God?

LUK 20:34 And Jesus answering said unto them, The children of this world [age / duration] marry, and are given in marriage:

LUK 20:35 But they which shall be accounted worthy to obtain that world, and the resurrection from the dead, neither marry, nor are given in marriage:

LUK 20:36 Neither can they die any more: for they are equal unto the angels; and are the children of God, being the children of the resurrection.

MAR 12:25 For when they shall rise from the dead, they neither marry, nor are given in marriage; but are as the angels which are in heaven.

MAR 12:26 And as touching the dead, that they rise: have ye not read in the book of Moses, how in the bush God spake unto him, saying, I am the God of Abraham, and the God of Isaac, and the God of Jacob?

LUK 20:38 For he is not a God of the dead, but of the living: for all live unto him.

MAR 12:27 ... ye therefore do greatly err.

MAT 22:33 And when the multitude heard this, they were astonished at his doctrine.

MAR 12:28 And one of the scribes came, and having heard them reasoning together, and perceiving that he had answered them well, asked him, Which is the first commandment of all?

MAR 12:29 And Jesus answered him, The first of all the commandments is, Hear, O Israel; The Lord our God is one Lord:

MAR 12:30 And thou shalt love the Lord thy God with all thy heart, and with all thy soul, and with all thy mind, and with all thy strength: this is the first commandment.

MAR 12:31 And the second is like, namely this, Thou shalt love thy neighbour as thyself. There is none other commandment greater than these.

MAR 22:40 On these two commandments hang all the law and the prophets.

MAR 12:32 And the scribe said unto him, Well, Master, thou hast said the truth: for there is one God; and there is none other but he:

MAR 12:33 And to love him with all the heart, and with all the understanding, and with all the soul, and with all the strength, and to love his neighbour as himself, is more than all whole burnt offerings and sacrifices.

MAR 12:34 And when Jesus saw that he answered discreetly, he said unto him, Thou art not far from the kingdom of God. ...

LUK 20:40 And after that they durst not ask him any question at all.

Mar 12:35 And Jesus answered and said, while he taught in the temple, How say the scribes that Christ is the Son of David?

MAR 12:36 For David himself said by the Holy Ghost, The LORD said to my Lord, Sit thou on my right hand, till I make thine enemies thy footstool.

MAR 12:37 David therefore himself calleth him Lord; and whence is he then his son? And the common people heard him gladly.

Matthew 22:23-46; Mark 12:18-37; Luke 20:27-44

E. Christ's Death and Resurrection

- A Collection of Scriptures Contained in the Gospels

MAR 8:29 And he saith unto them, But whom say ye that I am? And Peter answereth and saith unto him, Thou art the Christ.

MAR 8:30 And he charged them that they should tell no man of him.

MAR 8:31 And he began to teach them, that the Son of man must suffer many things, and be rejected of the elders, and of the chief priests, and scribes, and be killed, and after three days rise again.

MAR 9:9 And as they came down from the mountain, he charged them that they should tell no man what things they had seen, till the Son of man were risen from the dead.

MAR 9:10 And they kept that saying with themselves, questioning one with another what the rising from the dead should mean.

MAR 9:11 And they asked him, saying, Why say the scribes that Elias must first come?

MAR 9:12 And he answered and told them, Elias verily cometh first, and restoreth all things; and how it is written of the Son of man, that he must suffer many things, and be set at nought.

--- [shortly later after healing the epileptic]

MAR 9:31 For he taught his disciples, and said unto them, The Son of man is delivered into the hands of men, and they shall kill him; and after that he is killed, he shall rise the third day.

MAR 9:32 But they understood not that saying, and were afraid to ask him.

MAR 10:32 And they were in the way going up to Jerusalem; and Jesus went before them: and they were amazed; and as they followed, they were afraid. And he took again the twelve, and began to tell them what things should happen unto him,

MAR 10:33 Saying, Behold, we go up to Jerusalem; and the Son of man shall be delivered unto the chief priests, and unto the scribes; and they shall condemn him to death, and shall deliver him to the Gentiles:

MAR 10:34 And they shall mock him, and shall scourge him, and shall spit upon him, and shall kill him: and the third day he shall rise again.

MAR 14:21 The Son of man indeed goeth, as it is written of him: but woe to that man by whom the Son of man is betrayed! good were it for that man if he had never been born.

MAR 14:22 And as they did eat, Jesus took bread, and blessed, and brake it, and gave to them, and said, Take, eat: this is my body.

MAR 14:23 And he took the cup, and when he had given thanks, he gave it to them: and they all drank of it.

MAR 14:24 And he said unto them, This is my blood of the new testament, which is shed for many.

MAR 14:25 Verily I say unto you, I will drink no more of the fruit of the vine, until that day that I drink it new in the kingdom of God.

MAR 14:26 And when they had sung an hymn, they went out into the mount of Olives.

MAR 14:27 And Jesus saith unto them, All ye shall be offended because of me this night: for it is written, I will smite the shepherd, and the sheep shall be scattered.

MAR 14:28 But after that I am risen, I will go before you into Galilee.

MAR 15:33 And when the sixth hour was come, there was darkness over the whole land until the ninth hour.

MAR 15:34 And at the ninth hour Jesus cried with a loud voice, saying, Eloi, Eloi, lama sabachthani? which is, being interpreted, My God, my God, why hast thou forsaken me?

JOH 19:28 After this, Jesus knowing that all things were now accomplished, that the scripture might be fulfilled, saith, I thirst.

MAR 15:36 And one ran and filled a spunge full of vinegar, and put it on a reed, and gave him to drink, ...

JOH 19:30 When Jesus therefore had received the vinegar, he said, It is finished[518]: ...

LUK 23:46 And when Jesus had cried [again[519]] with a loud voice, he said, Father, into thy hands I commend[50] my spirit[520]: and having said thus, he *gave up the ghost*[521].

MAR 15:38 And the veil of the temple was rent in twain from the top to the bottom.

MAR 15:39 And when the centurion, which stood over against him, saw that he so cried out, and gave up the ghost, he said, Truly this man was the Son of God.

MAR 15:44 And Pilate marvelled if he were already dead: and calling unto him the centurion, he asked him whether he had been any while dead.

MAR 15:45 And when he knew it of the centurion, he gave the body to Joseph.

MAR 15:46 And he bought fine linen, and took him down, and wrapped him in the linen, and laid him in a sepulchre which was hewn out of a rock, and rolled a stone unto the door of the sepulchre.

[518] 'And Jesus cried with a loud voice, and gave up the ghost' Mar 15:37
I think Jesus cried "It is finished" with a loud voice because:
(1) in Mark 15:34-7 & Mat 27:46-50 it recounts crying out with a loud voice twice, the first being 'why have you forsaken me', then he received the vinegar, and then he cried again with a loud voice, and gave up the ghost.
(2) the only words recorded after receiving the vinegar are: "It is finished" (John 19:30) and (I think) "Father, into thy hands I commend my Spirit" (Luke 23:46) due to the immediacy of his expiring after speaking these words.

[519] 'Jesus, when he had cried again with a loud voice, yielded up the ghost.' Mat 27:50.
cf. previous loud voice 'My God, ...' Mar 15:34; Mat 27:46

[520] G4151 πνεῦμα pneuma pnyoo'-mah
From G4154; a *current* of air, i.e. *breath* (blast) or a *breeze*; by analogy or figuratively a *spirit*,...

[521] or *expired* (G1606) i.e. {G1537 from, out of} {G4154 to *breathe* hard i.e. a *forcible* respiration}. In my opinion, similar to H1478 [to *breathe* out, i.e. (by implic.) *expire*]. In Mat 27:50 Jesus yielded up (sent forth) the ghost (spirit). In John 19:30 Jesus gave up (surrendered/entrusted) the ghost (spirit).

MAR 15:47 And Mary Magdalene and Mary the mother of Joses beheld where he was laid.

MAR 16:1 And when the sabbath was past, Mary Magdalene, and Mary the mother of James, and Salome, had bought sweet spices, that they might come and anoint him.

MAR 16:2 And very early in the morning the first day of the week, they came unto the sepulchre at the rising of the sun.

MAR 16:3 And they said among themselves, Who shall roll us away the stone from the door of the sepulchre?

MAR 16:4 And when they looked, they saw that the stone was rolled away: for it was very great.

MAR 16:5 And entering into the sepulchre, they saw a young man sitting on the right side, clothed in a long white garment; and they were affrighted.

MAT 28:5 And the angel answered and said unto the women, Fear not ye: for I know that ye seek Jesus, which was crucified.

MAT 28:6 He is not here: for he is risen, as he said. Come, see the place where the Lord lay.

MAR 16:7 But go your way, tell his disciples and Peter that he goeth before you into Galilee: there shall ye see him, as he said unto you.

MAR 16:8 And they went out quickly, and fled from the sepulchre; for they trembled and were amazed: neither said they any thing to any man; for they were afraid.

MAR 16:9 Now when Jesus was risen early the first day of the week, he appeared first to Mary Magdalene, out of whom he had cast seven devils.

JOH 20:11 But Mary stood without at the sepulchre weeping: and as she wept, she stooped down, and looked into the sepulchre,

JOH 20:12 And seeth two angels in white sitting, the one at the head, and the other at the feet, where the body of Jesus had lain.

JOH 20:13 And they say unto her, Woman, why weepest thou? She saith unto them, Because they have taken away my LORD, and I know not where they have laid him.

JOH 20:14 And when she had thus said, she turned herself back, and saw Jesus standing, and knew not that it was Jesus.

JOH 20:15 Jesus saith unto her, Woman, why weepest thou? whom seekest thou? She, supposing him to be the gardener, saith unto him, Sir, if thou have borne him hence, tell me where thou hast laid him, and I will take him away.

JOH 20:16 Jesus saith unto her, Mary. She turned herself, and saith unto him, Rabboni; which is to say, Master.

JOH 20:17 Jesus saith unto her, Touch me not; for I am not yet ascended to my Father: but go to my brethren, and say unto them, I ascend unto my Father, and your Father; and to my God, and your God.

JOH 20:18 Mary Magdalene came and told the disciples that she had seen the Lord, and that he had spoken these things unto her.

MAR 16:10 And she went and told them that had been with him, as they mourned and wept.

MAR 16:11 And they, when they had heard that he was alive, and had been seen of her, believed not.

MAR 16:12 After that he appeared in another form unto two of them, as they walked, and went into the country.

MAR 16:13 And they went and told it unto the residue: neither believed they them.

LUK 24:35 And they told what things were done in the way, and how he was known of them in breaking of bread.

LUK 24:36 And as they thus spake, Jesus himself stood in the midst of them, and saith unto them, Peace be unto you.

LUK 24:37 But they were terrified and affrighted, and supposed that they had seen a spirit.

LUK 24:38 And he said unto them, Why are ye troubled? and why do thoughts arise in your hearts?

LUK 24:39 Behold my hands and my feet, that it is I myself: handle me, and see; for a spirit hath not flesh and bones, as ye see me have.

LUK 24:40 And when he had thus spoken, he shewed them his hands and his feet.

LUK 24:41 And while they yet believed not for joy, and wondered, he said unto them, Have ye here any meat?

LUK 24:42 And they gave him a piece of a broiled fish, and of an honeycomb.

LUK 24:43 And he took it, and did eat before them.

LUK 24:44 And he said unto them, These are the words which I spake unto you, while I was yet with you, that all things must be fulfilled, which were written in the law of Moses, and in the prophets, and in the psalms, concerning me.

LUK 24:45 Then opened he their understanding, that they might understand the scriptures,

LUK 24:46 And said unto them, Thus it is written, and thus it behoved Christ to suffer, and to rise from the dead the third day:

LUK 24:47 And that repentance and remission of sins should be preached in his name among all nations, beginning at Jerusalem.

LUK 24:48 And ye are witnesses of these things.

LUK 24:49 And, behold, I send the promise of my Father upon you: but tarry ye in the city of Jerusalem, until ye be endued with power from on high.

LUK 24:50 And he led them out as far as to Bethany, and he lifted up his hands, and blessed them.

LUK 24:51 And it came to pass, while he blessed them, he was parted from them, and carried up into heaven.

LUK 24:52 And they worshipped him, and returned to Jerusalem with great joy: ...

F. Eternal Judgment: A List of Parables/Analogies in the Gospels

	Parables/ Analogies	Notes	Matthew	Mark	Luke	John
1	The salt of the earth		5:13	10:49-50	14:34-35	
2	The narrow gate		7:13-14		13:24-30	
3	The fruit tree	not everyone … but he that doeth the will of my Father … Mat 7:21	7:18-19; 12:33		3:9; 6:43-45	
4	The unfruitful tree				3:9; 13:6-9	The vine 15:1-6
5	The house on the rock	… whosoever heareth these sayings of mine, and doeth them, …	7:24-27		6:47-49	
6	The harvest		9:37-38	4:26-29 (man waiting for …)	10:2 looking for workers	4:35-36 [v34 … & to finish his work]
7	He that taketh not his cross …		10:38; 16:24-25	8:34-38 judgement 10:21	9:23-24; 14:27; 14:28-33 tower, war	
8	The sower	… and he becometh unfruitful	13:1-23	4:1-20	8:5-15	
9	The tares		13:24-30,37-43; 15:13			
10	Treasure hid in a field. Merchant & pearls. The net.		13:44; 13:45-46; 13:47-50			
11	The unmerciful steward		18:22-35			
12	The camel & the eye of the needle.		19:24	10:24-25	18:24-25	
13	Parable where master gives 1 penny to workers even though some worked a whole day, and others only an hour. Then the labourers complained.		20:1-16			
14	One son said to father I go, but went not, other said no, but went.		20:27-32			
15	Marriage, but those invited didn't want to come. Brought poor people instead.		22:1-10		14:16-24	
16	Man without a wedding garment.		22:11-14			
17	The good man & the thief	need to be ready all the time	24:43-44		12:39-40 cf. v41-48	
18	The 10 maidens		25:1-13		cf. 13:25-29	
19	The talents given according to ability.		25:14-30			
20	Pound given to everyone the same.				19:12-27	
21	Dividing of sheep & goats		25:31-46			
22	Receive the kingdom as a child.	"But he that is greatest..." Mat 23:11	18:3-6	10:15	18:17	
23	The Man & the husbandmen, and his son.		21:33-46	12:1-9	20:9-16	
24	Man who went on a long trip, and left servants with work to do, and the porter to watch.			13:34-37		

	Parables/ Analogies	Notes	Matthew	Mark	Luke	John
25	Bread of life					6:32-40, & up to v69
26	Blind & the sighted; Blind leading blind.		15:14		6:39	9:39-41
27	Light of the world					11:9-10; 12:35-36; 12:46
28	Light of the body		6:22-23		11:33-36	
29	Mote in brother's eye		7:3-5		6:41-42	
30	Brother & sister & mother. Mother & brethren of Jesus - those who hear God's word and do it.		12:46-50	03:31-35	8:19-21	
31	No man, having put his hand to the plough, & looking back, is fit for the kingdom of God.				9:62	
32	The good Samaritan				10:30-37	
33	Waiting for the Lord to return from the wedding.	I suppose this was when the groom went on a trip to get his wife. Remember how can the children of the bride chamber mourn whilst the groom is with them? Mat 9:15			12:35-38 (&v40) 13:25-30	
34	The servant who cancelled part of the debt of his Lord's debtors.				16:1-13	
35	Stone which builders rejected	cf. Ps 118:19-23	21:42-46	12:10-12	20:17-19	
36	Born again					3:3-8
37	Water	cf. Isaiah 12:3,44:3, 55:1,58:11; Jer 2:13				4:10-14; 7:37-39
38	The wine in bottles, new cloth for old garment.		9:17-16	2:20-22	5:36-39	
39	The rich man & the bigger barns.				12:16-21	
40	Parable of the steward looking after the Lords other servants.		24:45-51		12:41-48	
41	Parable of thief breaking in				12:39-40	
42	The measure that you meet		7:1-2	4:24	6:38	
43	The adversary & the judge - put things right before its too late.		5:25-26		12:58-59	
44	The straight gate		7:13-14		13:24	
45	The lost sheep		18:12-13		15:4-7	
46	The woman and the lost penny.				5:8-10	
47	The prodigal son	"...: for this thy brother was dead, and is alive again; and was lost [cf. the lost sheep, the missing penny], and is found." Luke 15:32			15:11-24	

www.ingramcontent.com/pod-product-compliance
Ingram Content Group UK Ltd.
Pitfield, Milton Keynes, MK11 3LW, UK
UKHW050615260726
13967UKWH00008B/2877

9 780473 429522